Wanderings in Warsaw

with

Tony Konieczny

© Copyright Antony Konieczny 2019

The right of Antony Konieczny to be recognised as the author of this work has been asserted in accordance with the Copyright, Designs and Patents Act 1988, sections 77 and 78.

This book may not be reproduced in any form unless permitted by the author.

Thanks

Writing a book is hard, but enjoyable work and at times one can flag. My thanks go to my friends who read what I had done and motivated me to continue. In particular I would like to thank Andy Cox, Max Sassim, my daughter Samantha and partner Lin.

I would also like to thank all of those wonderful people with whom I had great conversations in Warsaw. You are mentioned in the book.

Contents

Introduction 10
    Poland 12
    Warsaw 15
    Language 16
    Money 19
    Transport 20
    The Pope 22

Travelling and Staying 23
    Travelling 23
    Staying 24

The Old Town 27
    Sigismund 30

Marie Curie 43

Długa – Plac Bankowy – Andersa 53
    General Władysław Albert Anders 58
    Monument to the Fallen and Murdered in the East
    60
    Ratusz Arsenał 61

Fountain Park 63

Partitions and Risings 65
    Partitions 65
    First Partition 66
    Second Partition 68
    Third Partition 68
    Kościuszko 69
    Great Poland Uprising 1806 73
    1830 Uprising (November Uprising) 74
    1863 Uprising (January Uprising) 77
    World War I 80
    1918 Poland Arises 81
    1920-21 Battle of Warsaw 81
    1939 -45 World War II 81

The Poniatowski Family 83
    Stanisław Antoni Poniatowski 84
    Josef Poniatowski 86

Polish National Anthem 90

Saxon Gardens and Plac Piłsudskiego 93

Krakowskie Przedmieście 96

Nowy Swiat 108
    Nowy Swiat – an Update 113

Frederyk Chopin..115

Chopin Quarter...120

Concerts..122

The Royal Route 131
    .Jan Paderewski...133
    Roman Dmowski...135
    Josef Piłsudski...137
    Łazienki Park...138
    Wilanów...142

Chopin in the Park..148

The Centre..158

The Jewish Quarter...167

Military Museum and Zloty Teras...................................181
    Muzeum Wojska Polskiego.......................................186
    Zloty Teras 189

Ulica Szucha..193

Katyn..199

Long Night of the Museums..204
    Sokrates Starynkiewicz...207

The Kopernik Experience..220

Pole Mokatowskie..224

Polish Air Force..234

Zoliborz..238
    Stanisław Maczek...240
    Krzysztof Komeda Trzcinski..245
    Citadel...246

Kabaty..250

Praga...255
    Josef Haller..259
    Saska Kępę...266
    Philharmonic...269

Monuments...270
    Monument to the Heroes of Warsaw (Nike)........270
    AK Monument..273
    Monument to the Polish Underground State and
    the Home Army...279

The Warsaw Rising..281
    Bór-Komorowski 282

Other Leaders in WW2...289
    Edward Rydz-Smigły..289
    Władysław Sikorski...292
    Stanisław Mikołajczyk..296

  Władysław Raczkiewicz...298
  Konstanty Rokossovski..299

Dentist...302

Hospital..307

Elecyjna..315
  Edward Szymanskiego Park...315
  Josef Sowinski Park..319
  Josef Sowinski. 319
  Orthodox Cemetery...320
  Skaryszewski Park..323
  Park Praski..325
  Park Szczęśliwicki..326

POLIN...328

Cemeteries..336
  Powązki..336
  Jewish..337
  Rising...338
  Bródno/Targowek...339
  Stefan Starzyński...340
  Prawosławny w Warszawie (Orthodox)................342
  Red Army Cemetery...343

Museums...345
  National..345
  Military..345
  Rising...345

    Diving..346
    Państwowe Muzeum Archaeologiczne
    (Archaeological)..346
    Castle...346
    Neon...347
    PRL Museum..347
    Rail Transport (Stacja Muzeum)............................347
    Katynskie, Oddział Martyrologiczny (Katyn)......348
    X Pawilionu Cytadeli Warszawskiej......................348
    Skwer Powstanców Styczniowych........................348
    Gasworks Museum...349

Parks...350
    Ogrod Saski (Saxon Gardens)................................350
    Uzadowski..350
    Lazienki..350
    Wilanow...350
    Pole Mokotowskie..351
    Skaryszewski...351
    Szymanskiego..352
    Krazinskich..352
    Marshal Edward /Rydza-Smigly............................352
    Szczęśliwica Garden Park....................................352
    Dolinka Szwajcarska..353
    Kazimierozowski..353
    Samuela Orgelbranda..354
    AK Rog..354
    RomualdanTraugutta...354
    Olympic Golf Club..354

Cemeteries...355
    Powstańców Warszawy (Warsaw Rising)............355
    Prawosławny (Orthodox)...355
    Wolski..355
    Powązkowski...356
    Zydowski..356
    Bródnowski..356
    Mauzoleum Zołnierzy Radzieckich.........................356

A Three Day Itinerary..357
    Friday Evening...357
    Saturday..358
    Sunday...359
    Monday..359

Timeline of Polish History..360
    Polish People's Republic..365

Conclusion..373

Alphabetical Index...374

Introduction

This is the book that I wish I'd had on my first visit to Warsaw. It is more than a travel guide that tells you about buildings and places to eat. It tells of history. It tells of the people behind the monuments and the street names. It tells of real encounters with real Poles. But it also provides some indication of what you can see in modern day Warsaw.

That is, Warsaw, Poland (population between one and two million), not Warsaw Indiana (population 13,559 in 2010). It is important to get that clear, because the Indiana Warsaw is often the default of search engines. This says something about American search engines!

I love Warsaw and the people. Warsaw was completely destroyed during World War 2. So badly that it made no economic sense to rebuild it. Poland had shifted to the west in the post war realignment of the country and it made sense to rebuild the capital further west as well. But too many Poles had fought and died defending Warsaw and had pledged that *Warsaw will never die* that there was no option but to rebuild. It is this obstinacy and can-do attitude that endears the Poles to me.

Today, Warsaw is a mixture of rebuilt old and modern new that makes it into the thriving and beautiful place it is today.

I have wandered in Warsaw for several years

and have grown to love it. Perhaps it is my heritage, for I am half-Polish on my father's side. Perhaps I go to Poland because he never could. He came to England in 1943, having had a "holiday", like many Poles, in Siberia for a couple of years, courtesy of the Russians, who spared all expense. The experience did not endear the Russians to him.

When the war ended, which he helped by repairing broken aircraft, the British Government did all it could to get the Poles to go back to their homeland. Many of those who took up the offer were shot shortly after arrival, or even (can you believe it?) sent to Siberia AGAIN, so it was as well that he remained in England.

This is not really a book about my father, but his experiences were shared by many, which helps to explain something about the Poles.

He was stubborn, like many Poles and refused work either in the mines, agriculture or factories, which were the choices offered. He was a surveyor and, through perseverance, got a job as a draughtsman.

He died in 1977. He would have loved to have seen the Polish Pope, who did not get elected until late 1978. Perhaps it was his love of his home country that enthused me to go. Whatever the reason, it is a great place. You should go. I have been annually for around five years now.

I have written this book because I would like to have had such a book with me as my own tour guide, with personal anecdotes.

I have always been fascinated by the names of

streets, parks and monuments, as these usually say something about the history of the area and a knowledge of history helps to explain the present.

Even if you are not planning to visit Warsaw (Poland), I hope that you find this book informative and entertaining.

Poland

If you have not looked for it on a map, you would get the impression that Poland is somewhere further north than Britain, because most people have heard of its cold winters. Actually, Warsaw has the same latitude as Milton Keynes, but don't let that put you off. It is a two hour flight due east of Luton.

It is roughly square-shaped, with Germany on the western side, Slovakia on the southern, Ukraine and Belarus on the eastern, and the Baltic Sea on the northern side, along with Kaliningrad (a Russian outpost) and Lithuania.

The southern side is determined largely by the Tatra mountains, which tail off in the east into the Bieszady – a range of smaller hills, but still the size of the best in England.

The western and eastern boundaries are mainly determined by rivers – the Oder in the West and the Bug in the east.

Warsaw is in the north-eastern quadrant.

Being in a land mass, it has a continental climate, which is to say (if you remember your school geography lessons) it has cold, wet winters and hot, dry summers, whereas Britain has a maritime climate of cool, wet winters and warm wet summers.

In May, when I usually go to Warsaw, the weather is similar to, but usually sunnier than, Britain's South East.

Even in winter, the temperature often only hits minus ten centigrade, which is cold, but not Arctic. However, there have been years when the temperature has dropped to minus thirty Centigrade.

Having the same latitude as Milton Keynes means that it gets exactly the same amount of light as Milton Keynes. It gets darker earlier in the evening because it is one hour ahead of Britain, whereas it should be nearer two hours ahead. So if it gets darker in the evening it must get lighter in the morning.

Poland has a population of around two thirds of that of Britain in a land area some third bigger than Britain. When you fly over Poland, you will see lots of land, laid out in strips reminiscent of the feudal system. Eventually these strips will coalesce into bigger farms for the purpose of efficiency, but it will take time.

So it is not a bad place to be and not too different from England.

Except that for most of its modern history (since 1795) it has been ruled by someone else.

From 1795 to 1918 it was partitioned between the Prussians, the Russians and the Austro-Hungarian empires.

From 1918 to 1st September 1939 it ruled itself, although from 1918 to 1920 the Russians tried to get its Polish lands back, but only ended up losing land on Poland's eastern borders, known as the Kresy.

From 1945 to 1989 it was part of the Communist Bloc, held there against the will of the people.

From 1989 it has been its own master, although in 2004 it joined the EU.

A more detailed timeline of Poland's history is provided as an appendix.

The Poles are fiercely patriotic, probably because this is what happens when you are ruled by a bigger, foreign country. Ask the Welsh, the Scots and the Irish.

They are also fiercely materialistic, having been poor for so long. Everybody wants a bigger flat, a car and holidays. Quite normal then.

This is why there are so many in Britain – there are more opportunities to save money.

It is said that the first question a Pole will ask a British employer is "How much overtime is there?"

Polish became the second most spoken language in Britain a few years ago, ousting Welsh from that spot. However, most Poles will also speak English, especially if they started Primary School after 1990, when Poland left the dominance of the USSR. Prior to this, Russian was the foreign language taught in schools. This means that most Poles have at least a smattering of English, if not a fluency, especially if they have spent time in England.

The converse side of this coin though is that older people do not generally speak English. This can be a problem when at a train or bus station. Smile sweetly at a youngster and see if they can translate for you.

Warsaw

Warsaw is the capital of Poland, but this was not always the case, as until 1596 Krakow (pronounced *Krakoff*) was the capital. Warsaw is better placed, being in the centre of what used to be Poland between the wars.

It is a thriving city of some two million people and every year I have been going to visit, there seems to be another skyscraper.

It is a green city, with about a quarter of its area being parkland or woodland. There is a massive forest to the north west, called the Kampinoski and a forest to the south called Kabaty. It has an almost unbroken park from the President's Palace to Łazienki within the city boundary.

It has a good public transport system of buses, trams, subway and urban railway.

The larger streets are laid out with tramlines in the middle of the street and buses on the pavement sides. To reach the tram stops you either use a (usually) light-controlled pedestrian crossing (known in England as Pelican crossings) or a subway. The light-controlled crossings don't let you hang about. It's a case of 'quick march', or you will hear the rapid bleeping before you reach the safety of the other side. If you dawdle, the rapid bleeping could be the last sound you ever hear.

If you use a subway, you will have to know roughly which direction your transport is going. From the Centre, north is towards Żoliborg or Młociny; South is towards

Mokotow or Kabaty; west is towards Ochota and east is towards Praga.

The metro has two lines: north-south and east-west, with the intersection at Swiętokrzyska, near the university.

It is best to leave the suburban railway alone, unless travelling from the airport to the centre.

The city is divided into east and west by the River Visła, which used to be called the River Vistula. Praga used to be a separate city on the east (right) bank of the river, but is now a suburb of Warsaw.

The main east-west road is Jerusalem Avenue, or Aleja Jerozolimskie.

Some way to the north of Aleja Jerozolimskie is another east-west road: Aleja Swiętokrzyska, and further north still is Aleja Solidarność.

The main north-south route is Marszałsowska and to the west is Aleja Jan Pawla II. Further west is Zelazna, heading north from Plac Starynkiewicza. Then further west is Towarowa, heading north from Plac Zawiszy

East of Marszałsowska is the Royal route: this starts at the Old Town and leads through Krakowskie Przedmiescie, Nowy Swiat and Ujazdowska to Wilanów.

You will not remember any of this.

Language

Polish appears to be a difficult language. It not only appears to be, but actually is. You are not going to learn Polish, because everybody under the age of thirty or so will have learned English at school. However, there is not always a young person around when you need a bit of translation, so it helps to know something about pronunciation, because there are a lot of words where you can guess the meaning if you get the pronunciation right.

Most letters are pronounced as in English.
There is no letter *x*. The Poles get this sound by using *ks* as in *seks*.
There is no letter *q*.
There is no letter *v*. The Poles get this sound by using *w* as in w*alisa* for valise or suitcase.
There is a new letter *ł or Ł* to get the sound of the English W as in the first letter of *wall*.
There is a new letter *ę* which sounds like the *en* in L*en*gth.
There is a new letter *ą* which is pronounced *on*. Just think of a French conversation as heard by English ears – hee hą hee hą hee hą hee hą
There is a new letter Ó or ó, which is pronounced as the oo in T*oo*th.
There are three versions of z, the non-accented one sounding as in English
ź which is pronounced like *azure* or the g's in *Gigi*
ż which is pronounced as in *buzz*.
ć which is pronounced as a cross between *ts* as in nits and *ch* as in Church.
Ś as in the sh of sheep
cz pronounced as the *ch* in *cheese*
sz pronounced as the *sh* in fre*sh*
So *szcz* is pronounced as the shch in fre*sh* *ch*eese
So now you know how to pronounce Łódz – as

Woodge.

And you can guess at words like *arkitekt (architect), dzem (jam), centrum (centre)* and so on. Once you get the hang of it, spelling is very precise, unlike English.

Now that you know how to pronounce Polish, try saying this Polish tongue-twister:

W Szczebrze szynie chrząszcz brzni w trzcinie. Which translated means *In Szczebrze the crickets chirp in the reeds.*

Now you can put your teeth back in!

Polish has no definite (the) or indefinite (a) articles. So a sentence in Polish might be "I buy ticket." Or "I catch tram." The meaning is usually clear. (We often say "I'm going to catch the bus to town." It is as though there is only one bus. What we really mean to say is "I'm going to catch a bus to town" because we don't care which particular bus it is as long as it goes to town.)

Polish also has only three verb tenses, which makes it easier, but it has perfective and imperfective versions to indicate whether or not an action is complete or ongoing.

And then it has seven cases of noun, each complicated by three genders, each with different word endings. Don't even try to to understand it! I have not found out why it is *Ulica Andersa* and *Plac Piłsudskiego*. (Anders Street and Piłsudski Square.)

Money

Poland has its own currency – the Złoty, divided into 100 Groszi. The value of a złoty is around five to one British pound, but this obviously varies.

By far and away the best place to change your British pounds is at a Kantor, of which there are lots in Warsaw. But all are not equal. I have found that those which offer Western Union facilities are the worst. At a time when the spot rate (money market rate) was around five to the pound, I was offered only four to the pound. It pays to know the current rate, which is why I search on the internet for 'sterling zloty conversion'. I will never get this rate, but I will get somewhere within ten to twenty Groszi of it.

The best practice therefore is to change as little money as possible to tide you over until you can get to a kantor. You can do this in Britain or try an ATM in Warsaw airport. Kantors are open during normal office hours, although they can vary.

There are good ones in Zloty Teras, Jerozolimskie near Nowe Swiat and Rondo ONZ. There will be others. Look at the spread – the difference between the buying price and the selling price. The smaller this is, the better the kantor. You can also try haggling – I was lucky once, but most times the rates are very good, so don't upset the person behind the counter.

Transport

One of the things you should know about Warsaw transport is that they employ a lot of inspectors to fine people who are travelling without tickets. At some stage you will get confronted and face a big fine unless you have a valid ticket. So make sure that you travel legally.

The best way to do this is to get a season ticket for your stay. All the information you need is available at ztm.waw.pl, where they have pages in English. You can buy these at the ZTM offices, or at automatic machines, or at a kiosk. As you will need a ticket to get you to the centre of Warsaw from the airport, it is prudent to buy a ticket from a kiosk at the airport, where they speak English. With a season ticket, you don't feel bad about hopping on a bus for one stop.

If you are aged seventy or over, then, like me, you can get free travel. All you have to have is a means of ID when travelling: something like a passport or driving licence with photo and date of birth.

I got a Warsaw Card. You can do this on-line and pick it up at the airport from the ZTM office at the airport. Just beware that when they say they want an image of your left ear, they mean a three-quarter shot of your face, where both your face and left ear are visible. When the system is satisfied that all is in order, it will tell you, so you know that the card will be waiting for you. You can then load your season ticket onto it by credit card.

When buying a ticket, you may be asked *Normalne*

albo Ogłowe? (Normal or discount). If you are a student or a pensioner, you can get the discounted ticket. Check the ZTM site for details (ztm.waw.pl, where there are English pages.

I find the ZTM maps very useful in finding my way around. Otherwise, for smart phone users, there is an app called Jak do Jade, which means "How do I get there".

If, like many tourists, you are going to be there over a weekend, beware that Nowy Swiat and Krakowskie Przedmiescie ban traffic at the weekend, so the buses which use those streets in the week take a different route on Saturdays and Sundays.

And whenever the President is entertaining a foreign visitor, which won't be you, so they won't tell you that the traffic ban is happening. You will just stand at a bus stop waiting until the cavalcade has passed, which could be some hours later.

Just keep your wits about you when approaching the Charles de Gaulle roundabout (the one with the palm tree) and get off the bus if it fails to go up Nowy Swiat.

The alternative routes can be discerned from the ZTM maps, but only if you are looking for the bus numbers in brackets. It is not very clear.

That said, I enjoy Warsaw transport. Just take a notebook and pen to have the buses you should be catching written down for your journey. A little planning can save a lot of time.

The Pope

When the Roman Catholic Poles talk of "the Pope", they mean John Paul II, or Jan Pawel II in Polish, after whom a main north-south street in Warsaw is named. He was the first Polish Pope and, with Lech Wałęsa, the architect of the liberation of Poland in 1990.

Travelling and Staying

Travelling

I have always travelled to Warsaw Chopin Airport and stayed in apartments. Wizzair and BA have been my favourites, but there are other airlines flying directly. By booking as far ahead as possible, you can get the best deals. I once bought a return trip, with small rucksack, for around £25, but that was a while ago. It is now more likely to be £100 return.

Wizzair and BA have around half a dozen flights a day from London airports, Wizzair favouring Luton and BA favouring Heathrow. This gives an indication of the popularity of going to Warsaw, mainly by Poles living in Britain, but also an increasing number of tourists, especially in summer.

Detractors of Wizzair will tell you that they fly rubbish planes. This is untrue. The only thing rubbish about their modern, new planes is the garish pink that forms the colour of their brand. The benefit is that the planes are hard to miss.

Wizzair has grown on the back of the migration of Central Europeans to Britain. It is a Hungarian enterprise that has grown rapidly. It must be one of the main customers of AirBus, as it buys new, most efficient planes to keep the costs down.

Like any low cost airline, it charges for any deviation from its system, so make sure that the information you provide is correct and that your baggage meets their specifications.

I have not heard any horror stories like I've heard about Ryanair, with staff seeming to want to spot deviations so that they can charge extra. Wizzair staff, in my experience, are kind and reasonable. However, I did see them stop a woman with a large suitcase (and I do mean 'large') from taking it into the cabin. They charged her £56 for putting it into the hold.

On another occasion, two women were stopped from trying to take a couple of bottles of vodka in their hand luggage. As they had already checked in their hold baggage, there was no place for the vodka to go, except to the Wizzair staff.

Talking of vodka, I love the flavoured vodkas (more later) and on one trip decided to bring some back. I filled a large suitcase with eleven vodka bottles, each wrapped in an item of clothing. The suitcase weighed 23Kg – just on the limit of what was allowed. It was so heavy that it could not be hurled around by the baggage handlers and every bottle arrived intact.

Staying

I always stay in apartments. And I don't like anything less than hotel quality, so I tested apartments on my first visit to Warsaw, I was using Warsaw as my arrival point in Poland, but I was going on to Lublin after a couple of days. Let's face it, I was in the Scouts, so could rough it for two days if needed.

There was no need to worry. I had arranged to rent an apartment literally one minute away from the Sigismund Column in the Old Town. I did this trough Bookings.com and Warsaw Best Apartments. It was an apartment in number 7 Senatorska.

I had been in contact with Jaroslaw, the agent, through email, so he knew when I would be arriving. Sure enough, he was waiting as I arrived. He carried my case up the two flights of stairs to the apartment, which had an astounding array of locks and a steel plate over the door. The last time I had seen this sort of door was at my daughter's flat when she was at Uni. It later transpired that drug addicts congregated in the ground floor of her block. Fortunately she was on the 20th floor. Even more fortunately, she encountered no problems with the addicts. Even more fortunately, she did not do drugs.

So I now wondered about this apartment. Was it reasonably priced because the building was stuffed with maladjusted families? Should I go now?

"Don't worry about the door. As keys were lost over time, new locks were added. This is the only key you need for the door."

"And the steel plate? I asked.

"This goes back to Communist times, when there could have been a few problems, but all is well now."

Reassured, we entered the flat. It was quite large. There was an entrance area, large bathroom with loo, washing machine, corner bath and shower. There was a small kitchen area, small dining table with two chairs, sofa and TV and separate bedroom area with double bed. It all looked clean, but dark, as the view from the windows looked out onto other apartments very nearby.

No problem. It was a nice flat and the electric lights cured the lack of light. Besides, I planned to be out in Warsaw most of the time.

By modern standards, the WiFi was primitive as Broadband had to make its way to the rented apartments of Warsaw. But it would do for emails and light web browsing. I hasten to add that the quality of WiFi has improved in line with technical improvements, so now the WiFi is of high standard.

The emails were important, because Lin, my partner, who was not accompanying me, was worried for my safety, so I had bought a new laptop computer so that I could send emails at least once a day. Smartphones were not the thing in those days and phone calls home were a task that involved a mortgage broker. I had bought a basic phone on a previous journey, with a Polish SIM card, as this gave me emergency contact home as well as the ability to call Polish numbers if I needed to check on facilities. In the end, I needed neither.

I should say at this point that Warsaw is a safe city. I have never seen anything that caused me concern, other than hearing some drunken British louts swearing and generally being obnoxious.

When Jaroslaw left, I unpacked. That is to say, took out the things I would need for my short stay in Warsaw, which was not much. I then went out to explore.

The Old Town

The Old Town is the tourist hot spot in Warsaw. It is known as *Stare Miasto* in Polish. Don't worry about missing the stop when arriving by public transport, because the announcement on the bus or tram will say *Old Town*.

Being one minute away from the Old Town Square on my first visit, this was the place to start. Indeed, it is the obvious starting point for any tourist, given that one will arrive at this point if you travel by public transport from the Krakowskie Przedmieście direction, or from the Stare Miasto stop below.

There is no public transport within the Old Town, so you will need to walk or use a wheelchair. The nearest public transport is on the east-west route from *Ratusz Arsenał*. Both trams and buses stop here on their way to and from Praga, on the other side of the river, so services are frequent.

When alighting the tram be aware that you are in the middle of the road, so do watch out for cars. My experience has been that the drivers are careful and wait while passengers alight, but you never know, yours might be the first accident on this spot!

Having safely left the transport, take a moment to look at the tunnel you have come through. This is a recent construction, being officially opened on 22nd July 1949. It was a technical marvel, being built by a cut-and-fill method along Leszno Street. It allowed for an east-west route across the city, whilst at the same time preserving the atmosphere of the Old Town. The town walls are original.

If coming from the Stare Miasto stop you can either climb the steps either side of the road, or, on the right side, through glass doors, there is a communist-era hall leading to escalators. In the winter, the huge radiators belt out quite a bit of heat. The Poles are very good at closing the glass doors to keep the heat in, so I always follow suit. In the summer, there is no need as the heating is provided directly by the sun.

The escalators are noteworthy in that they were the first to be installed in Poland and Poles visited the area just to see them.

When I first visited Warsaw, back in 2012, I don't recall a lift. At that time it seemed that Warsaw was unprepared for wheelchair users. Every place I went seemed to have at least a few steps, just to make wheelchair travel impossible. Happily to say, things have now improved enormously and there are lifts or ramps at most places where there are stairs.

This escalator hall is also useful to know about, because at the top of the escalators, to the left, there are public toilets down some stairs, at the bottom of which is a Russian control panel. I don't know what it controlled, or even if it is still operational, but it is a magnificent piece of kit. Were it not for the Russian writing, it could have been a control panel for a Boulton and Watt steam engine. It is worth a look while you go for a natural break.

If coming to the Old Town from Krakowskie Przedmieście, the buses all turn off before getting to the Old Town, leaving you with a bit of a walk. The nearest stop is Plac Zamkowy, but you might have to get off your bus at Uniwersitet (University) if your bus does not go to Plac Zamkowy.

The obvious starting point for exploring the Old Town (Stare Miasto) is the Sigismund Column. It cannot be missed as it stands 22 metres high at the approach to Castle Square (Plac Zamkowy).

Warsaw is in the province of Mazowie and this used to be a separate country until the last of the Mazowian princes died in 1526. It then got incorporated into the Kingdom of Poland and, following the Act of Union with Lithuania in 1569, parliament moved to Warsaw. In 1596 King Sigismund III Wasa (he of the column) moved the capital of Poland from Krakow to Warsaw. Hence his veneration, especially by his son, King Władysław IV Wasa, who commissioned it.

It was based on a column that Władysław had seen on a visit to Rome in 1625 and was erected between 1643 and 1644. The original column was made from red marble.

"But you said that Warsaw was destroyed by the Nazis," I hear you say. "Surely the column could not have escaped?"

True. The column did not escape the Nazis. Prior to the Nazis it did not escape the attacks by the weather, for it was renovated several times , until in 1887 it was replaced with a granite column.

The Nazis used the column for artillery target practise on 1st September 1944 and blew it up.

The original columns can be seen by the southern wall of the castle nearby.

Sigismund

Sigismund reigned Poland when it was at the height of its powers, but then presided over a decline, so it is not known whether to praise him or condemn him. What is sure is that his life was not dull.

He was born in prison in 1566, which you will remember is when Elizabeth I was on the English throne. His parents were Duke John of Finland and Catherine Jagiellon, a Polish princess. They were imprisoned in Sweden by King Erik the Fourteenth, who was a protestant. Sigismund, however, was brought up as a Catholic.

In 1567, Erik released the family from prison and in 1568 he was deposed and Sigismund's father became King John III of Sweden. From prison to palace in two years!

All this action and the young Sigismund was only two years old!

In 1587, when Sigismund was twenty-one, his uncle, Stephen Bathory, elected King of Poland, died and Sigismund was elected King of Poland, with the support of many strong Polish nobles. It is quite possible that he received this backing on conditions, these being that he would give up some royal powers to the Sejm (parliament), which he did immediately on gaining power. He also made a political marriage with Austria by marrying Anne Habsburg in 1592.

However, all was not smooth. There was somebody else who thought he would make a better king and this was Archduke Maximillian III of Austria.

Sigismund was crowned King of Poland in Krakow on December 27 1587. In doing so, he became "by the grace of God, King of Poland, Grand Duke of Lithuania, Ruthenia, Prussia, Masovia, Samogitia, Livonia and also hereditary King of the Swedes, Goths and Wends."

Ruthenia is an indeterminate area of land to the east of Poland. Maslovia is the north eastern area of Poland which has Warsaw as its capital. It stretches from Łódź to Białystok.

King of the Goths is a title historically used by the kings of both Sweden and Denmark and refers to tribes centred on the island of Gotland.

The Wends historically inhabited the western Slavic lands adjoining the Baltic Sea.

So Sigismund ruled over vast swathes of lands.

Or he would have done had Maximilian not been a poor loser and decide to fight for the throne. He invaded Poland in early 1588 and entered into battle with Hetman Jan Zamoyski at the Battle of Byczna.

Zamoyski took Maximilian prisoner. It was only in 1589, when Maximilian renounced all claim to the Polish throne, that he was released.

For a few years, relationships soured between the King and his Chancellor, Jan Zamoyski, but were happily resolved and Poland entered into a short period of prosperity and peace.

in 1594 Sigismund was pronounced King of Sweden and appointed his uncle, Duke Charles, to rule Sweden as regent, while Sigismund stayed in Poland. However, tensions grew in Lutheran Sweden as they were suspicious of their Catholic King.

In 1598 things came to a head, with the death of Anne and a rebellion led by his uncle, Duke Charles, in Sweden. After a good start, winning many battles, Sigismund lost the Battle of Stangebro and he retreated to Poland. He was deposed as King of Sweden and his uncle was pronounced King of Sweden in 1600. Many minor wars followed between Sweden and Poland.

There was also a war opportunity with Russia, as the various groups there were fighting a civil war. It was an opportunity for the Poles to invade Russia, along with the Swedes, who were a bit ambivalent.

At one point, the Boyars of Russia, the aristocratic group of families, invited Sigismund's son, Władysław, to become Tsar. Sigismund wanted Russia for himself, so disallowed it.

At one point in the conflict, Hetman Stanisław Zołkiewski captured Moscow and the Kremlin, but this made it impossible to have any future union between the Poles and the Russians.

Poland was engaged in wars on several fronts during Sigismund's reign: in the north against Sweden; in the east against Russia; in the south against the Ottoman Empire. From 1618 there was the Thirty Years' War, finishing in 1648. It was one of the most destructive wars in human history, with 8 million deaths from violence, famine and plague, as well as military engagements. (In Germany the proportion of its population killed was only exceeded by the period between January and May 1945. The results of this war became a justification for the 1871 creation of the Empire). The war mainly involved the Holy Roman Empire, but Poland was drawn into it to a relatively minor extent.

It was in 1632, during this war, that Sigismund died and his son, Władysław IV Wasa was elected as king.

When we talk about electing kings in this period, we are not talking about universal suffrage, but an electorate which comprised a small group of wealthy nobles, known collectively as the *szlachta*.

When the Thirty Years' War ended in 1648, Poland was drawn into the Khmelnytski Uprising, which continued until a Hetmanate had been established in what is now part of Ukraine. The rising was conducted by the Cossacks and Tartars. There was some religious element to this war as the Orthodox rebels resented the Catholic rulers and the Jews, who were extensive lessees of most lands in the area. There was extensive slaughter. Władysław did not live to see the end of the war, for he died on May 20th 1648, to be replaced by his younger brother, John II Casimir Wasa.

Heading past the column, which is a popular meeting point, on the ground is a line of dark-coloured tiles, marking the line of the old city wall. Back in the day of Władysław, it was not permitted to erect statues to mortals within the city walls, which is why the column was placed outside the city walls on a column which was tall enough to peep, and be seen, over the city walls.

Walking onwards towards the restaurants in the square, you come to Piwna, or Beer Street. It is narrow, with narrow pavements, and small shops and restaurants aimed at tourists. It is one of two parallel roads that lead off the Castle Square (Plac Zamkowy), the second being Swiętojańska (Saint John Street).

(There is another street beyond Swiętojańska, which is a continuation of Plac Zamkowy that turns into Kanonia.)

Going down Piwna, one is in a cobbled street. One year, when I was there in the winter, I saw the cobbles in this street being relaid, to give a smooth surface for wheeled traffic. Not cars, but mobility scooters, cycles, wheeled suitcases and that sort of wheel.

The buildings have been rebuilt after the war, but you would not know it as they have been rebuilt so well. Now, instead of crafts, the ground floors of the buildings have restaurants and tourist shops, often advertised with signs of the old-fashioned sort made of wrought iron or painted steel sheet. The rendered fronts of the buildings are decorated with designs and coloured paints.

In Piwna is the old church of Saint Martins,

opposite which is a narrow alley going through to Saint John's cathedral. Enjoy the view, but carry on down Piwna to Zapiecek (Baker Street), which you can take to get to the Old Town Square, or Market (Rynek).

In 2018 my daughter treated me to a visit to Warsaw so that I could show her what was so fascinating about the place. We stayed in a flat at the top of a building in Piwna. Those three flights of stairs to climb every day added to my general exhaustion, but I think it made me fitter!

I had seen photos of the square taken in 1945 and it was then a scene of total devastation. None of the buildings had roofs. Where there had been wooden windows, there were holes (assuming there was any wall left to show where the window holes were). All the wooden floors were gone and any paintwork had been burnt off.

I did hear one amusing story of the

reconstruction period, which was that concerning a former wine merchant's house. As the workers cleared the rubble, they found a stash of wine bottles, most of which had, miraculously, survived the flames and the falling masonry. As these were communist times, the workers kept the secret to themselves and enjoyed the present from the past as they toasted the future.

The scene as I approached the square for the first time, and subsequently, is one of timelessness. It looked as though the square had been there since the Middle Ages. It was beautiful. Unsurprisingly, it is a UNESCO World Heritage Site.

In the middle of the square is the Warsaw Mermaid. Said to be the sister of the one in Copenhagen, this one had further to travel along the Baltic, before swimming upstream in the Visła to Warsaw. She was found by fishermen, whose nets were being tangled and torn by, what they thought, was some kind of animal. It was the mermaid and they immediately fell in love with her, letting her go. She was then captured by a rich merchant, who imprisoned her. On hearing her cries, the fishermen released her. Since that time, armed with sword and shield, she has protected the inhabitants of Warsaw.

Given what happened in the 20th century, she must have been asleep or with her sister in Copenhagen.

A favourite occupation while in Warsaw is to spot the mermaid, for images appear all over the city.

The south-eastern wall of the square nearly was no more, as the authorities planned to demolish what remained of it to open up a view of the Visła. When he heard that an official visit was to be made, Professor Jan Zachwatowicz ordered that a single-storey wall be built in front of it. When President Beirut visited the site, he assumed that reconstruction was under way and, obviously, what had been built by Polish workers could not be destroyed.

On the north-west wall of the square is the Warsaw Museum, opened in September 2017 after extensive renovation. It is worth a visit. I found the films of the inter-war period particularly fascinating.

In 2019 I had the perfect opportunity to visit this museum with my friend Max, who is a lover of museums and art. It is well worth a visit. A veritable rabbit-warren of a building, there are stairs and rooms all over, each room containing different groups of objects: some have clothes; some have portraits of past dignitaries; some have gilt tableware; some have books, maps and sheet music. There were plenty of interesting artefacts.

At the top of the building is a viewing gallery with views in several directions, one of which is over the market square.

Just beyond the north corner of the square are the stone steps. These are picturesque and worth a trot up and down.

Turning right at the bottom of the steps on Brzozowa (Birch Street) brings one to a viewing point, where can be seen the river and Praga. The road bridge is the Śląsko-Dąbrowski bridge.

It is one of the best viewing spots in Warsaw, which is why all of the walking tours stop there.

Retracing one's steps slightly brings you to Cielna and a route back to the Old Town Square at the north-eastern corner.

After absorbing the atmosphere of the Old Town Square on my first visit, I wandered up Nowomiejska at the western corner of the square. This led me to the Barbican – a lovely brick structure on the old city walls. From this point it is possible to walk along the walls, but for now I would walk into the New Town beyond the Barbican.

I heard tell that one of the restaurants on the right, as you exit the Barbican, was as it was in communist times, complete with ambience of surly staff with no understanding of 'customer service'. I kept meaning to go in to see what it was like, but its lack of appeal kept me away.

Following the road past the Barbican led me past the house of Maria Skłodowska, better known as Marie Curie. The house is at 16 Freta and used to be covered in garish paintings, mainly featuring Polonium and Radium – the two elements she discovered. Thank goodness that it has now been repainted more or less as it was in her day.

One year (when it had the garish outside) I went round the museum. The exhibits were mainly photographs and information boards. This is not surprising, given that it will be difficult to get hold of any of her possessions, but it was a pleasant visit to the house where she grew up. More about her in the next chapter.

For this initial trip, I retraced my steps and turned left into Krzywe Kolo along the old walls. Eventually this led me to a part of Warsaw that could have been straight out of the TV series *The Polish Officer*. This came out at the Old Town Square, which was a suitable place and time to search for some food and a beer.

That first evening I missed out on seeing Kanonia – the street that is at the rear of the cathedral – and which is even more *The Polish Officer*, with arches, a little square and buildings which would have been identical to those at the start of the second world war.

There is a bell in the centre of a little square which, so the tourist guides will tell you, is to be walked round three times while touching it. If you do this, then you will return to Warsaw. You will see many parties being led by a tour guide who do this. Personally, I have never done it and I have returned to Warsaw several times. But it seems to keep the tourists and the guides happy.

There is a house in the corner of the buildings near the bell, with narrow windows. This is reported to be the smallest house in Warsaw, but the myth is laid bare when you go round to the other side, to see that it splays into a much wider house with views over the viewing spot you have just come from.

The brick building that you see in Kanonia will

remind you of a building in Swiętojańska – the cathedral – for what you see here is the rear. Going under the arch brings you to the side of the cathedral. If you are there at around 2:15 in the afternoon, you might want to go in to listen to an organ recital. I went once and it was an accomplished performance, although I have heard better organs, which is not to say that this is a bad one – it's just that I have heard better ones.

The cathedral has been well restored, given the level of destruction it received during the war, so is well worth a visit. Just make sure that there is not a service! This might not be an easy thing to do, given that many important events take place in the cathedral.

Whichever exit you choose from Kanonia, you will end up in Castle Square.

The most important building in Castle Square is the castle. It nearly was not so, for after the 1944 Rising, Hitler ordered its complete destruction, along with the rest of Warsaw. His outright hatred of the Poles can be realised when you appreciate that he was facing the advancing Anglo-American troops in France and that the army divisions held in Warsaw could have been very useful on the Western Front.

The castle, being of very solid construction, as a castle should be, could not be bulldozed, so holes were drilled into the walls and dynamite was inserted. It took some time to destroy it.

Every night, brave resistance fighters would search through the rubble and retrieve fragments. It was from these fragments that the reconstruction became possible.

It is well worth visiting the interior of the castle. The entrance is via the door on Castle Square. Tickets are obtained from a separate ticket office and not at the entrance to the castle, which can be confusing. Tickets to the right, entrance to the left.

It is recommended that you get the audio guide to get the full experience. This will point out every significant object as you take the tour along the corridors and through the rooms.

Remember that this was totally destroyed and what you see is the result of painstaking research, exquisite craftsmanship and heroism shown by those who saved the fragments. Funding was done by appeal to the Polish diaspora.

You have only to look at the marquetry on the floors, the mouldings on the doors and mirrors, and the chandeliers to realise how many fragments had to be retrieved, in the dark, after curfew and with an ever-present fear of death if seen. This knowledge should add excitement to what you see. I have been round the castle three times and each time I have been humbled by what the Poles did to retrieve one of their historic monuments. The only other time I felt like that was while touring the inside of Windsor castle a few years after the devastating fire.

There is one story that I particularly like. It concerns the silver Polish eagles behind the throne in the Throne Room.

All of the silver eagles had been lost. There were

photographs of the Throne Room showing the eagles, but not in enough detail to allow them to be reproduced.

Then an ex-Gestapo man, presumably riddled with guilt, sent an eagle that he had stolen from the Throne Room as a souvenir. From that eagle the others could be reproduced and placed where the old photos showed them to belong.

One last thing to see, before going off to find refreshment, is the Copper Roofed Palace, or, as the literal Polish translation would have it: the Palace Under Sheet Metal. You cannot mistake it. It is the white palace with the green roof.

There is more to see in the Old and New towns, but now it is time to get some food and perhaps a beer.

Marie Curie

Marie Curie was probably the most amazing woman in history. Born Maria Skłodowska (pron. *Skwodoffska)* on 7th November 1867, she lived in the house at 16 Freta Street, with her four siblings: three sisters and a brother.

At the time she was growing up, Warsaw was part of the Russian empire and sensible people with government jobs did not upset the ruling elite. Unless you were Maria's father. He backed the wrong side in the 1863-4 uprising aimed at restoring Poland's national independence. As a result the family fell on difficult times.

She went to live with some relatives who owned land, working as a governess. It was here that she fell in love with the son, Kazimierz Zorawski, but his parents forbade him to marry such a penniless woman. Although he became a professor of Mathematics at Warsaw Polytechnic, he never achieved her greatness and he never lost his love for her. Theirs is a story ready for Hollywood treatment.

She moved to Paris in 1891, aged 24, to join her elder sister, Bronisława. She continued studying at the University of Paris, but always had the intention of returning to Poland.

It is worth noting at this point that neither Oxford nor Cambridge accepted women students at this time.

Her first work in Paris was a commission to investigate the magnetic properties of various steels.

She was introduced to Pierre Curie by a mutual friend, who had heard of her need for laboratory space and thought that Pierre had some. Unfortunately, he did not have much, but that did not stop him from letting her squeeze in to his lab. She was still planning to return to Poland, so she refused his first offer of marriage. However, she failed to get a post at Krakow university because she was a woman, so she returned to France and married Pierre in 1895 at the age of 28. Pierre was some eight years older than Maria.

Pierre was pretty bright, gaining his bachelor's degree in maths at the age of sixteen.

With his brother Jacques, he discovered piezoelectricity, which is the electricity generated by compressing crystals. To go further in this work, some sensitive measuring devices were needed, one of which was the piezoelectric quartz electrometer.

In 1881, the brothers demonstrated the reverse effect - namely the deformation of crystals when subjected to an electric field.

For his doctoral thesis, Pierre studied magnetism of various types and discovered Curie's Law, which showed that the amount of induced magnetism in a material was equal to the strength of the applied magnetic field and inversely proportional to temperature. That is to say that the induced field reduces as temperature increases.

As part of this equation he found that the

material in which the induced field was created had a value that indicted how much induced magnetism could be generated. This value became the Curie Constant, specific for each material.

He also discovered that there was a temperature, above which ferro-magnetic materials lost their magnetism. This is the Curie Temperature.

As the forces being measured were e very small, he developed a highly-sensitive torsion balance. This balance would be of great value in their work on Radium, which they first published in 1898.

Pierre's magnetometer would later be used to determine that there were three types of radioactive radiation, depending on how they affected a magnetic field. These were the alpha, beta and gamma radiations.

At Maria's insistence, Pierre submitted his work on magnetism for his doctorate thesis, and he obtained his PhD in the same year that they married – 1895.

In 1895 Wilhelm Roentgen discovered the existence of X-Rays, although the mechanism of their production was not known.

The following year, Henri Becquerel discovered that uranium salts gave off rays similar to X-Rays.

Henri Becquerel had detected radioactivity (although he did not call it that). He had been working on phosphorescence, which is the emission of light from something that is illuminated by light of a different colour. He knew of the work of Rontgen and wondered if phosphorescent salts, like those of uranium, might emit X rays when subjected to strong sunlight. (He could never have done this work in Glasgow!) He one day fortuitously left a piece of uranium on a piece of unexposed film in a drawer and found that the film had an image of the uranium. After a lot of experimenting, he came to the conclusion that the emissions were coming from uranium itself. As applying a magnetic field was in vogue, he passed the emissions through a magnetic field and found that the beam deflected up, down or not at all, concluding that there were three parts to the radiation: positive, negative and neutral.

Maria took these two pieces of research and decided to investigate further, with a possible thesis at the end.

Using Pierre's electrometer, she found that the amount of radiation from uranium depended only on the quantity of uranium present. She hypothesised that it was the uranium atom that was the source of the radiation and not the interaction of molecules. At a time when the belief in the scientific world was that atoms were indivisible, this was some leap of imagination.

In 1897 her daughter Irene was born, but still Maria continued working. The laboratory where she and Pierre worked was little more than a large shed that was cold and damp in winter. She was also working with materials that were radioactive (although the term was yet to be invented and the damaging effects of radiation were unknown at the time.

And then, to cap it all, she was not given a research grant, but had to do research on behalf of metallurgical and mining companies.

So there she was, with baby, working in a damp and cold shed, lecturing to make some income and doing research with dangerous materials when her work involved two minerals – pitchblende and torbernite.

Her work with the electrometer showed that pitchblende was four times as active as uranium metal and torbernite twice as much. She concluded that these minerals must contain a highly radioactive substance in addition to uranium.

She then systematically searched for other substances that emitted radiation and found that thorium did. She did not get the credit for this as a German scientist had published his work on thorium two months earlier, in which he described its radioactivity.

In July 1898, she and Pierre jointly published a paper announcing the existence of a new element, Polonium, named after Maria's home country. This was relatively easy, because Polonium resembles Bismuth, and there was no bismuth in the ore, so it was easily separated.

In December 1898, they announced the existence of a second element, Radium,. However, Radium (which she named after the Latin for 'ray') resembled Barium, and the ore contained Barium. She only obtained a salt of Radium by a process of differential crystallisation, something that Pierre was expert in. The task was enormous, with a ton of ore yielding only one-tenth of one gram of radium chloride. It took another eight years (to 1910) to get the pure metal.

They also coined the word 'radioactivity'.

She shared the third Nobel Prize ever awarded in Physics, with her husband, Pierre, and the great Henri Becquerel. This was in 1903.

There had been three previous winners. In 1901 the first awarded physics prize went to Wilhelm Conrad Roentgen for his work on X Rays. The citation read "in recognition of the extraordinary services he has rendered by the discovery of the remarkable rays subsequently named after him." The power of X Rays is still measured in Roentgens.

The 1902 prize was shared between Hendrick Lorentz and Pieter Zeeman for work on the Zeeman effect. This is the effect on a spectrum line when a magnetic field is applied to light. (No, I don't really. understand it either.). There is a Faraday Effect when rays are passed through a magnetic field and the Magneto-optic Kerr effect that describes light that is reflected from a magnetic surface. It just goes to show how much fun physicists can have with magnets and light, only to spoil it for the rest of us by explaining what they see in terms of mathematical formulae that make no sense to a non-physicist.

Anyway, we digress.

Having awarded the 1901 prize to one person, and the 1902 prize to two people, it was time to award the 1903 physics prize to three people. However, this was only at the insistence of Pierre, who told the Nobel committee that his wife had done as much work as he had and that, if they could not name her on the award, then he would be unable to accept it.

They relented.

One has to remember that women would only be accepted into Oxford University on a par with men, as medical students in 1917, and other disciplines only accepted women as the equals of men in 1920. Dorothy Hodgkin (1910-1994), Britain's only female Nobel Prize winner in chemistry (1964), experienced obstacles to studying chemistry, starting with her grammar school in Beccles only allowing two girls to study chemistry. Between 1927 and 1957, the number of women students at Oxford University was limited to a quarter of the men.

Becquerel's citation read "in recognition of the extraordinary services he has rendered by his discovery of spontaneous radioactivity."

The citation for Pierre and Marie Curie read "in recognition of the extraordinary services they have rendered by their joint researches on the radiation phenomena discovered by Professor Henri Becquerel."

In 1906, Pierre Curie was killed in a street accident, when the wheel of a horse-drawn carriage ran over his head, crushing his skull. Maria was devastated.

It was for the discovery of Radium and Polonium that she won the Nobel Prize for Chemistry in 1911 – the eleventh person to do so in eleven years, as there was only one winner each year.

Only six laureates have won more than one prize:

International Committee of the Red Cross – 3 times for Peace

UNHCR – twice for Peace

John Bardeen – twice for Physics

Frederick Sanger – twice for Chemistry

Linus Pauling – for Chemistry and Peace

Marie Skłodowska-Curie – for Physics and Chemistry

Polonium is difficult to isolate because it does not last long. It has a half life of only 136 days as it decays into lead. This makes it highly dangerous, as Mr Litvinienko found out when he was poisoned with it in London on 1st November 2006. He was poisoned with approximately one-millionth of a gram, which was enough to kill him slowly over a three week period. Had more been used, he would have died quicker. Polonium is ten million times as lethal as cyanide,

Polonium occurs in uranium ores in small quantities, where it is a product of decaying Uranium 238, before the Polonium itself decays into lead. These days it is produced by bombarding Bismuth with neutrons.

Maria's daughter, Irene, won the Nobel Prize for Chemistry with her husband, Jean-Frederique Joliot. He was the youngest laureate ever to be awarded the Nobel Prize for Chemistry, at the age of 35. She is commemorated with a bus stop named Joliot-Curie. It is in the region of Radio Poland, near the M1 station of

Wierzbno.

Maria's immediate family therefore had five Nobel Prizes between them: Maria (2), husband Pierre (1), daughter Irene (1) and son-in-law Jean-Frederique (1)

Maria designed a mobile X-ray unit in the First World War for the French army that led to many lives being saved.

She also set up two Radium institutes – one in Paris and the other in Warsaw. These looked at uses of Radium, especially in the treatment of cancers.

She died of radiation exposure in 1934 and was buried with her husband. However, in 1995 the French Government decided that she and Pierre were to be given the highest honour by being buried in the Pantheon. During the preparations, the radioactivity of her body was measured to see if it would be safe to handle. Radium has a half life of sixteen thousand years, so any radium in her body would have hardly decayed. Her body was only slightly more radioactive than the average Parisian cellar. Polonium has a half life of 136 days, so any Polonium in her body would have almost entirely decayed, but it was concluded that her death had been caused by radiation from the mobile X-ray units, as she had taken many X-rays during WW1 without protecting herself.

In April 1995, the bodies of her and her husband were transferred, with full State fanfare, to the holy of holies that is the Pantheon in Paris.

An amazing woman, the like of which we are unlikely to see again.

And she lived for a time in Freta Street, Warsaw.

She is commemorated in Warsaw by a lovely statue in the New Town, which overlooks the Vistula. There is also a commemorative statue in the Maria Skłodowka-Curie park on Ul. Wawelska by Ul. Marii Skłodowkiej-Curie near the department of Chemistry at the University of Warsaw.

Długa – Plac Bankowy – Andersa

From Freta you can take a walk, as I did, down ul. Długa. Długa means 'long'. There are no buses or trams along this straight road, so you should find it relatively quiet, except for the cars, but even they are not numerous.

Długa is straight and tree-lined, going in a south-westerly direction from the New Town.

On the left is the church of the Holy Spirit. There has been a church associated with the care of the sick and travellers since the fourteenth century. Originally built in the Gothic style, it was demolished during the Swedish invasion of 1655-60, but rebuilt some fifty years later in the current Baroque style. It was almost completely destroyed in the Warsaw Rising of 1944 and rebuilt by 1956.

As you walk down Długa, you will leave the tourists, who tend to walk from the Old Town to the New Town and back along the same route.

After the government offices behind the church, there is Ulica Jana Kilinskiego, named after the prominent burgher of the early 1790's who formed a unit of the National Militia in 1794 and led them against the occupying garrison of Russian soldiers. This was the Warsaw Uprising of 1794 and part of the greater Kościuszko Rising, which ultimately failed and Kilinski found himself a resident of the :Peter and Paul Fortress in St. Petersburg for a couple of years. He never got on with the Russians after that and they later forcibly removed him to Russia, where they could keep a close eye on him. They returned him to Warsaw, presumably when he was no further danger, and he died there in 1819. There is a statue of him, waving a sword, on Podwale by Ulica Kapitulna.

You can get to Podwale down Ulica Jan Kilinskiego and turn right to his monument, but if you do this, as you enter Podwale, you should be facing my favourite monument in all of Warsaw. It is the monument to the Little Insurgent, or Pomnik Małego Powstańca.

This statue is rife with inaccuracies, but it captures the heart of the observer, with the helmet that is too large and the sub-machine gun which is held, more as in a movie rather than in war. In the Warsaw Rising of 1944, youngsters played a very important part in carrying messages and acting as observers, but they never used weapons, presumably because there were not enough to go round and what were available would be more useful in the hands of someone older.

The artistry of the sculptor, Jerzy Januskiewicz in 1946, is perfect in its portrayal of sadness (you have a feeling that he is not really a soldier and will be doomed under the might of the Nazis); the portrayal of inclusivity (for every Warszavian can play a part in the Rising) and the horror of war, when such small people are dragged in to the conflict.

On several occasions I have seen Scout neckerchiefs around his neck, for Boy Scouts played a significant role in the Rising and the Little Insurgent is their, and my, hero.

If you carry on, past the Little Insurgent and get to the statue of Jan Kilinski, turn right up Kapitulna and at the end you will be facing Pałac Paca on Miodowa (Honey Street). Turning right brings you to the Archbishop's Palace.

Walking past this, one comes to the Aleksandra Zelwerowicza theatre school. Founded in Łódź in 1946, presumably to go with the film school there, and moved to Warsaw in 1949. It is a public seat of higher education, specialising in the theatre arts and has many distinguished Polish actors who were trained there.

Opposite is Schiller street. Not named after the German poet, but the first Rector of the Stage School: Leon Schiller. He was rector from 1946 to 1949. He was a theatre and film director, as well as a theatre theoretician. As if this was not enough, he wrote screenplays for radio and theatre and composed music.

In 1955 the school gained a patron, Aleksander Zelwerowicz, but did not receive its current name until 1996. Zelwerowicz was an actor, director and teacher and is one of the Polish Righteous Among the Nations – an award given to people who have saved Jews from extermination during the Holocaust. Over a quarter of the twenty-six thousand people awarded this honour, are Polish, which is truly amazing, considering the retribution handed out by the Nazis to anybody who helped Jews escape the Final Solution. It is a proud record that should not be underestimated.

The theatre school was demolished after the 1944 Rising and rebuilt after the war.

Walking onwards you come back to Długa, where, on the corner, is the garrison church of the army in Warsaw and the representative cathedral of the whole Polish army.

Like most buildings in Warsaw, it was severely damaged in the 1944 Rising, being targetted by the Luftwaffe. It was fought over because of its western tower, which was a good observation post, and its crypt, which was made into a field hospital. The Nazis destroyed it after the 1944 Rising and it was restored between 1946 and 1960 to its former glory.

Opposite the field cathedral is a square with two monuments to the Rising of 1944.

There is the communist-brutal heroic representation of charging Polish soldiers attacking the enemy. This is in the shadow of the new building that houses the supreme courts of justice.

Then there is the moving sculpture, showing resistance fighters emerging from the sewers via a manhole, while colleagues look out for approaching Nazis.

During the week, there are usually parties of schoolchildren at these monuments as they are taught Polish history. It is very unlikely that the Poles will forget their history.

The ugly new building is the Supreme Court and the phrases on the pillars are taken from the Constitution.

The name of the square is Płac Krasinskich, which gives a clue as to the name of the old palace opposite the Supreme Court. It is Krasiński palace with its large gardens behind that are entered through a gate to the left of the palace.

The palace was designed by the Dutch architect, Tylman von Gameren, who designed many of the buildings of that period (late seventeenth century). Krasiński Palace was constructed between 1677 and 1683 for Jan Dobrogost Krasiński, a man who came from a privileged background.

When I was last there, the palace was undergoing renovations, courtesy of funding from the EU and the Norwegian State Fund. No doubt it will be lovely when finished.

The gardens are wooded, with a lake. Warszawians like feeding the ducks on the lake, which is reached by walking away from the palace. On the lake is a sculpture.

Continuing the walk away from the palace brings one to the "Heroes of the Ghetto" Street. This commemorates the April 1943 uprising in the ghetto of the Jews. This is not to be confused with the Warsaw Rising of September 1944.Ghetto Rising

The Ghetto Rising came about when the remaining Jews in the walled ghetto realised for certain that the people who had been taken from the ghetto had not gone to a better life, but to Treblinka, where they were murdered. Supplied with arms by the AK, the Jews fought a hopeless fight against the might of the Nazis, who fought with machine guns, artillery and flamethrowers. At least they died fighting.

After the ghetto rising was over, Hitler ordered the complete destruction of the ghetto. I have seen photos of the result. The whole area is flattened to rubble, except for St. Augustine's church on Nowolipkie, which was used as a warehouse.

General Władysław Albert Anders

Crossing the street brings a small park and in this park is a monument to the Battle of Monte Casino. The main road beyond is Andersa, named after a superb general of the second world war. General Władysław Albert Anders was born in 1892 and is renowned for two things: letting me be born and winning the Battle of Monte Casino.

My father was one of the Polish Army held in Russian prisoner-of-war camps, who was moved south to Tehran, rather than being incorporated into the Russian Army, where they would almost certainly have died.

When Poland was partitioned between the Nazis and the Russians in 1939, according to the provisions of the Ribbentrop-Molotov Pact of August 1939, members of the Polish Army in east Poland were taken by the Russians to labour camps in Siberia and Kazakhstan. My father was one of these to be sent to a remote camp in Siberia, where they worked to make a railway in the Pechora River area. Of the 60,000 prisoners sent there, only 20,000 survived.

When Hitler attacked the Russians in 1941, the fate of these prisoners was a problem. Stalin wanted them to form a Polish subsection of the Russian Army, whereas the Poles wanted to be a separate army. How General Anders negotiated the exodus of the Polish Army and accompanying civilians to Persia is a mystery, but it was pure genius.

Many of the army went on to fight at Monte Casino – a monastery built at the top of a hill that blocked any movement of the Allied Army up the Italian peninsula. Four different groups had tried to capture this hill, and it was only at the fifth attempt, by the Poles under the command of General Anders, that it was captured., but with great loss of life

The monument in the park commemorates this battle.

General Anders was much decorated by Poland and other countries, including Britain, who awarded him (amongst other honours) with Honorary Companion of the Order of the Bath.

He was married twice and his daughter Anna Maria by his second wife, entered Polish politics and had a successful career.

Walking north through the park, parallel to Andersa, one emerges at the transport stops for Muranow. If feeling energetic, walk to the next major intersection. If feeling a little tired, then take any tram to the next stop of Muranowska, named after the road that joins Andersa at this point. The road changes its name to Stawki on the western side of Andersa.

The road splits into two parts at this point and in

the middle of the two sections is the Monument to the Fallen and Murdered in the East.

Monument to the Fallen and Murdered in the East

The monument and its title pull no punches and for obvious reasons could not have been erected during the post-war Russian dominance of Poland. It was unveiled on 17th September 1995, on the 56th anniversary of the invasion of Poland by Russia.

It was designed by Maksimilian Biskupski in 1991. Construction started a month before its official unveiling.

The monument is moving. It consists of a flatbed rail wagon with lots of crosses stacked on it: most vertical; some horizontal. The whole edifice is rough and coloured charcoal grey. It looks unfinished, as though a tale had to be told and there was little time in which to do it. The immediate impression is death while working on a railway.

In front of the wagon are sleepers, each one of which denotes a transit point or a destination in the *gulag* where Poles died or were murdered. Katyn is included, as well as the notorious Lubianka prison. I recognised a couple of places my father had been. It was very emotional.

One sleeper, without a name on it, shows hands – as though the people being buried below the sleeper are striving to get out

As a monument, it is exactly right for what it

depicts.

During the time that Poland was under the control of the Russians (until1989), there was never mention of the deportations and murders, so it was necessary for the Polish population to be educated in the real history of Poland. This monument pulls no punches: it accuses Russia of murdering Polish citizens and members of the armed forces at a large number of locations.

I have visited this site three times – once at night and once in the sunshine. On both occasions it was moving. The night experience was more eerie as the crosses took on shadows and you feared that, had you been alive in those years, you could be represented by one of the crosses. The daytime experience showed quite clearly that there was death.

The third time I visited was with my daughter in 2018, when it was being renovated. This was very unfortunate, as I wanted her to experience the monument up close.

I was grateful to General Anders for getting my father out of that Hell so that he could be my Dad and my daughter's Grandfather.

Ratusz Arsenał

It is time to visit Ratusz Arsenał, which is at the end of Ul. Długa.

To do this, take any southbound tram for two stops. As you travel, reflect that the distance between Stawki and Ratusz Arsenał is approximately half the length of the Jewish Ghetto of 1940.

We left Ul. Długa at Miodowa so that we could wander through Krasiński gardens. What we missed we need not worry about. The main building on this part of Długa is the Archaeological Museum.

I haven't been to the Archaeological Museum, because it is not really my thing, but while I was at the Tourist Information Office, a British couple arrived and seemed most concerned that they could visit the Archaeological Museum, to the exclusion of all other attractions. They were quite old, but not old enough to be of interest to archaeologists. But if they had come all the way to Warsaw for that museum, it must be worth visiting, so perhaps that is a joy to have on another day.

Outside the museum, which is at the corner on Długa, there is a tribute to those who gave their lives for others. Ratusz Arsenał is a busy transport interchange, with Metro on the M1, or north-south line, and Ul. Solidarność to the east and west and Marszałkowska to the south, all of which have trams and buses. It is a useful interchange for going to the Old Town and Praga. It seems that I end up visiting it several times every time I go to Warsaw.

Fountain Park

Throughout the summer months on Friday and Saturday evenings after dusk, which means at 9pm or 9:30pm, depending on month of the year, there is a performance at the Fountain Park lasting approximately half an hour. So what can you expect?

Firstly, crowds. This is a popular event amongst Warszawians, who bring the family. There are therefore many children. And where there are children, there are street vendors. Be prepared to see lots of children with brightly coloured glowing sticks, bracelets, swords and other shapes about their persons. Until the show starts, these are the only means of illumination. It might be worthwhile to do as prescient Poles do and bring along a torch.

Because it is popular, it is wise to arrive early and try to find somewhere to sit near the north western end of the pool.

So where is it?

It is on the left bank of the Visła, north of the Old Town, next to Wybzeża Gdańskii, where the nearest bus stop is Boleść. However, I have always approached it from the Old Town from the Market Square. Go down the Stone Steps just off the north eastern corner of the square and turn left at the bottom. The road is Bugaj and it leads onto Ul. Mostowa. You turn right and should follow this downhill until you see Ul. Rybaki on the left. There should be plenty of crowds to guide you. Rybaki takes you into the park and you will come to the fountain pond on your right. You need to try to get a spot at the far end of the pond.

I have seen a couple of shows, so I give you an idea of what to expect.

Firstly, everybody wants a seat around the perimeter of the pond, especially children, so hope that the child who sits in front of you (unless you decide to sit on the wall round the pond) to be of the small variety.

Secondly, there is quite a long session of testing the fountains and lights, so this gives you a chance to move your position if required.

The show will start fairly promptly, following an announcement in Polish and English. The narration of the show will only be in Polish and will be accompanied by a spray wall of water, onto which is projected scenes from the story and the other fountains will shoot jets into the air, accompanied by light changes.

It is all very spectacular.

After the show, lots of people will make their way along the path the way you came and the few lucky ones will try to manipulate their cars out of the limited car park, adding to the chaos.

If you make it back to the Market Square, it is probably time for a beer, or other refreshment.

Partitions and Risings

While having a well-earned beer, it might be a good time to catch up on some of the earlier history of Poland, so that the rest of this book falls into context.

Poland was partitioned three times in the late 1700's. Unsurprisingly, there were uprisings. The main ones were in 1830 and 1863. Poland did not become a country again until 1918, so some knowledge of this 123 year period will help to understand a lot of the present.

Partitions

Until 1772, Poland was actually part of the Lithuanian-Polish Commonwealth. This had been in effect informally since 1386, when the Polish queen Hedwig married the Lithuanian Grand Duke Jogaila, who then became crowned king Władysław II Jagiełło of the Polish-Lithuanian Union.

The Poles and Lithuanians were allies in many joint battles, including the Battle of Grunwald (15th July 1410), also known as the Battle of Tannenburg. This battle was the culmination of Lithuanians rising against the Teutonic Knights, who were invading the country and generally causing trouble. In this the Lithuanians were supported by the Poles. The knights were defeated, but managed to withstand the siege of their capital city at Malbork.

However, the arrangement was not formalised until the Union of Lublin was signed in Lublin in July 1569. This made the Commonwealth into the largest and most populous country in Europe, with an area that would eventually extend to a million square kilometres of land, and a population of some 11 million.

The Union of Lublin was one of the major achievements of Sigismund II Augustus. Yes – he of the column fame.

The Commonwealth had many attributes regarded as common today. It was a constitutional monarchy with checks on the monarch. This was enacted via the Sejm (parliament) controlled by the Szlachta (nobility).

It was characterised by a wide ethnic diversity and religious freedom, even though the recognised religion was Roman Catholicism. This was enshrined in the Constitution of May 3rd 1791 – more of which later.

The period between the Union of Lublin and the first partition was regarded as the most prosperous period of Polish history to date, although if one was a peasant in that feudal period, one might have disagreed with this statement.

First Partition

The first partition of the Lithuanian-Polish Commonwealth took place on August 5th 1772. This came about due to a combination of factors – the growing weakness of the Commonwealth and the growing might of Russia, especially after it had defeated the Ottoman empire in the Russo-Turkish War of 1768-1774.

The Poles had become weakened by a civil war (1768-1772), caused by the Bar Confederation wanting to defend Poland against internal and external attacks. The founders of the Bar Confederation included wealthy families with names like Krasiński, Radziwiłł and Pulaski. Meeting at Bar, a fortress located in what is now Ukraine, the nobles vowed to oppose Russian influence and the reforms of Stanisław II Augustus, which would have reduced their power.

Austria was particularly concerned about the shift in power to Russia and contemplated attacking Russia, but the French intervened and suggested things might settle if Austria took a bit of land from Prussia, Prussia took a bit of Poland to compensate and Russia took a bit of eastern Poland to stop its antagonism towards Austria.

In this first partition, the commonwealth lost 30% of its land, 50% of its population and Prussia controlled 80% of its exports through the port of Danzig (Gdansk). Prussia then applied steep duties on trade and this brought about the speedier demise of the Commonwealth.

Powerless to resist the partition militarially, and with no other country prepared to come to its aid, the Sejm had no option but to sign the Partition Treaty, which it did on September 18 1773.

Second Partition

By 1790, the Commonwealth had been further weakened. At the same time, Prussia was fearful that it could be attacked by an Austro-Russian alliance, so the two countries signed the Polish Prussian Pact, which was valuable to the Commonwealth because it wanted to carry out some internal reforms without interference from foreign powers.

On 3rd May 1791, these reforms were encapsulated in the Constitution, which extended the franchise to the bourgeoisie, much to the annoyance of the Szlachta, who saw their influence (and quality of life) diminishing. With the help of Russia, the Szlachta defeated the pro-constitution side. The Szlachta thought that Russia would restore for them the Golden Age of prosperity. No such thing. The Prussians failed to keep the Polish Prussian Pact, saying that they were not consulted about the Constitution and the Russians accused the Poles of radical Jacobinism and invaded. The Prussians and Russians clubbed together and each took as much of Poland as they wanted. Poland was left with one third of its 1772 population.

Third Partition

After the Second Partition, the Poles were left with no Constitution and ruled by foreign powers. (Even what was left of the country was garrisoned by Russians.) Led by Tadeusz Kościuszko and Josef Poniatowski, the

Kościuszko Uprising began on March 15th 1794. This was earlier than he had anticipated because the Russians were planning to run down the Polish army and incorporate the rump into the Russian army. General Antoni Madalinski, commander of 1,500 cavalrymen, refused to demobilise. This defiance happened near Krakow. The Russian army in Krakow was despatched to handle the rebellion, which had ignited other rebellions throughout Poland.

Kościuszko had been planning to attack the Russian garrison and steal their arms. Instead, he announced the revolution on 24th March 1794.

Kościuszko

It is worth diverting from history to learn more about Andrzej Tadeusz Bonawentura Kościuszko. After all, he is more important than Warsaw. Warsaw Indiana that is. Kościuszko County is located in Indiana. In 2010 it had a population of 77,358. Its county seat is Warsaw, which in 2010 only had a population of 13,559. So he must have been quite a character to have a whole county named after him, whereas the capital of Poland only has a small city named after it.

He was born on 4th February 1746 in a manor house on the Mereczowszczyzna estate near Brest-Litowsk, which was in Lithuania. It is unimportant to know the name of the estate, but I had to include it as it contains a goodly collection of z's. It will also be fun for you to try to pronounce it, now that you are getting used to Polish words.

Anyway, our digression is digressing, so back to the man.

At the age of 20 he graduated from the Corps of Cadets in Warsaw. That would be in 1766. The civil war of the Bar Confederation started in 1768 and Kościuszko moved to France in 1769 to continue his studies, returning to the Commonwealth in 1774, just two years after the first partition.

There was no sign of a military career, for he entered the house of Jósef Sywester Sosnowski as a tutor, and shortly after tried to elope with his employer's daughter, which was not a good move as it resulted in him being beaten up by his employer's retainers.

He returned to France and then joined the Continental Army to fight in the American War of Independence in 1776. He had the rank of colonel.

An accomplished military architect, he designed and oversaw the construction of several state-of-the-art fortifications, including those at West Point in 1783.

He returned to the Commonwealth in 1784, where he became a major-general in the Polish-Lithuanian Commonwealth Army in 1789 and after the Second Partition of Poland in 1792. In March 1794, as commander-in-chief, he organised an uprising against the Russians

Now back to the Third Partition and the Kościuszko Uprising...

Catherine the Great ordered the deployment of

the corps of Major General Fiodor Denisov to attack Krakow and his and Kościuszko's forces met at a village called Raclawice. Kościuszko won and there are locations in Warsaw named after the battle, some of which you will pass on the way to the airport.

Meanwhile, in early April, those Polish forces which were being sent to join the Russian army, were based around Lublin: They revolted and joined the revolution.

Meanwhile, in Warsaw, the Russians were rounding up those they suspected of supporting the revolution. They also disarmed the weak Polish garrison in Warsaw. However, General Stanisław Mokronowski attacked the arsenal on Ul. Miodowa. This was the precursor to an attack on the Russian garrison in Warsaw, led by Jan Kilinski. (Remember his statue on Podwale?) Over two days of heavy fighting, the Russian garrison, originally 5,000 strong, lost between 2,000 and 4,000 men.

One black mark against the insurgents was the killing of unarmed Russian soldiers who were attending an Easter service. This was the excuse for vengeance later.

Kościuszko was not only a soldier, but he was a reformer. On 7th May 1794 he announced the Proclamation of Połaniec, in which he recognised that peasants were part of the Polish nation (for the first time in its history), partially abolished serfdom; granted civil liberties to all peasants and provided them with state help against abuses by the nobility. Although opposed by the nobility, it did result in attracting many peasants to the ranks of the revolutionaries.

On 6th June Kościuszko was defeated at the Battle of Szczekociny by a combined Prussian-Russian force. On 8th June the Poles lost the Battle of Chełm.

Kosciusko withdrew all Polish forces to Warsaw. On 15th June. Krakow was taken by the Russians unopposed.

Opposition in Lithuania was crushed by the Russians, but in Greater Poland there was more success. Jan Henryk Dąbrowski (note the name – it comes up later) won the Battle of Bydgoszcz on 2nd October.

The Russians founded a new corps and sent it into Poland with the aim of joining with the corps of General Fersen, who was already there.

In an attempt to stop the forces from combining, Kościuszko sent General Sierakowski to prevent this from happening. At the Battle of Maciejowice, Kościuszko was wounded and captured. He was sent to Saint Petersburg, where he was held a prisoner until the death of Catherine the Great in 1796, when he was pardoned by her successor, Tsar Paul I. He went to live in the United States, where he was friends with Thomas Jefferson, but returned to Europe, where he lived in Switzerland until his death in 1817.

With the loss of Kościuszko, the resistance was taken over by Tomasz Wawrzecki and (at a time like this) a power struggle developed between the Poles on the left (the Jacobins) and those on the right (the nobility).

On 4th November 1794, the Battle of Praga was won by the Russians after four hours of hand-to-hand fighting. The Cossacks were let loose on the population and 20,000 Poles were murdered. Poland was broken. The Third Partition took place as the remainder of the country was shared out between the three occupiers. It would disappear as a country from the map for 123 years.

Great Poland Uprising 1806

This was a military insurrection led by Jan Henryk Dąbrowski to help the advancing French army advance through Prussia and thereby liberate Poland from Prussian occupation. It was one of the most successful uprisings in the history of Poland.

This was helped by the number of Poles in the Prussian army, who did not need much encouragement to desert and join the Polish army under Dąbrowski.

However, when it came to appointing the Chief of the War Office, where the two contenders were Josef Poniatowski and Dąbrowski, Napoleon, wanting to ensure the support of the Polish aristocracy, so chose Poniatowski.

The result of the battles and skirmishes was that the Duchy of Warsaw was recognised by the Kingdom of Prussia. The Prussian army, once thought invincible, had been wiped out, so that the only country facing the French was Russia.

Unfortunately, it was only as long as the French

had the upper hand that the Duchy of Poland survived. It did not survive beyond the Congress of Vienna in 1815.

1830 Uprising (November Uprising)

The Treaty of Vienna created the Kingdom of Poland, which was an area around Warsaw in the Russian Partition. It was semi-autonomous, with its own constitution. It also had its own parliament, army, courts and treasury. But the Tsar gradually diluted these. In 1815 the Tsar appointed Grand Duke Constantine Pavlovitch as Viceroy. Four years later, in 1819 he curtailed the freedom of the Press and introduced censorship. To go with this, he also introduced the secret police, who infiltrated resistance organisations. It got so bad that in 1825 the parliamentary sessions were held in secret.

On 24th May 1829, Nicholas I crowned himself King of Poland.

Meanwhile, Grand Duke Constantine was making himself unpopular with the army, especially the officer corps. He planned to use the Polish army to fight in the July Revolution in France and the Belgian Revolution in Belgium. This was a violation of the Constitution. On 29th November 1830 a group of officer cadets of the army school, led by Piotr Wysocki, started the armed struggle. They took arms from their garrison and attacked the Belweder Palace, the main home of the Grand Duke. However, he escaped, dressed as a woman.

The rebels then took the main city arsenal and, with newly-armed Polish civilians, they forced the Russian troops, based in the city, to the north of Warsaw.

The Administrative Council of the Sejm took control of the situation and men like Prince Adam Jerzy Czartoryski and Josef Chłopicki planned to negotiate with the Grand Duke so that matters could be settled peacefully. However, Maurycy Mochnatski and other radicals were having none of it. They wanted a national uprising.

Czartoryski agreed to let the Grand Duke depart with his troops, but Mochnatski distrusted this and set out to create what he called a Patriotic Club that would henceforth dictate the course of events. He planned to start a military campaign in Lithuania, so as to spare Poland the devastation of war and also to protect local food supplies. As a start, he would attack the Grand Duke and his troops (who had not yet departed). The Polish army joined the revolution.

To legalise the uprising, on 5th December Mochnatski appointed Chłopicki as Dictator of the Uprising. Chłopicki thought the whole thing was mad, but went along with it in the hope that he could avoid fighting breaking out.

He sent Prince Franciszek Ksawery Drucki-Lubecki to St. Petersburg to negotiate with the Tsar, but the Tsar was having none of it and gave no concessions. During the prince's absence, the Sejm had gone radical and demanded the complete freedom of Poland.

The prince returned on January 7th 1831. Chłopicki resigned the following day.

The radicals were now in control and on 25th January 1831 the Sejm effectively declared war on Russia by passing an Act of Dethronement to remove Nicholas as king of Poland.

Russia takes time to mobilise, but on February 4th 1831, 115,000 Russian troops marched into Poland. The first battle was on Valentine's Day, close to the village of Stoczek, which the Poles won. But it is difficult to stop a Russian steamroller and the Russians fought the Poles in three battles –Dobre, Wawer and Białołęka – on their way to Warsaw.

40,000 Poles faced 60,000 Russians at the Battle of Olszynka Grochowska, which lasted from 25 – 26 February. Losses on both sides were high, with some 7,000 Poles killed and 7,000 plus Russians killed.

The Poles were on their own. Although many of the populations of Europe had great sympathy for their cause, their governments offered no more than supportive words. Palmerston in Britain did not want to see a rising France, so maintained friendly terms with Russia (which could be a counterbalance). The Austrians and Prussians showed neutrality, but closed their borders to the passage of arms and ammunition to Poland.

In spite of risings in outlying parts of the former Polish-Lithuanian Commonwealth, one of which was by Emilia Plater (more of whom later), the Russians quickly exterminated these little local risings. A notorious slaughter of the inhabitants of the village of Ashmiany in Belarus occurred in this period.

A new Russian force arrived in Poland, but suffered many defeats in battle. However, the toll on the Poles was great, with the loss of 8,000 Polish lives.

The government did not help matters by not giving the peasants more rights, fearing that this would deter foreign governments from helping. So the enthusiasm of the peasants naturally waned and the tide fell in favour of the Russians. They encircled Warsaw.

Despite heroic resistance by General Józef Sowiński (more later), Wola fell to the Russians on 6th September. The army and the government retreated to the Modlin fortress. New plans were made, but not executed because news reached them that a crack unit of Poles, unable to join up with the main army, had crossed the Austrian border in Galicia and laid down their arms. On 5th October 1831, 20,000 men crossed the Prussian border and laid down their arms rather than submit to the Russians. The uprising was over. Russia took away what autonomy there was in Poland and made it into a province of Russia with direct rule from Moscow.

1863 Uprising (January Uprising)

All went quiet for a generation. The nobility increasingly hankered after the conditions that existed before the 1830 Uprising, but could do nothing about it. But then Russia had a bad time of it in the Crimean War of 1853 to 1856 and was weakened as a result. It took a more liberal attitude towards its subjects.

Polish youths' imagination was fired by the independence movement in Italy and the prospect of doing something similar in Poland took hold.

The Russian army in Warsaw applied a heavy hand to demonstrations, in which lives were lost in 1861 and 1862 at demonstrations. Leaders were rounded up and sent to Siberia. It was not a happy time.

The Polish underground government planned an organised strike against the Russians to start no later than the Spring of 1863.

However, Aleksander Wielopolski, the pro-Russian Pole who headed the civil service administration in the Russian partition, got wind of the trouble afoot and decided to do something about it. He had planned to introduce conscription into the Russian army to divert youth from resistance, and now he brought forward these plans to January 1863.

His plan backfired and, instead of defusing the situation, it triggered it. Some 10,000 men, mainly from the lower classes, rallied round the revolution.

At the time there were 90,000 soldiers of the Russian army in Poland. The resistance took the form of guerilla fighting.

This time round, the underground government decreed that all Poles were equal and that peasants who tilled soil would henceforth own that land, with compensation being paid by the government.

The government appealed to other countries for help. Governments did nothing, this being a rare peaceful time in Europe and governments did not want to upset this state, but citizens responded. It was estimated that those in the Polish cause rose to 35,000, but the Russians also raised the stakes by providing an army of 145,000 in Poland.

However, things had gone too far to give European governments a quiet life. Things were hotting up.

On February 8th 1863 the Prussians and Russians had signed the secret Alvenslaben Convention in which Prussia and Russia would jointly put down the Poles.

Napoleon III was seeking an alliance with Austria against the Prussians.

Britain did not want a Franco-Prussian war, which fortunately became less likely when Austria rejected Napoleon's advances as being against the interests of German-speaking people.

Britain then focused on ensuring that the French did not become allies of Russia, which seemed unlikely as Napoleon was supportive of the Poles.

France, Britain and Austria then started diplomacy and managed to agree on some limited concessions by Russia to Poland, but these fell well short of Polish expectations. Negotiations between Russia and the three western powers ended in September 1863.

On 17th October 1863, Polish General Romuald Traugutt managed to unite all the disparate groups under one national banner. Fighting continued throughout the winter of 1863-4, but there was no outside support.

Traugutt was taken on the night of 10th April 1864 and executed on 5th August by hanging in the Warsaw Citadel.

The Russians then ruined the Szlachta by taxing them heavily and giving their land to the peasants.

Russia was harsh in reprisals. Tens of thousands had been killed in some 850 battles and skirmishes. Hundreds of men were hanged; around 80,000 people were exiled to Siberia or other remote pars of Russia. Whole villages were burned down. The Szlachta lost lands and possessions through confiscation and exorbitant taxes. The whole population was Russified with the intention of destroying the Polish language and culture.

World War I

At the outbreak of World War I, the partitioning powers in Poland were on different sides. Russia was part of the Triple Entente of Britain, France and Russia, while Prussia and Austro-Hungary were part of the Triple Alliance, with Italy. For a Pole, whose side you fought on depended on where you lived. Two million Poles fought; 450,000 died. Poland as a county did not exist, so it was not on anybody's side.

1918 Poland Arises

Point thirteen of Woodrow Wilson's Fourteen Point Plan for what was to happen after the end of World War I was the creation of an independent Polish state. The inclusion of this was largely as a result of the personal friendship that existed between Ignacy Paderewski of Poland, and President of the USA, Woodrow Wilson himself.

1920-21 Battle of Warsaw

Not everybody agreed with this. Vladimir Lenin saw the route to world socialism passing to the West through Poland and drove his Bolshevik army through Poland towards Germany, where he was expecting a revolution. Perhaps he also wanted to recover the lost lands of the third partition. However, the squabbling Poles managed to unite themselves long enough to defeat the Russians at the Battle of Warsaw and to gain lands in Ukraine.

One of the generals on the losing side was one Josef Vissarionovitch dze Jughashvili, later to be known as Josef Stalin.

1939 -45 World War II

As far as Poland was concerned, the invasions of September 1939 could be regarded as an attempt to restore the partition. Although Britain declared war on Germany when the Nazis invaded Poland, in

practical terms little changed for some time.
More on the later wars later...

The Poniatowski Family

Now that we have an appreciation of some Polish history, we can see how one of its great families fitted in. This family has been very influential in Polish history and deserves some mention.

The first reference to the family appears to be in 1446, where they appeared in Poniatowa, a village some 40 kilometres west of Lublin. However, it was not until the late eighteenth century that they came to prominence, rising in the space of three generations from gentry to the elected king of Poland.

Stanisław Poniatowski (1676 – 1762) was probably the first to find fame in the classic way of being a military genius and winning battles.

Stanisław had many children. Two of his daughters are noteworthy because of who they married.

Ludwika Maria Poniatowska married Jan Jakub Zamoyski, a landed family based around Zamość, near Lublin and also very influential in Polish history.

Izabella Poniatowska married Jan Klemens Branicki, the last male survivor of the wealthy Branicki family. At the time of his marriage, he owned twelve towns, 257 villages and seventeen palaces. Izabella was his third wife and they had no children.

Interestingly, his first wife was Katarzyna Barbara Radziwiłł, a member of a prominent Polish-Lithuanian family. (Jackie Kennedy's sister, Lee, married into the

Radziwiłł family by marrying Stanisław Albrecht. He died in London in 1976, aged 62 and was buried in Fawley Court near the Thames in Henley, England.).

Stanisław Antoni Poniatowski

Stanisław's fifth son, Stanisław Antoni Poniatowski, was born 17th January 1732 and became King of Poland in 1764 at the age of 32, with the name Stanisław II Augustus

At the age of 23, he had arrived at the Russian Imperial Court in Saint Petersburg and became romantically involved with Catherine the Great. With her connivance he was elected King of Poland.

At that time the three adjacent empires of Prussia, Russia and Austria-Hungary, together with the Polish nobility (who wanted to retain their privileged lifestyle) wanted a weak Commonwealth. They all therefore opposed Stanisław's attempts at strengthening the Commonwealth.

The first action of the Polish nobles was to form a Confederation at the fortress at Bar in 1768. Its aim was to defend the internal and external independence of the Commonwealth. Externally against increasing Russian influence and internally against King Stanisław II, who was trying to limit the power of the wealthy magnates.

For some time, Russia had effectively controlled Poland, treating it as a vassal state. The nobles saw the weakness of the king in not standing up to the Russians, while at the same time undermining his powers.

The Confederation declared war on Russia and attacked Russian forces dotted around the Commonwealth.

Stanisław tried to mediate between the Confederation and Russia, but failed, so he attacked the confederation. It was civil war that lasted until 1772.

Not wanting to miss an opportunity, the Prussians and Austro-Hungarians carved slices of the Commonwealth for themselves, in what was to be known as the First Partition of Poland.

Although he won the civil war, Stanisław II was in a weak state. He tried to reform the country by adopting a new Constitution on May 3rd 1791. This enraged the nobles, whose powers were further reduced, so they formed a Confederation at Targowek in 1792. In the war that followed, Prince Josef Poniatowski bravely fought a rearguard action until told to desist by King Stanisław.

The Confederation won. As a result, King Stanisław II formally joined the Confederation.

Russia then invaded Poland and brought about the Second Parturition of Poland.

In 1795, the Third and final Partition of Poland took place and Poland effectively ceased to exist as a country.

Stripped of all power, Stanisław abdicated in November 1795 and spent the last years of his life as virtual captive in Saint Petersburg, where he died on 12th February 1798.

Modern-day feelings about him are mixed. He was,

after all, the king at the time of Poland's Third Partition, in which Poland ceased to exist as a country. But then he was king at the time of the 3rd May Constitution in 1791. By doing the right thing with the Constitution he alienated the powerful ruling class, who wanted to pursue their own selfish lifestyle, thus making him weak when the neighbouring empires decided to strike. Perhaps we should blame the ruling class for the Third Partition.

In fairness, he did inherit a bad hand in that Poland was weakened by bad government for the best part of one hundred years. The army was run down to some 16,000 men, whereas the great powers on either side and to the south had armies with some 200-300,000 men each.

Another thing that made reform difficult was the ruling that any one member of parliament could veto any legislation, so little got done.

It was against this backdrop that the Great Sejm (Parliament) of 1788-1792 tried to introduce a new constitution on 3rd May 1791. However, there were too many rich Poles who were doing well under the old system, plus foreign powers who wanted a weak Poland, that it was thrown out.

The only other notable Poniatowski is the one on his horse in front of the Presidential Palace.

Josef Poniatowski

Born 7th May 1763 and died 19th October 1813.

For someone with a major bridge named after him, and a statue of him on a horse outside the

President's Palace, one expects someone special.

He had a good start, being a nephew of King Stanisław II Augustus. When his father died, his brother, the king, brought him up and the two enjoyed a close personal lifelong relationship.

As a 17 year old, he joined the Austrian army, rising to the rank of colonel by the time he was 26. He then returned to Poland, where he reached the rank of Major-General. He won the Battle of Zieleńce in the Polish-Russian War of 1792

He became a Polish leader, military General, Minister for War and army chief. These were turbulent times. In 1795, Poland was partitioned and in the early 1800's Napoleon was having his battles.

He seemed to be a reasonable general, winning the Battle of Zieleńce against the Russians in 1792

In 1794 he took part in the Kościuszko Uprising, which was a failed attempt to rid Poland of Russian domination after the Second Partition. Josef was in charge of the defence of Warsaw, an act for which he was exiled by the victorious Russians. However, in 1798 he was permitted to return, with an offer by Tzar Alexander I to join the Imperial Russian army, which he refused.

In 1806, after the creation of the Duchy of Warsaw, he was appointed Minister for War.

By 1809 he commanded an army of 16,000 men, which fought in the Austro-Polish War. He beat the larger and more experienced Austrian army at the Battle of Raszyn. He followed this up with an advance into Galicia. As a result, he recovered lands for the Duchy of Warsaw that had been lost in the Third

Partition.

A big supporter of Napoleon, he took part in the French invasion of Russia, and fought in the 1812 Battle for Moscow, in which he was injured. He returned to Warsaw, where he planned the reconstruction of the Polish armed forces with a view to fighting Prussia.

When Napoleon lost the Battle of the Nations at Lepzig in 1813, Poniatowski covered their retreat. He was repeatedly wounded and eventually drowned in the Elster River near Leipzig.

So much potential! No wonder that he got his statue in front of the President's Palace!

Totally unconnected is Poniatowski in Wisconsin. Named after Josef, its claim to fame is that it is less than a mile from one of the four 45 degree latitude, 90 degree longitude points on Earth. This one is 45N and 90W. Half way between the Equator and the North Pole and quarter of the way round the earth from the Greenwich Meridian. Yes. With that as a main claim to fame, you can imagine what a sleepy place it is!

The Poniatowski Bridge in Warsaw is another matter. An extension of Aleja Jerozolimskie, it was built between 1904 and 1914, only to be destroyed in World War One. It was rebuilt and then destroyed in WW2, before being rebuilt, but lack of funds after the war meant that it was not built as nicely as it had originally been. However, a beautification programme in 2004 made it into its present state.

It is 506 metres long with eight spans.

North of Poniatowski is my favourite bridge – the Swiętokrzyski bridge. This is a cable-stayed bridge, which is to say that it has tall (90 metre) pillars to which 48 cables are attached to hold up the bridge. It was built in the year 2000 and is 479 metres long.

It is best seen from the nearby suburban rail bridge, or else from the Kopernik Centre.

Polish National Anthem

During the Kościuszko Rising of 1794, we came across the name of Jan Henryk Dąbrowski. In this chapter we will learn more about him and why the Polish National Anthem is sometimes known as the Dąbrowski Mazurka.

The words are attributed to an adjutant of Kościuszko, Jósef Wybicki, and the music attributed to Prince M.K. Oginski (1765 - 1831)

I do not have the facilities to provide the music, but can provide the lyrics and their translation into English.

Jeszcze Polska nie zginęła Póki my żyjemy Co nam obca przemoc wzięła Szablą odbieremy.	Our dear Poland shall not perish, While her sons are living. What the foe took, we'll replenish, There'll be no forgiving.
Marsz, marsz Dąbrowski *Z ziemi włoskiej do Polski* *Za twoim przewodem* *Złączym się z narodem.*	*March, march Dombrowski,* *From Italian valleys* *Lead us to our homeland* *Till our nation rallies*
Przejdziem Wysłę, przejdziem Wartę Będziem Polakami Dał nam przykład Bonaparte Jak zwyciężać mamy.	Cross Vistula, cross Varta, Then be Poles for ever, We shall win like Bonaparte And our bondage sever.
Marsz, marsz Dąbrowski *Z ziemi włoskiej do Polski* *Za twoim przewodem* *Złączym się z narodem.*	*March, march Dombrowski,* *From Italian valleys* *Lead us to our homeland* *Till our nation rallies*

There are more verses. I don't know whether the Poles are better with their national anthem than the Brits are, where hardly anybody is even aware that there are more verses than the first, let alone what the words of the second verse are, but two verses are probably sufficient to get the drift.

The chorus mentions Dąbrowski and marching from Italian valleys. Why?

Dąbrowski was born in 1755, which made him 40 at the time of the third partition. A professional soldier, he was promoted to the rank of general in Kościuszko's Uprising, but after the third partition he threw himself into the cause of promoting Polish independence abroad. He was the founder of the Polish Legions in Italy, serving under Napoleon Bonaparte from 1795, participating in the Napoleonic wars, including the French invasion of Russia.

Following the defeat of Napoleon in 1813, he accepted a senatorial position in the Russian-controlled congress of Poland and was one of the organisers of the Army of Congress Poland. He must have been a fantastic diplomat to get himself such positions after having fought against the Russians. It was more normal to pick up a bullet rather than an influential position. Perhaps it was because he picked up many military awards from several different countries that showed him to be a professional soldier, who could be an asset to any country that employed him, that helped him survive and prosper until his death in 1818.

Saxon Gardens and Plac Piłsudskiego

If you are going to venture to the second biggest square in Warsaw (the biggest being Plac Defilad by the Palace of Culture and Science), then you may as well go and look at the Saxon Gardens and the tomb of the unknown soldier.

The square is big. Pope John Paul II gave a mass there in 1979 to a congregation estimated at half a million. It was a lot anyway. (According to my rough calculations, the square is some 31,000 square metres, whereas Plac Defiliad has some 43,000 square metres. At ten people per square metre standing, this would make less than a third of a million people seeing the Pope in the square itself.)

The square was originally called Saxon Square after the Saxon Palace which was located at the western end. The tomb of the unknown soldier is in all that remains of the Saxon Palace, following its destruction by the Nazis in WW2.

Then, in the Second Polish Republic between the wars, it was called after Marszal Piłsudski. With Poland under the iron boot of Hitler it became Adolf Hitler Plaz (no surprise there then!).

From 1946 – 1990, it became Victory Square to celebrate the victory of the Allies over Nazism. It got its present name when Poland became free of the Soviet Union in 1990.

From the middle of the square you can admire

the Warsaw skyline, which is about as much fun as you can have in the middle of the square. It is then advisable to move to the arches of the Tomb of the Unknown Soldier.

The tomb is guarded at all times by an eternal flame and two soldiers, impeccably dressed and behaved. Every so often they will, on some unknown signal, perform a march to keep their circulation of blood to the feet going. It is advisable to stand clear at this time, because those soldiers don't look as though they take prisoners once they get going.

The guard is changed every hour, on the hour, every day of the year. It is worth watching.

The location of the tomb has been in the same place since 1925, when the Saxon Palace was still there. The present colonnade joined two symmetrical wings of the palace, which was damaged in the fighting of 1939, but quickly repaired. The palace was systematically destroyed by the Nazis following the end of the 1944 Warsaw Rising. There were plans to restore the palace, but these seem less likely to happen as the years progress. (The footprint of these two halves can be seen on the ground.)

On each face of the pillars are lists of battles that the Poles have participated in. Most are army battles, but the Air Force and Naval battles make interesting reading. The Battle of Britain is there as well as the D Day landings, when the navy is also mentioned. In fact, a large part of the history of Poland can be found on these columns. It makes interesting reading. Hopefully you will recognise some of the battles from what you read in this book.

The gardens behind the tomb are delightful, especially on a summer's day, when the leaves of the trees provide a much-needed cooling shelter. Unfortunately the trees do not provide much shelter from the rain, as I found out one afternoon in a downpour.

Krakowskie Przedmieście

This is one of my favourite streets in Warsaw, if only because I like pronouncing its name. Like all Polish, you pronounce it as written – Krakoffskiyeh Prshedmee-esh-see-eh.

It is a beautiful road and popular with tourists, probably because it runs from the Old Town to Świętokrzyska, where it turns into Nowy Świat *(New World Street)*.

Beware if you go at the weekend, because the road is closed to traffic, including buses. It also has a habit of being randomly closed when a foreign delegation is visiting the President, who has a house near the Old Town.

Krakowskie Przedmieście starts at Plac Zamkowy, where the Zygmunt III column is located.

From the square, there is a good view over the Visła river to the National Stadium and Praga.

For a better view there is a viewing tower (*widok*), where you can climb a large number of stairs to the viewing gallery and have a view over the Old Town and the river. Most of the publicity photographs of Warsaw are taken from this tower. I once had a pleasant half hour up there trying to avoid a teenage couple who were seeing whose tongue could go furthest down the other's throat.

I took my daughter up this tower a few years later and was not impressed to find that I was so much less fit than the first time. In fact, it was quite a struggle to climb the stairs to the top and, even worse, to gingerly descend.

Whilst up there on the first visit, I had a bird's eye view of the street performers. One was a fire eater and the other was a group of young male street dancers. Both were good, but the dancers seemed to be having the most fun, as each took turns to show off some amazing dance/acrobatic moves, only to be eclipsed by the next performer.

Next to the tower is the church of Święta Anny, where daily organ recitals occur at noon. I have not been to one of these, but I have been to a half hour organ recital at the cathedral. These happen around 2:15pm so if you want, you can get both recitals in the same day.

Saint Anny was the mother of Mary and grandmother of Jesus, just in case you were wondering!

The church is built in a neoclassical style, unchanged from 1788, when it was ordered by Stanisław August Poniatowski, except for the partial rebuild after WWII. In the seventeenth century it was reconstructed several times, not only because of the damage following the Siege of Warsaw in the 1650's.

During the Warsaw Uprising of 1794, Bishop Josef Rossakowski was executed in front of the church to great applause, as he was considered to be the traitor of the nation.

At Number 66 Krakowskie Przedmieście is the building which used to be the Ministry of Industry and Agriculture in Maria Skłodowska's time. Her cousin,

Josef Boguski ran the laboratory there and he let her use part of it to further her practical training. Josef's claim to fame was that he had been an assistant in St. Petersburg to the Russian chemist Mendeleev, he of the Periodic Table fame.

Further down the street is a shady copse with a statue of the Madonna and Child. It is known as the Madonna of Passau. Erected in 1683 to commemorate King John Sobieski's victory over the Turks at the Battle of Vienna in 1683, it is the second oldest column in Warsaw, after Zygmunt's Column.

Next is the Herbert Hoover monument, celebrating the American President, although what he did I don't know. But then the Poles love America and seem to want to be American. They have almost entirely taken over Chicago.

The Adam Mickiewicz statue is next. This statue was originally erected in 1898 on the 100th anniversary of his birth. He was probably Poland's greatest poet. Unfortunately, in 1942 his statue upset the visiting Nazis and they destroyed it. Only the head and part of the torso remained to enable reconstruction after the war. It is a sight to see, day or night.

Most foreign poetry does not translate well. Mickiewicz is no exception, so I will not attempt it here. It would only make you wonder what was great about his poetry.

There is then a car park with a church behind it. This is the church of the Assumption and Saint Joseph.

The President's Palace, which is next, was

undamaged in the war, because it was used by the Nazi top brass and the occasional visiting Hitler. Presumably the hotel next door, the Hotel Bristol, Warsaw's finest, was not good enough.

In front of the President's Palace is a man on a horse. It is Josef Poniatowski, of whom we read earlier.

I once had the fortune to be at the President's Palace at noon, when the changing of the guard takes place. It is worth watching if you like men in smart uniforms stamping their feet, marching and slapping rifles. I can never get enough of it.

It is a favourite stopping point for the walking tours of Warsaw. These start from Sigismund's Column at eleven in the morning, so the noon changing of the guard fits in well after a tour of the Old Town. You may therefore experience the changing with a lot of cameras accompanied by people.

Next door to the palace is the Hotel Bristol, a fine, expensive luxury hotel where diplomats and top business people will stay if they are not invited to stay at the palace. There are usually several very black, very large, very clean cars waiting outside.

Needless to say, I have never stayed there and have never packed the clothes I would need to feel comfortable in even their coffee lounge. Somehow, I feel that my Regatta Adventure trousers with Slazenger polo shirt would be a little too common. However, my friend Max is determined to have coffee and cake there next time we visit, Adventure trousers or not.

Moving on, we come to the delightful square

named in honour of Jan Twardowski (1915 - 2006), a poet and priest. He wrote humorous verses and ones which combined nature with philosophy.

The next church is where Cardinal Wyszynski (1901-1981) preached and there is a statue of him.

My mother used to revere Stefan Wyszynski, for it was he who ensured the continuation of Christianity in Poland during the years of the Communist rule (1945-1989). He opposed totalitarian government, whether Nazi or Communist, which made him popular with Poles, but not with those in power, for which he served three years in prison.

When war broke out he was preaching at the Catholic Seminary at Włotsławek and was soon wanted by the Nazis. Not because they wanted to support his work, you understand? So he moved to Laski, near Warsaw.

During the 1944 Warsaw Rising he became chaplain in the Żoliborz military district of the AK.

After the war he returned to Włotsławek to oversee reconstruction work, but shortly after, at the end of 1948, he became the Primate of Poland.

He trod a careful line with the communist rulers, agreeing to give the State choice of bishops from a list of three candidates, and the prohibition of religious indoctrination in public schools. In return he managed to separate religion from politics and for the church to keep a reasonable amount of land and buildings.

In 1953 a wave of persecution of the Roman Catholic Church was supported by the Communist rulers. Ever since the end of the war, the main opposition to Communist rule had been the Church. By 1953, the authorities had had enough and tried to outlaw the Catholic Church. This led to the internment of priests. Wyszynski was interned in the Bieszczady mountains – a remote part of Poland. He was released after three years in 1956.

1956 was the year of the Polish October, when the oppressive political system was eased a bit. This followed from the death of Stalin in 1953 and Khruchev's denunciation of Stalin in 1956; Polish communist leader Bierut's death in March of that year and the rise of reformist leader, Gomulka. The liberalisation did not last long before it was tightened by the Russians.

In 1966 he celebrated Poland's thousand years of Christianity, but the communist authorities would not allow a visit by the Pope.

He was instrumental in persuading Cardinal Karol Wojtiła to accept his election as Pope in 1978. This was followed by the spectacular visit of Pope John Paul II to his native Poland in 1979.

Civil unrest started in 1980, but, aware that it could turn into a bloodbath, Wyszynski urged moderation on both sides. There had been enough examples of communist suppression since the war to make this a real fear.

It is almost certain that he will become a Saint.

On the other side of the road, next to Krolewska that leads to Plac Piłsudskiego, is a glass cube set at an angle. The cube is made of sheets of glass, all bonded together. Underneath the top sheet is a copy of a painting of the church opposite. The cube is located at the exact position where the artist stood in the eighteenth century. It was from paintings like this that many Warsaw buildings were recreated, including this church, after the war. (It makes a change from paintings of churches to have churches built from paintings!)

Whilst on this side of the road, contemplate that it might be time for a bite to eat, because the building with seats outside is Brawarnia, a beer restaurant. They have a selection of beers that are worth sampling. I have been there several times for beer and food, none more welcome than one afternoon when I got caught in a downpour while in the vicinity of Plac Piłsudskiego. That schabowy was divine.

Now talk to any Pole who has been away from Poland for some time and Schabowy is one of the things they miss. Along with Zapiekanka. Schabowy is a thin piece of pork, covered in breadcrumbs and fried. Served with chips and salad, it makes a good meal. Probably derived from Wiener Schnitzel, but distinctly Polish. Like zapiekanka. Zapiekanka is a slice of baguette covered in a sauce of some description, such as mushroom and sweetcorn, covered with a generous lashing of ketchup. There is just something missing in a visit to Poland for a Pole if there is no schabowy and no zapiekanka.

Anyway, moving on from Brauwarnia, on the opposite side of the road is Palac Tyszkiewiczów. This is on of the seats of the Polish-Lithuanian family of Tyskiewicz. It was a well-connected family.

One of its recent members of note was Stefan Tyszkiewicz (1894-1976) who was an engineer, inventor and early pioneer of the Polish Automotive industry. Not only that, he was a decorated veteran of both World Wars. In the Second World War he was arrested by the Russians and taken to the notorious Lubijanka prison, where he managed to get his release in October 1941. He immediately went to join General Anders, who was forming the Polish Army in Russia prior to its move south to Persia. He followed Anders to Britain, where he lived until his death. Some history! Some life!

The palace now houses the Museum of the University of Warsaw.

The next building is also a palace. This time it is of Uruski. There was a baroque palace on this site until the new one, in Renaissance style was built between 1844-47. This was burned down in the 1944 Rising then rebuilt between 1947-51. It is now the Faculty of Geography of the University.

After passing the next building, which is owned by the University, we come to the square in front of the Staszic Palace. It contains the statue of Nicolas Kopernikus, the famous astronomer, who was the first person to be credited with saying that the Earth moved round the sun, rather than the other way round.

Not only is there a statue, there is, on the ground, the planets circling round the statue, as though Kopernikus was the Sun itself.

Kopernikus' home town is Toruń. I took the

opportunity on one of my visits to take a day trip there. It was a delight.

It started with the early train ride from Warsaw Centralny, where I happened to share a compartment with a delightful young lady who was on her way to some lectures at the university. Apparently she did this journey every week, sharing her studies between Warsaw and Toruń. We talked about a variety of subjects as her English improved immensely, which did little for my Polish.

It was nice having her company, even more so at the end, where she made sure that I got off at the right station and caught the bus to the town proper (for the rail station is some distance away from the town over the modern bridge. She even paid for my bus ticket, which I could not refuse as she had bought it along with hers. We bade each other farewell as she left for the university and I left to explore the Mediaeval town that had remarkably been spared destruction in two world wars.

Of course, I saw the house of Nikolas Kopernik, but there were crowds of schoolchildren, so I resisted the urge to spend time with them and walked on to ensure that I explored every part of the old town before returning to Warsaw.

So now I was standing before the statue of the man in Warsaw.

One winter visit, the whole of the Staszic Palace was the screen for falling snowflakes projected upon it. It was magical.

In the square is another of those glass cubes.

The picture is of the Holy Cross Church.

There is an iconic photo of this church in World War 2 standing there looking very battered, with smoke rising behind. The focus of the picture is the statue of Christ holding the cross.

This church has its place in history. There has been a church on this site since the fifteenth century, when it was located well outside the bounds of the Old Town. The present church was built between 1679 and 1696 after the original church was damaged beyond repair during the Deluge.

From 1765 the church was the one most attended by King Stanisław II Augustus.

Of more importance, since 1882 an urn containing the heart of Frederick Chopin was immured in a pillar.

The front steps and statue of Christ bearing the

Holy Cross were added in 1889.

During the Warsaw 1944 Rising the Nazis detonated two Goliath tracked mines in the church on 6th September 1944 and these severely damaged the church. To make sure it was properly damaged, the Nazis blew it up in January 1945. It was reconstructed after the war between 1945 and 1953 , with the main alter being rebuilt between 1960 and 1972.

The reconstruction was greatly facilitated by the painting you can see in the glass cube near the Copernicus statue.

Krakowskie Przedmieście narrows between the University Language School on the right and the Copernicus Square on the left. At this point it becomes Nowy Swiat. It does not change its name at the next intersection, which is with Świętokrzyżka, a main east-west road crossing Warsaw.

This is probably a good point at which to leave this tour, as there is a metro station just round the corner of Świętokrzyżka.

You may have noticed that the church and Świętokrzyżka have the same name. Unsurprisingly, the road was named after the church.

For a number of years, this road (Świętokrzyżka) was closed to traffic as the east-west second metro line was built using cut and fill methods. It seemed that all the sand from all the deserts in all the world was used as there was so much of it.

Turning east along Świętokrzyżka eventually brings you (after a few turns) to Most Świętokrzyżka, perhaps the most easily recognised bridge in Warsaw.

A road suspended by steel cables stretching either side of two high pillars, it has an artistry about it. It is illuminated at night, so is worth seeing at any time of the day or night.

Nowy Swiat

This is a lovely street. Its name means New World Street.

For many visits to Warsaw I rented an apartment just off Nowy Swiat at Warecka, about half way down. So this street is rather like home from home.

There is a homely feeling about the buildings, all of which were destroyed in the Second World War, but reconstructed afterwards.

In the summer there are large tubs of flowers all the way along the pavements, which are broad enough to accommodate the tourists and Warsawians who stroll up and down this street, looking in the fashion shops or eating at the many restaurants along its length. Being near the university, it also has many students. Being relatively free from traffic, with only buses passing along it, there are cyclists and skateboarders.

At the corner of Warecka is a "24 hour" shop that closes only between 4am and 6:30am that provides all the basics in food and household items. It is also a good place to get alcohol for an impromptu party.

At the Świętokrzyżka end of the street is a sushi restaurant, that I have often thought of trying, but never have, always being tempted away by one of the other restaurants, like Zapiecek, one of a chain of restaurants specialising in the Polish dish of pierogi – a dumpling pastry rectangle folded over a filling and served with a sauce. Rather like large ravioli.

[Pedant's Note: both *pierogi* and *ravioli* are plural words.]

They do several sizes, depending on the number of pieces required. Although I am a granddad and there is a Granddad size of eleven dumplings, I found that the Grandma's size was more comfortable, especially if ordered with a *duze piwo,* or large beer.

Then there is a recent arrival in Warsaw – North Fish. It was the Nowy Swiat branch of this fish restaurant chain that I first experienced the varieties of fish they serve. Worth trying, but beware, there is no waiter service.

Along the street is a branch of Sphinx. One of my favourite steak restaurants. All male waiting staff, the service can be a bit variable, but I never had a bad meal there, although on recent visits I have had an indifferent meal twice at the Wilanów branch.

There is also a traditional Polish restaurant that does not appear to be part of a chain, although it may well be. This is well worth a visit.

In fact all the restaurants on Nowy Swiat are good, so, unless you rent an apartment near here, you will have the unenviable task of deciding which one to go to on your visit.

As you walk from Swiętokrzyżka south, you will see the shops and restaurants and then arrive at Ordynacka on the left. This is the main artery into the Chopin Quarter. Here is the house where Chopin lived and which is now a museum.

I must confess that my experiences of this museum have not been good. I have tried to go round the museum, but failed for one reason or another, such as the museum was closed, or there are too many people in already, or we don't like the look of someone who wears Regatta Adventure trousers.

I have tried to go to concerts held there, but failed, probably because I did not go on line two years earlier to acquire tickets off the Polish-only website.

This would not be so bad were it not for the disdainful manner in which the female guardians of the memory of Chopin treated me. Perhaps they only like people who look wealthy, or can argue in Polish, or wear the sort of clothes a Chopin pianist would wear. The attitude did not change even when I picked up a boxed set of the Complete Works of Chopin by an unknown pianist (well, unknown to me). It was priced at the sort of sum that would provide the pianist with a decent-sized pension pot, but instead of being excited at the thought of selling something so expensive, the staff were thinking that, as I could not afford proper clothes, I would not be able to afford that set.

They were right about me not buying it. Not because I could not afford it, but because I did not want it. I had a copy of pieces by Katarzyna Kraszewska, which were lovely and I would buy a boxed set (if I wanted one) from Empik rather than the museum.

So my experience of the Chopin Quarter was not

good and only improved when I went to the Frederick Chopin University Music School for their concerts (more of which later).

During the walk from Ordynacka to the next street on the right, Foksal, one passes number 39, which is famed for being the house of Josef Conrad, the author of novels like *Heart of Darkness*. Quite remarkable that a native Polish speaker could write such good books in a foreign language, namely English.

Number 49 was the site of public hangings by the Nazis in WW2, designed to instil terror in the population. The gallows were not reconstructed after the war.

I have been down Foksal many times and assumed that it came to a dead end at the rather swish restaurant at the end. However, one day, while gazing at this restaurant, I saw an elderly man walk through the gates and turn right. I figured that wherever this elderly man was going, two elderly men could also go, so I followed him.

I found myself in a park located on a scarp. It was well wooded, so the views were limited, but it was very pleasant. I walked on, leaving the elderly man, who had gone into some flats near the restaurant.

I walked in the direction of where I thought I would meet Ordynacka and came out of the park near the Music School on Okolnik.

I had never known that park existed. It was a lovely discovery.

Opposite Foksal is Chmielna, a very fashionable

traffic-free road, running from Nowy Swiat to Marszałkowska at Centrum.

Just before Nowy Swiat meets Aleja jerozolymskie, there is Palac Branickich, one of three palaces of that name in Warsaw. It stands roughly opposite the bus stop at Foksal, which is why I know of it, for I have often looked at the magnificent wrought-iron gates while waiting for a bus.

In the same way that you would expect Nowy Swiat to start at Swiętokrzyska and not at the Kopernikus monument, so one might expect it to end at Jerozolymskie, but it continues across the road, past the Charles de Gaulle roundabout. This roundabout is distinctive because of its palm tree. Not an actual palm tree, because a real one would last hardly any time at all, given the severity of the winters, but is artificial, made from synthetic organics and natural materials.

It is an artwork known as "Greetings from Jerusalem Avenue" by Joanna Rajkowska, following a visit to Israel in 2001.

On the other side of the roundabout is a collection of posh shops. One that I found particularly amusing was Pinko.

Moving on, one comes to Płac Trzech Krzyży. This is almost impossible to say, as somewhere in the attempt, one's teeth, lips and tongue get out of sync. To hear how it should be pronounced, take any bus that passes through and listen to the announcement. The man on the recording makes it sound so easy to say.

The square takes its name from three crosses – one atop the church and two atop columns.

The church is in neoclassical form, and named after Saint Aleksander. It was designed in 1818-25 by Chrystian Piotr Aigner, a Polish architect of the time.

The square and its buildings were completely destroyed during the 1944 Warsaw Rising.

Adjacent to the square is the Polish Stock Exchange, a modern steel and glass structure which has been its home since 2000. Following the fall of communism in 1990, in a delicious piece of irony, the Polish Stock Exchange took over the building of the Central Committee of the Polish United Workers Party – the governors of Poland between 1948 and 1989.

And here ends Nowy Swiat.

Nowy Swiat – an Update

I cannot recall in 2018 being touted to go to a strip club, yet one evening in 2019 I walked from Warecka down Nowy Swiat to Chmiena and then down Chmielna and back along the same route to Warecka. In that time I was approached five times to go to a 'Gentlemen's Club'. For a start, this is an oxymoron: people who go there are not gentlemen and they have not clubbed together to fund the establishment. The last touter was a very pleasant young lady who offered me free entry and free drinks all night for 49zl (around £10). Now these operations are expensive to run and 49zl for an insatiable thirst is not going to pay its way. There must be some other money-taking operation alongside it.

It is probably a sign that Warsaw has become a

tourist centre.

    Meanwhile, I did find a reasonable pizza restaurant and had a tasty pizza and beer while watching the lovely young girls walk by with their friends, having an evening out. Nowy Swiat in the evening is a delightful place to be (as are numerous other locations in Warsaw). I have never seen an aggressive drunk there, but I have seen loud groups of young men, usually foreigners, at bars around the area, but these are mercifully few.

Frederyk Chopin

There seems to be something about Paris that attracts great Poles, for the two most well-known Poles went there to continue the work for which they are famed. And one of them nearly did not become Polish!

I am, of course, referring to Fryderyk Chopin.

Have you ever wondered why his name is not spelled in the Polish way of Szopan? Wonder no more, for all will be revealed.

Fryderyk Franciszek Chopin (1st March 1810 - 17th October 1849) was born in Żelazowa Wola, some 29 miles west of Warsaw, to Nicolas Chopin and his wife Justyna Krzyżanowska.

Nicolas (1771-1844) was born in a village in the Vosges mountains in north-east France.

Now bear with me while I introduce Fryderyk's grandfather, for he has a great influence on the young, unborn boy.

Grandfather Chopin, François (1738-1814) was the village administrator. The owner of the village, and the large estate, was a Polish-Lithuanian nobleman, Michał Jan Pac. He had driven into exile when the Polish Bar Confederation, which, comprising other powerful nobles, failed to overthrow the king. He bought the village and estate in 1780 and left its running to his steward, Adam Weydlich, whom he had brought with him from Poland.

It was inevitable that the village administrator and the estate administrator would have a close relationship. In fact, this relationship was so good that Nicolas became a sort of son to Weydlich and his Parisian-born wife, Françoise-Nichole, nee Schilling. He taught Nicholas rudimentary Polish and she taught him music as well as French and German literature, calligraphy, etiquette and accounting.

When Pac died in 1787, Weydlich decided to return to his native Poland. He obtained a position as a supervisor of a tobacco manufacturing plant in Warsaw. Nicholas, at the age of sixteen, was employed as a personal assistant of Weydlich and a tutor for his children.

The timing of the emigration was fortuitous, for in 1789 the French Revolution happened, and because of this, Nicholas stayed in Poland. But all was not peaceful in Poland, for in 1792 the Second Partition took place and the tobacco company closed.

Nicholas was now unemployed at a tough time. Since 1789, there had been a mass migration of French aristocrats to Central and Eastern Europe and there were so many of them offering their services as tutors that even relatively modest Polish families could employ one. The fact that Nicholas could find employment as a tutor on a large estate in the countryside, spoke volumes about his education.

He obviously felt secure enough to get married to a poor relation of the estate owners, the Skarbeks. She was employed by them to run the household.

A year later, they had a daughter and in 1810, they

had their only son, Fryderyk.

Things did not go well. Count Skarbek fell heavily into debt and left the area. As his children had reached the age when they no longer needed a tutor, and given the precarious financial position of the Countess, it was obvious that Nicholas's employment would be coming to an end very soon. He therefore moved to Warsaw, where he obtained a position teaching French at the Warsaw Lyceum, located in the Saxon Palace.

He achieved promotion to the position of professor and held his position at the Lyceum until 1833.

So Fryderyk grew up in relative stability.

Both of his parents were musical – his father played the flute and the violin, while his mother played (and taught) the piano. Although his mother did give him and his eldest sister piano lessons, he was taught from 1816 to 1821 by the Czech pianist Wojciech Żywny.

It was obvious that he was a child prodigy. He gave his first public performance at the age of seven, at an age when he also composed his first two polonaises (G minor and B flat Major). Neither of these compositions survive.

Poland at that time was very much a vassal state of Russia and in 1817 the Russians commandeered the Saxon Palace and the Chopins were evicted. Do not feel sad for them, for they re-established themselves in the Kazimierz Palace at 26/28 Krakowskie Przedmieście. Well, not quite in the palace, but in a building next door.

This less-than-sumptuous abode did not deter the Russian ruler of Warsaw, the Grand Duke Constantine, for Fryderyk was often invited to the Belweder Palace as a playmate for his son.

Having an eye for what was good for him, Chopin composed a march for the Grand Duke.

Chopin continued his education at the Warsaw Lyceum and studied under a number of prominent musicians.

In 1830, at the age of 20, Chopin might have got wind of the November 1830 Uprising, because, in the October, he moved to Paris, where he supported himself by selling compositions and giving piano lessons.

Although he only gave thirty public performances in the last eighteen years of his life, word must have got around about his genius, because he became friendly with Franz Liszt, and contemporaries like Robert Schumann held him in high regard.

He must have been happy in Paris, because in 1835 he obtained French citizenship.

But all was not well. He was engaged to Maria Wodzinska from 1836 to 1837, but it was broken off.

He then began a troubled relationship with the writer Amantine Dupin, who wrote under the pen name of Georges Sand.

They went to Majorca in 1838-39, which proved to be Chopin's most productive period, but emotionally difficult. He returned to Paris, where a Scottish admirer, Jane Stirling, supported him financially for the remaining years of his life, arranging for him to visit Scotland in 1848.

But his health was failing and he died, probably of tuberculosis in 1849.

Fortunately, he left over 230 compositions, mainly for solo piano, but also a few with other instruments or the human voice. This gives a wide choice for the performers at the summer Chopin concerts in Łazienki Park.

Chopin Quarter

I don't think this is an official name for part of Warsaw, but it is a convenient label for a pleasant area in the city.

The area is centred on the Chopin Museum on Ul. Ordynacka, just off Nowy Swiat. Nearby is the Music University on Okólnik and running parallel to Okólnik is Kopernika, named after the astronomer and running north for some 300m to the Kopernik monument outside the Staszic palace.

Some 850m due east of the museum is the Visła river and 450m due south is Jerozolimskie.

Roughly bisecting the area in a north-south direction is Ul. Leona Kruczkowskiego, named after the poet and writer. He lived from 1900 to 1962. His left-leaning views endeared him to the Communists and he was awarded the Order of the Builders of People's Poland and the Stalin Prize for Strengthening Peace among Peoples. Prizes which had names almost as long as one of his poems. This road turns into Topiel in the north. Topiel means 'deep water', which adds nothing to our understanding.

Further east we have the street named after Julian Smulikowski, born 1890, died 1934 and renowned for being a socialist activist and a member of the Polish Teachers' Union.

Near to the Chopin Museum is the monument to the Golden Duck (Złoty Kaczka). This is the subject of a fable, where the duck can only be returned to human form if somebody can spend a fortune everyday for three days. The fortune in this case is 100 ducats. In one version of the legend, a poor shoemaker finds the duck and fails to spend the money, but finds happiness. In the second ending, a soldier finds the duck and spends all the money, save for the last penny, which he gives to a beggar, at which point the duck disappears.

Not the best Polish legend, but presumably designed to make people happy with their lot, rather than striving for riches.

North of the duck is Ul. Juliana Bartoszewicza, named after Julian Bartoszewicz *1821-1870), a Polish historian who wrote a history of Kopernik.

Concerts

The nice thing about a capital city is that there is always something going on. One way to find out about what is going on in Warsaw is to call into the Information Office at the Palac Kultury i Nauki (the Stalin monstrosity). It is located on the Emilii Plater side. The people in there are invariably nice and all speak English. They have access to a vast mount of information about what is going on in Warsaw, but this tends to be short notice stuff, so it is best to go in every couple of days to see what is about to go on.

It was through them that I learned of the forthcoming concert at the University of Chopin Music School. I was shown where it was on one of the free maps they give out, so that evening I went there. The concert was advertised to start at 6pm, so I arrived about twenty to in order to be sure of a seat. You see, the concert was free and Poles love anything that is free, so I was expecting a queue. There was none. In fact, when I asked at the information desk, neither of the two women who worked there knew of either the concert, nor where the concert hall was. So I asked a passing student, who spoke perfect English in response to my appalling Polish.

I found it and opened the door. The concert was already under way, but at a suitable gap, I walked into the hall and sat down in one of the many empty seats.

The concert started again. It felt as though they

had been waiting for my arrival. It was a Mozart piano piece for piano and string orchestra. It sounded wonderful and then it stopped. A young woman, who looked like a cross between a Rocker and a chic model entered the hall and walked up onto the stage. She greeted the other pianist and the string section and went to the other piano. It was a rehearsal. Presumably for twenty minutes until 6pm?

No. The rehearsal lasted about half an hour more.

The young male pianist kept looking at me and sought my approval every time they stopped. I put my thumb up, because it was fabulous stuff. If only they didn't keep stopping.

But there was method in their madness. This was all about entrances and exits. The strings would play a bit until the piano, or two pianos, came in, when they would do a few bars together then stop.

It also dawned on me that there must be somebody sitting behind me who knew more about music than I did, so I could relax and not worry about approving something that in a musicians eyes may have been awful.

At six fifteen, the string section came off the stage and started packing their violins. Only the two cellists were male and one of them was wearing the sort of neck support beloved of Mrs Tishell in *Doc Martin*. Obviously, cello playing was not without its dangers.

The violinists and viola players were all young ladies, presumably students. The leader was impossibly thin and serious. All were attractive and spoke impeccable English. It was from them that I learned that there had been a misprint of the time in the programme and that it started at seven, as always. "Time for a beer, then" I said to one of the viola players. "Yes, time for a beer" she smiled back.

I actually found a restaurant on Nowy Swiat that served me a dark beer and a traditional Polish meal, wolfed down in record time before rushing back to join the fragrant Polish glitterati. I even managed to go for a safety pee before the start.

There were lots of people in the hall when I entered with a couple of minutes to spare. The stage was empty, except for the chairs for the strings and the two pianos at the front of the stage.

High up on the rear wall was a bust of Chopin, gently and tastefully illuminated by a spotlight.

Then the strings entered, elegantly, dressed in black concert clothes, walking in single file, carrying their instruments. We applauded. Presumably the applause at the beginning of a concert is to give the performers confidence, or just to let them know that we are there and awake.

Then the male pianist entered, dressed in dinner suit, shirt with winged collar and bow tie where the strap is visible all around the neck. He too received applause.

The concert was magic. The strings were fantastic, whereas I thought the pianist was not up to the strings' high standard. The stress of the real performance took away the jollity that had been there in rehearsal, which detracted from the performance. At least it did from the perspective of one person, who had attended both rehearsal and performance.

There was a piano piece with strings to open. This was one movement of very Mozart music. It was all over too soon.

The second piece was a Mozart cello concerto, with a nervous soloist, who was slightly out in timing and finger work. I can only assume this to be nerves, because she looked as though she could eat Mozart for breakfast. Unfortunately, this was dinner time

The final piece was the Mozart triple piano concerto (two piano version).

Before describing this, mention must be made of the two gentlemen in grey suits, black shirts and black gloves, who, after the first piece, moved one piano to one side of the stage and the other to the other side. Why they did not position one piano to the side of the stage before the start of the concert was beyond me. Perhaps it would have looked asymmetric and ungainly. They then brought in a dais about two metres square, plus chair for the cellist to sit on.

After the cello concerto, they reversed the process, wheeling the pianos back so that their curvy sides interlocked.

It was this setup that we had for the twin piano concerto.

The strings had gone off after the cello concerto and now they came back, followed by the male pianist and the Rocker pianist, now dressed in a magnificent scarlet evening gown.

I had not heard this piece before, (except in the parts I had heard in rehearsal), but it was pure Mozart. The two pianos and strings interacted and played with each other, all the time developing the refrain. Wonderful stuff. Those girls in the strings are going to go far – if only they treat the performances as a rehearsal!

Warmed by this wonderful experience, I made my next visit to the Information centre and looked out the next performance at the university. It was singing. OK. Not my favourite, but I went anyway.

Well, my ignorance did not take long too come to the fore.

The first on was a soprano, Ewa Leszczynska, who opened with four pieces from a work by the famous polish composer/pianist/prime minister, Ignacy Jan Paderewski. In French. She had a wonderful voice and competed well with the pianist, who was doing his best to drown her out.

At the end of the four songs, the audience did not clap, but waited for her to do four songs in German by Karol Szymanowski. Thank goodness there were only four songs, for, according to the programme, the whole Szymanowski work consisted of twelve songs.

At the end of the fourth Szymanowski song, the audience gave her a proper round of applause to make up for their lack of humanity at the end of the Paderewski set.

We then had a young soprano who did a Samuel Barber and a Richard Strauss. I was now getting the distinct impression that all these songs were sounding the same. It was as though there was a formula that forbade any originality. Barber's Adagio for Strings is exquisite. I can only assume that he recycled his reject notes from the adagio and made them into songs.

We carried on. Another soprano gave four pieces and the man in the seat next to me applauded wildly, having filmed it all on his smart phone. Either he is her husband or else he is a stalker.

Then we had a baritone intoning a few pieces and finally another baritone who had hair somewhere between Jedward and a half Chopin. He sang numerous songs (well he intoned it that way, but they were either in German or Italian, so I didn't get the gist). His pianist, a nice looking youngster, did in spades what I came to realise, was what all the other pianists had done – either upstage the singer or try to put the singer off by playing a different tune, or else drown them out by crashing ten finger chords from a great height.

I was glad when it was all over and nobody asked for an encore.

On the way back from the second concert, I walked up Ordinacka to Nowy Swiat and would have normally turned left to go to Chmielna, then walk along Chmielna to the flat. This time I thought I would cross straight across Nowy Swiat and walk up Warecka, where in other visits I had rented an apartment.

During the daytime there is normally a flower seller at Warecka, but they had long gone, as it was now past eight in the evening and it was starting to get a little chillier, although still pleasant.

A short distance up Warecka is Winnie-the-Pooh street, or Ulica Kubusia Puchatka. At the beginning of the little street is a charming plaque that shows a little figure of Winnie-the-Pooh.

Walking through the usual range of buildings, one comes to Plac Powstancow Warszawy, or Warsaw Rising Square, commemorating the Warsaw Rising of August and September 1944.

As I stood facing the square, I could see the iconic Prudential building that had been the focus of resistance during the Rising. It has now been restored and is Hotel Warszawa, but its solid construction helped the Resistance to hold it for a while, even though it was the focus of Nazi attack.

It was time to turn left down Szpitalna.

At the corner of Warecka and Szpitalna I saw the E. Wedel Chocolate Shop cafe. A smart young couple were entering this throwback to a gentler age. The windows were surmounted with elegant canopies, each bearing the legend 'E. Wedel'.

Now you have to be remarkably detached in Warsaw if you never come across E Wedel, for they are famous for making chocolate. This site used to be the location of the business in 1865, when Emil Wedel was given the company as a wedding gift. It stayed in Szpital Street until it moved to Zamoyski Street in 1931.

In 1989 there was a flurry of acquisitions of Polish companies by western mega corporations.

Poland sold out its prospect of prosperity. In the case of Wedel, they sold out to PepsiCo, who probably bought it because it was cheap, rather than a strategic acquisition, for Pepsi knew nothing of luxury chocolate. This became quickly apparent and they sold the chocolate part of company in 1991 to Cadbury – a much more sensible choice of owner. However, Kraft Foods, having taken over Cadbury in the meantime sold out to the Korean conglomerate, Lotte, So although it is considered to be Polish, like many other Polish companies, it is owned by foreigners.

There is a long list of Polish companies that have been sold out to foreign owners:

Zywiec, the brewer, now 61% owned by Heineken of Holland. This includes Warta.

Tyskie, the brewer, including Lech, bought by SABMiller in 1999 and sold to Asahi in December 1916

Coffee Heaven, the cafe chain, formed in 1999, the first Polish company to be listed on the London AIM Market, bought in 2009 by Costa Coffee, a subsidiary of Whitbread.

These are just a few companies of which I have heard.

Now on the evening of the concert I had already eaten and did not feel that a chocolate indulgence would have done my digestion a favour, so I had to wait for a later visit to sample the delights of this establishment. It was worth the wait.

The interior is pure second republic Poland

(between the world wars). It is truly lovely. Three giant paintings of the Wedel owners hang on one of the walls, which are painted in a sort of antique gold colour.

My waiter was an exceedingly polite and pleasant young man, who could sense my excitement at having actually made it to the restaurant.

I chose chocolate cake with a glass of chocolate milk with ice cream. The calorie count was going to be off the scale, but, after I had indulged, I thought it well worth the experience.

From the Wedel Chocolate Shop it was a short distance to the apartment, where I could curl up round my stomach and go to sleep.

The Royal Route

On my first visit to Warsaw I walked the Royal Route one day (well, at least as far as Łazienki Park). It was a long way from the castle in the Old Town to Łazienki. I took the bus to the end of the Royal Route at Wilanów Palace.

The name of the route implies that it was a road followed by royalty, from the royal castle to the royal palace. Today it passes by some elegant properties.

We have already been to the Old Town and followed Krakowskie Przedmieście and Nowy Swiat to Plac Trzech Krzyzy, so now we can see what is down Al. Ujazdowski.

Almost the first building on the right is the New Zealand Embassy. This is followed by the Lawyers' Association, so now you should be getting an idea of the types of people who live and work along this route.

On the left is a doorway with two enormous male figures holding up the lintel above the door. They are giants and the restaurant is aptly named as "Under the Giants"

Later there is the Lithuanian Embassy, the Bulgarian Embassy and the United States Embassy. Then the Palace of Aleksander Rembelinski and the Swiss Embassy.

Then Ul. Piękna, or Pretty Street. Obviously, nowhere else in Warsaw could be perfect for the

French Embassy!

Another palace and the Hungarian Embassy. By this time one is getting a little tired of spotting embassies and trying to work out which one they are from the flags they display.

A street named after Frederik Chopin comes into view. It was on the corner of this street on February 1st 1944 that the assassination of Franz Kutschera took place.

Kutschera was appointed as Head of SS and Police in Warsaw on September 25th 1943 at the age of 39. and was responsible for increasing the number of round-ups and public executions of Poles.

Wisely, his movements and locations were kept secret, but he was found by Polish Intelligence in a story that is worth retelling. Aleksander Kunicki (code-named Rayski), the head of Polish Intelligence for anti-Gestapo operations, was performing regular observations on the Gestapo offices on Aleje Szachta in December 1943, when he noticed an Opel Admiral limousine enter the driveway and an officer, with insignia of *Brigadefuhrer* exit the car. Intrigued, he monitored the arrivals and departures of this man and filed a report. It was later confirmed that it was Franz Kutchera, and plans were made to kill him.

At 9:06am on February 1st 1943, Kutschera's Opel, followed by an open truck filled with soldiers and armed SS men marching alongside, entered the boulevard. Its arrival was signalled by a woman who pulled up the hood of her coat and crossed the street. A car then came from nowhere and smashed head-on into the convoy.

One assassin ran down the right side of the convoy and emptied his Sten gun into the Opel. A second man appeared from the other side and did the same. Both attackers were shot by Nazi gunfire, but gunfire and grenades from fellow Poles enabled the two attackers to be retrieved and taken away in two waiting cars.

The two injured were treated that night by a surgeon, but they died. Death certificates gave tuberculosis of the liver as the cause of death and funerals were carried out by a regular undertaker.

The Nazis investigated deaths around that date and exhumed the body of one of the attackers, finding the cause of death to be falsely recorded. But they never found the organisers.

In retribution, the Nazis murdered 300 Poles.

Moving on, we come to the entrance to the park that has been tempting me for some distance. This is Ujazdowski Park.

The magnificent gates open directly onto a statue. I walk up to it and discover that it is the statue of Ignaci Jan Paderewski, the only Prime Minister of a country to have been a concert pianist and composer

.Jan Paderewski

Born in 1860, his claim to fame was meeting President Woodrow Wilson and obtaining the explicit inclusion of an Independent Poland in the Peace Terms to end World War I. An independent Poland was point 13 of the Fourteen Points. Paderewski had obtained international renown through his piano playing and became very wealthy. With some of this wealth he funded the erection of the Battle of Grunwald monument in Krakow in commemoration of the 500th anniversary of the battle.

In 1913 he settled in California, where he planted Zinfandel vines to make wine. Although he represented Poland in many diplomatic talks, he never returned to Poland to live. But in the ten months he was Prime Minister in 1919 he achieved more than many politicians achieve in a lifetime. This is why he deserves his statue in a beautiful park.

I didn't just stop at the statue when I first visited the park, but carried on to see what else there was.

To my delight there was a very beautiful young lady and an attractive, older lady in the park. From what the older lady was carrying, I could see that they were on a photo-shoot, for she was carrying not only a camera and camera bag, but also a collapsible reflector. Wearing a camera myself, I was curious to see what they were doing, so I kept a polite distance away as I walked round the park. The camera lady knew all the most photogenic spots, which saved me from having to find them. Every now and then I would develop a close interest in some uninteresting flower or bush as they took a photo. After they had walked on, I would photograph the beauty spot they had stopped at. Some rocks by a stream; a glade with a view of the lake and so on.

I would have been a groupie, but it would have

been rude to interfere, so I settled for distant views of their activities for ten minutes or so, before deliberately going my own way.

I could imagine newly-wed couples being taken to these places by their photographer a couple of days after their wedding.

On my wanderings I came across Ujazdowski Castle. Unfortunately for me it was being refurbished. (Yet again, for it had a long history and several refurbishments.) Some time after 1674, when it was rented by King Augustus II, an extension was designed by the noted architect of the time, Tylman of Gameren.

I also found out later that the pre-stressed concrete bridge over part of the lake was designed by the Victorian, English engineer, William Lindley – he of Filtry fame. More of which later.

I was fortunate on the day I visited the park in that there were few people around and I could enjoy the peace and tranquillity.

But there was walking to be done.

I left the park and walked over a main road - Aleja Armii Ludowi, or People's Army Alley. For a very brief time, this was renamed Aleja Lech Kaczyńskiego, named after the President who died in the air crash at Smolensk in 2005.

Roman Dmowski

Emerging on the other side of the bridge, one can see the statue of Roman Dmowski (1864 - 1939). He was a contemporary of the famous Marshal

Piłsudski and a politician.

He saw how the Germans were aggressively Germanising those parts of Poland under German control at the end of the 19th century/beginning of the twentieth century, and how this was a threat to Polish culture. One of the ways that the Germans were diminishing Polish culture was in the way they insisted on all school lessons being taught in German from 1908. (The Russians had been doing the same in their partition, except that they were Russifying that part of the population.)

Dmowski founded the National Democracy movement. He saw no problem with gaining the help of one of Poland's other occupiers – Russia – and sought to reach an accommodation with them.

During Word War I he was very influential in promoting the cause of Polish Independence.

His views of what Poland should be differed markedly from Piłsudski. He thought that Poland should be populated only by Polish-speaking, Roman Catholic people. This led him to be anti-Semitic, as the large Jewish population of the time was mainly Yiddish-speaking. Piłsudski, on the other hand, believed in a multi-national, multi-racial Lithuanian-Polish Commonwealth consisting of lands between the Baltic and Black Sea. Dmowski never held office, except for a brief period as foreign minister in 1923, but was extremely influential amongst opponents of Piłsudski.

Walking on, I came to the Botanical Gardens, part of the university. Not being knowledgeable about plants to the extent required of a meaningful visit to a botanical garden, I gave it a miss and carried on to the main entrance of Łazienki Park.

Josef Piłsudski

But before going in, it is better to walk a little further and visit the statue of Josef Piłsudski. The authorities must have had a sensitivity to place him a distance away from his arch opponent, Roman Dmowski. But then Piłsudski is everywhere. There is Plac Piłsudskiego near the Old Town – the second biggest square in Warsaw.

There is almost certainly a road named after him in every town or city of significant size in Poland.

Not bad for a man born in what had been Lithuania in 1867.

He was a good forecaster, forecasting that Polish independence would have to be won by military means, he formed the Polish Legions in 1914. He forecast that Russia would be defeated by the Central Powers (mainly Germany and Austria) and that the Central Powers would in turn be defeated by the Western Allies.

In 1917, he saw Russia faring badly, so he withdrew the support of the Polish Legions for the Central Powers and was consequently imprisoned in Magdeburg by the Germans.

When Poland gained its independence in 1918, he became Chief of State, when, between 1919-21 he also commanded his forces against six border wars.

On the verge of defeat in August 1920, he rallied the troops and threw back the Russian army in the Battle of Warsaw. The result was that Poland gained land on the eastern borders of the country. This new border land became known as The Kresy.

Piłsudski retired from politics when the government was dominated by his opponents (mainly the National Democrats). However, in May 1926, he organised a *coup d'etat* which saw him returned to power. Until his death in 1935 he concerned himself mainly with military matters and foreign affairs.

He had two main objectives: one was the breakup of the Soviet Union into its component countries; the other was the formation of a federation of states between the Baltic to the north and the Black Sea to the south, stretching east-west between Russia and Germany. This, he thought, would provide protection for Poland's borders. This second objective was known as the *Intermarum* from the Latin *between the seas*.

He never achieved either.

It is easy to recognise Piłsudski because he had a large moustache of a sort still beloved by Polish men of a certain age.

Łazienki Park

The main entrances around this area lead to the park. It is a big park of seventy six hectares, which equates to an area of 900 x 800 metres..

Bearing left takes one to the ornamental lake and the Chopin memorial, but it is far better to enjoy this at a concert (see later).

Going in as straight a line as possible from the gates by the Piłsudski statue takes one past the Belweder Palace, built in 1660.

The gardens contain many buildings and statues, but, unless you want to spend the whole day there it is best to visit the highlights, top of which is the palace on the water.

I stumbled upon this on my first visit and fortuitously approached it from the best viewing end of the lake, by the Jan Sobieski III monument, which is on Ul. Agrikola at the north of the park. I recall that there was a storm of flowers from the trees, that gathered in any spot sheltered from the wind.. There was also the inevitable school party with a teacher. As well as teaching the children Polish history, he was also trying to impart some English. He was trying to tell the children that Łazienki Park was called *Royal Baths Park* but was having problems enunciating *Royal*, so I helped him get the right pronunciation, for which he was profoundly grateful, getting me to pronounce it to all the children. I felt pretty good about my contribution to Polish Education.

The teacher and I had a brief conversation to give him a chance to speak some English with a native, before he went off with the children and I stayed behind to examine the Sobieski monument. This is a rather fanciful monument, with our hero riding a prancing horse while waving encouragement to his troops and vanquishing the enemy.

I also took some photos of the palace on the lake.

Not very good ones because the tree florets made it look as though the image had been burned with spots due to radiation.

On this occasion I did not go in to the palace as it was a fine day and I was getting tired and hungry, but I did go round on a later visit.

One expects every building in Warsaw to have been destroyed by the Nazis in World War 2, so to find an original is pleasantly surprising. The Nazis did drill holes in the building ready to hold the dynamite, but for some reason they never got round to it. Perhaps they exceeded the dynamite budget on the Royal Castle.

I visited the interior on a winter visit and remember the warmth as I entered the palace. It was all very civilised, with a space to hang one's coat and hat to go unencumbered round he building.

The general impression of the building is that it is stark in that there is no sign of anything that can be considered homely. It is the sort of building you would have if you wanted to impress, but did not quite have the budget to do it properly. There were statues, ornate plasterwork, gilding and some heavy baroque furniture, but nothing soft.

There was a dance hall where Michael Portillo danced with some teenagers who were preparing for an end-of-term dance (or some such) and I envied him when I saw the TV broadcast, for he has researchers to find the best places to visit and the power of the BBC to open otherwise closed doors. When I visited, there was me and a few other tourists wandering from room to room, peering at the various objects and reading the notes, but it was not the same as having a personal guide and a very pretty teenage girl to dance the Polonaise with. And he was getting paid to enjoy this!

Having had my fill of the palace, I collected my hat and coat and went outside to the gloomy mid-winter mid-afternoon and made my way towards the main road and the bus. On the way I passed a number of silhouettes of period couples outlined in lights that would form a spectacle as Christmas approached. Michael Portillo would have been taken there when they were lit. Or even have them lit for him.

I did not know it at the time, but subsequently found out that somewhere round that area – probably the very path with the silhouettes, there are gas lamps of the old fashioned variety, that are lit by a gas lighter, presumably on a bicycle, to show how all of Warsaw's streets were once lit.

There is an orangery in the park, which is a lovely building near the White House (not the American one), which in turn is on the route back to the road from the palace on the lake.

You may see the park referred to as Łazienki Królewski. The Królewski means 'Royal', so it is properly titled Royal Baths Park.

There are many buildings and statues in the park. One of these buildings is the exotic Grecian-styled temple *Świątynia Sybilli*, which is a short walk from the Belweder Palace.

Bearing ever-so-slightly right should bring you

to the bust of Maurycy Mochnacki. He was a a literary, theatre and music critic, whom we met earlier in the 1830 Rising. Born in 1801 and died in 1834, he had a short, but apparently busy life.

He joined the November Uprising of 1830 and took part in several battles. This gained him promotion to the officer class.

Mochnacki subsequently went to France where he later died.

Wilanów

When having had one's fill of Łazienki park, do not despair! There is another park and palace to see further out of Warsaw, but on the same bus route, the 180 or 116. This is Wilanów. Wilanów palace is a little confusing to find when arriving by bus. The bus will pull into a sort of bus station on the opposite side of where you want to be. When I made my first visit, I was confused as to where this important palace was, for there was no sign of it from the bus station. However, there was a very large zebra crossing and everybody on the bus was making for it, so I followed.

The pedestrian traffic led me past a few restaurants and cafes to a church. This church is Saint Anny of Wilanów. (Not to be confused with Saint Anny of Old Town. As if you would!)

It was worth a look, so I circumnavigated it before finding my way to a path that led to the palace.

The view of the palace is breathtaking. For a start, this is a royal palace built for King John III

Sobieski in the late 1600's. (He of the statue at the end of the lake in Łazienki Park.) It was successively owned by many of the greatest families in Poland, most of whom added to the building.

Secondly, it survived the partitions of Poland and both world wars. Although damaged in World War II, it was not demolished and was renovated after the war.

It was also fortunate that the interior items, which had been looted in the war, were mostly repatriated after the war, so the interior is quite something.

But that is for later.

The approach to the palace is perfect.

The palace is a wide building with two wings coming towards you. In the middle is an oval of lawn. The view, on a sunny day, is perfect. No wonder it is one of the national treasures of Poland and is a must-see for any discerning tourist.

Outside the sides and back of the palace are formal gardens, with neatly tended plants and low hedges dotted with statuary.

At the back of the middle section of the palace is a very large patio leading away to paths that will take you on a walk to the canal. Walking along the canal gives glimpses of the back of the palace through the trees.

It is a fabulous place. Tasteful yet opulent with just enough gold leaf to stop it from looking like bling.

From the inside one can look out over the gardens, where the formality of the layout is more apparent.

I have now been several times, the last time being with my friend Max. It was not the best of trips.

The bus we got to go to Wilanów from Łazienki, post concert, was caught at a sprint as we crossed the road before it could leave. We made it, but had to stand all the way. There were two teenage girls seated together who let down Polish youth by not offering us oldies their seats. (Not that I would have wanted them, but offering is what I expect.)

Anyway, we stood the whole way.

It was getting on, so we voted to eat first. There was a Sphinx restaurant, so we sat at one of the outside tables in the sunshine so that we could watch the world go by. In this case it was families in their Sunday finery. It was like a fashion parade. Very nice.

I think Sphinx is going downhill. I chose BBQ ribs and they seemed underdone. This is the second time I have had an indifferent meal there. Time to move on.

We made our way to the palace via the church and its ceremonial bells on the ground. As we approached the gates, Max saw the palace and was duly impressed, if not to say gobsmacked.

We bought our tickets to go on a couple of the tours. The cashier looked pissed off when, having rung up two full price tickets, was told by me that I wanted discount. Maybe I am wearing well for my age!

Anyway, they had a timed ticket system so we had quarter of an hour to wait. The lady told us about the bookshop down the corridor, so we meandered there to have a mosey.

There was a pretty young lady behind a counter, looking a bit bored. The place was empty and looked as though its purpose was to amuse people who were waiting to go round the palace on their timed tickets.

So I went up to her, found that she spoke good English and asked her about finding a hospital to get the stitches taken out of my leg (see the full story in *Hospitals.*). She didn't go to hospitals, but the surly man next to her did, so she directed my question at him in Polish. He replied with a comment something like "Fucked if I know", which she interpreted as "My colleague does not know either, but I think I know of one near the centre. She wrote it down, having found its location on the internet. "It is near the National Museum. She pointed at the national museum on the screen's map. "You come back here..."

"..To the Charles de Gaulle roundabout?" I interjected.

"Yes. You know Warsaw well."

"I should do. I'm writing a book about it."

"You must let me know when it is finished. I will buy a copy. I will email you. I will be your stalker."

"Oh good! I have always wanted a stalker. Here is my email address." I wrote my name and email address and the book title. If I ever get an email from her, this part of the book is dedicated to you, Katarzyna.

Having spent enough time in the book area, we went into the palace interior through the turnstiles. .

Quite frankly, it was boring. A few rooms of

Chinese objects followed by some indifferent country works. It was lifeless. I also lost Max at this point, so walked quickly round the route again. Up the stairs and follow the rooms again to ascertain that he was not there before going downstairs and into the second exhibition area, which is mainly paintings and gilt and glass.

It was not exciting. Until, that is, we came across a few erotic paintings of nude women draped around men.

There was a painting that showed two young girls holding recorders in front of a man who looked as though he was explaining things to them. He, the teacher, was dressed in a diaphanous piece of cloth that just covered his own pipe and cymbals.

"You are supposed to hold it gently in your fingers and blow", I heard him say.

"But our last teacher told us to suck on the pipe as we put it in our mouths."

"No. You can suck my pipe later. For now you must blow your recorders."

The next painting had a woman with bare breasts reclining in front of a man. She was holding what appeared to be a couple of plums, but on further examination it could have been a fig.

Senses now tuned in to erotica, the next painting showed a scantly clad woman holding a tobacco pipe in a rather suggestive manner.

Having had as much fun as we could over the erotic (or our imagined erotic) pictures, we left the palace and went round the gardens. These are

Italianate in style and pretty.

We walked past the shallow pond and down to the long lake, before returning to the palace formal gardens and off for the bus, pausing only for ice creams.

We almost caught a 180, but it arrived as we were trying to cross the road and departed soon afterwards, before we could get there. We did catch the116 and found that it went to the Plac Powstania, near where we were staying

But we had to walk past the flat and get provisions from our local shop. Which was closed. We were in a dilemma, because the lift had failed that morning and we did not fancy a hike of ten flights of stairs every time we needed something.

Max spotted a cafe that looked like a convenience store, which it was. Presumably the cafe marking was a ruse to get round Sunday trading laws. Anyway, we got our beers and vodka plus bread and crisps to eat. (All our healthy eating – where did it go?)

Anyway, stoked up, we found the lift had been fixed to arrive back tired but provisioned.

Chopin in the Park

Whenever I come to Warsaw between May and September, I always include at least one weekend so that I can go to the Chopin recitals in Łazienki Park on the Sunday. There are two performances, these are at noon and at 4pm. They started in 1959.

The one I am first writing about was the performance at noon on 20th May 2018, given by Joanna Różewska *(Roojeffska)*.

She is a shapely young lady, but, more importantly, she is an exquisite pianist. Her performance was not only technically superb, but the programme was well though out, with a mixture of familiar and less-familiar pieces.

It was a bright, sunny day – seemingly typical for these May performances – at least in my limited experience. I had arrived around 11am in time to get a good position on a bench behind the Chopin monument. When I arrived, I was in the shade, but within half an hour I was getting the sun on my legs.

I spent a pleasant half hour listening to and watching, the piano tuner at work. The piano is transported to the park and placed under an awning that looks like a big Pringle next to the Chopin monument. At the end of the day it is transported back again and unloaded at wherever it is stored, ready to be brought back the next Sunday.

As you can imagine, this puts it out of tune. Not

so that you and I would notice, but the performer certainly would. Hence the tuning. I don't know how long it takes, but it is always underway when I arrive. My guess is around the hour.

The Chopin monument has an interesting history. Chopin (or *Szopan* in Polish) is Poland's composer, even though he spent the last half of his life outside of Poland and his father was born in France (see earlier). As such, the Nazis wanted to destroy anything to do with Chopin, in case it acted as a revolutionary focal point. The bulk of the monument was destroyed, but the head was kept and found after the war in a railway shed in Wrocław. Even more surprisingly, the mould, from which the rest of the monument was made, was also found intact. So the one in the park is sort of original.

It shows a contemplative Chopin sitting under a willow tree.

Anyway, there is a whole industry round Chopin as any visit to the Chopin area at the end of Ordinacka will show. There is the Chopin museum in the house where he grew up, the Chopin University Music School, an annual Chopin competition and so on. Somehow Goretski doesn't have the same ring.

I once tried bashing out Chopin on the piano and I can tell you that it is difficult. (But then any playing of the piano is difficult for me.)

Now it is said that, if you want to be top in your profession, you need to put in between ten thousand and twenty thousand hours of study and practise. I could certainly believe this in the case of Joanna. She, like the forty one other performers in the 2018 season, is at the top of the tree when it comes to playing Chopin. The pianists come from all over the world to play underneath the Chopin statue before one of the largest concert audiences around. Typically there will be some three to four thousand people gathered for these free concerts. Loudspeakers convey the music to most of the audience because the open air, trees and birdsong makes the piano itself unable to travel to such numbers. After so many years of these performances, the technicians know where to place the speakers for best effect.

After sixty years the concerts themselves run quite well. A delightful young lady, with beautiful Polish, introduces proceedings by telling us how long the concerts have been running and who the sponsors are. She then says the same in beautiful English. Her Polish is so good that I can almost understand every word, so the English translation is not a surprise.

She then introduces the pianist with brief CV and lists the pieces we are about to hear. It is pointed out, very politely, that recordings and media are the sole preserve of those who have been accredited. The pianist comes from behind where I was sitting, to rapturous applause and settles at the piano to begin the performance.

At the end of the performance, the announcer takes a small bunch of flowers to the pianist, who walks back alone, leaving the announcer to either remind the audience of the four o'clock performance, or to thank those at the four o'clock performance for attending..

Now in 2014, before the media ban came into effect, I had been sitting in pole position near the piano and recorded a few of the pieces as they were played by a lady called Katarzina Kraszewska and I had got round to making a proper video of the event before I came to Warsaw in 2018. I wanted to get a copy to her, so I approached the announcer and asked if she could find out whether I could get it to Katarzina through her. She agreed to find out and let me know when I came back for the afternoon performance.

I am writing this between performances, having grabbed lunch at a restaurant near the flat. (Yes, it really is that easy to get back to the centre of Warsaw between performances, have lunch and do some typing.)

I shall now go back and see what the four pm audience is like, presumably after they have had alcohol with lunch.

Well, it was quieter, perhaps because of the blazing sun that was high in the lightly-clouded sky.

Surprisingly, I sat in the exact same place as in the morning, even though I had arrived only half an hour before the start of the performance.

The pianist this time was Edward Wolanin, who, on paper, seemed to be the bees' knees.

His repertoire consisted of angry Chopin pieces. Lots of loud chords and energetic glissandos. Even the nocturnes got energetic. Perhaps it would not have been so bad had the timing been better.

It seemed to me that the rest of the audience did not approve it as much as the morning's performance, but perhaps that was just my wishful thinking.

I approached the young announcer at the end of the performance and she assured me that I could leave the DVD with her and she would ensure that Katarzina received it. I felt sure that she would appreciate it.

It had been another lovely day of Chopin.

The only sad thing about the concert is the intrusion of modern manners. It seems that a small percentage of the population has to photograph everywhere they have been and to tell all their 'friends' on Facebook about it. There was a gang of silver-tops taking selfish selfies as the pianist performed; there were the fat people who blocked out the view of the pianist as they moved as close as they could to take their pikshers; the Japanese tourists (who can be forgiven, because it is in their DNA) taking pictures of everything; the walkers, who scrunch on the gravel paths as they walk and the occasional talker, who has to share with their neighbour something that can easily wait until after the performance. There is no point doing a surreptitious recording of the concert, because these things make it unwatchable.

In spite of all these intrusions, it is a really lovely day, which is why they are so popular among such a large number of people year after year.

Even getting away from the concerts is easy. Most people travel back on public transport. Yes, the buses are crowded, but it seems that everybody gets back to town without too much delay.

The third concert I'll mention was when I came in September 2018 with my daughter to one of the last concerts of the season and, although she is no great fan of Chopin, thoroughly enjoyed the music and the atmosphere of the event.

I then came with my friend, Max, to the first concert of 2019.

The pianist was Krzysztof Jabłoński. From the moment he hit the first chord we knew we were in the presence of a master. His first piece was the polonaise in A flat Opus 53, which is served with mothers milk to all Poles. But is was brilliantly performed and received rapturous applause before he went into the etude in C minor Op.10 Nr.12, known to all as The Revolutionary. This too received rapturous applause. It was then that I realised that the park was fuller than normal. This could either be because it was the first performance of the season and Poles had been waiting six cold, dark months for the season to start again, or they could have known that this performer was world class. Or a combination of both.

But while we are diverted from the performance, it is worth noting two new innovations in the sixtieth year of the Chopin concerts. One was the printing of the programme. Previously this had been announced for the benefit of those with what passed for a memory. The second was the availability of deck chairs. Whether one paid for these or not I did not find out. But they were heavily utilised.

While still diverted from the performance, it is worth noting that the crowd are very knowledgeable and will heavily applaud a performer whom they consider worth it.

Back to the concert where Krysztof was on a roll, now giving the crowd the scherzo in B Minor op. 20. He aced it and he and the crowd knew it.

On to Ballade in G minor Op. 23 and more appreciation. Not even the persistent walkers and fat people that insisted on blocking one's view could detract from this performance. The cognoscenti were lovin' it.

On to Andante Spianato and Grande Polonaise in E flat major Op. 22. A truly delicate piece performed with all the skill and dexterity of a leading brain surgeon.

And that was Krysztof. Dressed modestly like, as Nigel Farage would say, "a bank clerk". But this was no nonentity. This was a genius.

My favourite announcer came on to announce what would happen next. She was going Goth. All in black. A short leather jacket. Hair now in a long bob, Short tight skirt and legs in black nylon. Even a hint of dye in her hair. Delicious!

She announced that Mrs. Rita Chen would be joining Krysztof to play a Grande Concertatante in E Major for piano and cello adapted for four hands. Krysztof duly went to fetch her and bring her to the piano with him while the announcement was made and piano stools arranged. Mrs. Chen appeared, dressed in a silver metallic dress. She was short with long black hair and bowed to everyone.

Krysztof seated her and reassured her before they started. While this was going on, Max did the lip reading and translated it for me:

"Have you been through the music yet?"

"I had a quick look at it. It seems OK."

"How are we going to start this? Will you play the top notes?"

"I'd better, as I am already in front of them."

"Do you know how it starts?"

"I have an idea. Let's just see how we get on."

"I thought you were going to start? Oh well. 1-2-3-4 go."

And a lovely piece it was.

At the end there was a standing ovation and an encore. The first encore I have ever heard at the concerts. Well deserved.

After the performance I took Max to have a look at Wilanów palace and gardens and to find something to eat, so we missed the four o'clock performance.

But I did go the next week, after Max had flown back home, to see a 'beginner at the start of his international career'. This was an understatement, for the 'beginner' had been gold medallist, finalist and winner of other awards in his career so far. Perhaps he was a beginner because he was still studying and was currently at the Royal College of Music in London. His name was Łukasz Krupiński. His repertoire started with a nocturne (C Minor op. 48 No. 1) of which I was unfamiliar, but it was sublime. Then a ballade (F minor Op. 52), which was enthusiastically received, followed by three familiar waltzes, the first (E Flat Major Op. 18) opening with what sounds like Morse code on one note.

The three waltzes were played as though for a Viennese version of Pride and Prejudice. The music actually danced. It was just perfect.

Finally, we came to his masterpieces – the Barcarole in F Sharp Minor Op.60) and Scherzo in B Flat Minor Op.31. They were perfect.

Having never seen an encore until the week before, I was about to see one now as the crowd continued to clap until he came back and played a short piece by Grieg, at which point they let him go. Either because he had now satisfied them, or because they had come to see Chopin and not Grieg. I don't know. Perhaps, like me, they had let him know how much they loved him and now it was time to let him go.

Except it wasn't. Someone had brought out a table and chair for him to sit at while people queued to offer him their felicitations. I last saw him standing as an elderly matron was kissing him on both cheeks. It might have been his mother, I suppose, but all the other matrons in the queue could not be.

It was yet another wonderful day of Chopin on a sunny day in the park. But it was time to go back to the flat as nature was calling and there were too many people about to be able to hide in the bushes! I was also getting chilly as I had come inappropriately dressed in shorts and polo shirt and, although sunny, there was quite a stiff breeze blowing that had a chilling effect.

The Centre

The centre of Warsaw is probably obvious: there is a transport interchange called *Centrum* at the intersection of *aleja Jerozolymskie* and *Marszałkowska,* two of the busiest roads in Warsaw. It is therefore always busy with people swapping transport. From here it is possible to get on a tram, a bus, the Metro and the suburban railway. It is the place you can easily get to from Chopin airport, either by 175 bus or suburban railway.

One stop west of Centrum is the Central Railway Station and north between these two stops is the iconic Palace of Culture and Science (*Palac Kultury i Nauki)* or PKiN. This is the building most people think of when referring to Warsaw. It was a 'present' from Josef Stalin to the people of Poland. A present they did not want. For this reason it is sometimes referred to as 'Stalin's dick'.

It is 237 metres high, including the 43 metre high spire. If Poland had been in the EU in 1990, rather than from 2004, then this would have been the tallest structure in the EU. At present it lies eighth, which just goes to show how many skyscrapers have been built since 1990. In 2018 it is still the tallest building in Warsaw, but probably not for much longer.

It has a distinctive style that cannot be mistaken. There are seven other buildings in Moscow in the same style – each different, but each bearing the characteristics of the others. The seven buildings in Moscow are often called the Seven Sisters and the one in Warsaw the Eighth Sister..

Each building has a tall tower, because Josef Stalin wanted buildings to be as impressive as the skyscrapers in America. Unfortunately, Russian technology was not as good and the buildings were inefficient.

These towers have a similar look, being of square cross-section surmounted by another tower of smaller cross-section. Round the top of the supporting tower, there are decorations, especially at the corners, in the form of statues, turrets or spires. Atop the second tower is a third tower surmounted by a spire.

The windows are oblong and inset, so that the supports appeared as long columns, giving the distinctive brand look.

The towers are surrounded by shorter, wider buildings. The one in Warsaw consists of four low buildings, making it look pretty much the same from any side, were it not for the circular Congress Hall located on the western side.

The Warsaw building was 'given' to the people of Poland by Josef Stalin, probably in recognition for the Poles keeping their Russian brethren warm with Polish coal sold at five percent of market value for many years. Some four thousand Poles and three and a half to five thousand Russians were employed on the project, which lasted from 1952 to 1955.

Naturally, the Poles, being the hosts, had to provide the Russian workers with the sort of accommodation they could only dream of at home, so housing was provided, while Poles were still emerging from the post-war devastation that had befallen their city

Four 21 metre high clock faces were added for the Millennium celebrations in 2000.

It is still the tallest tower in Warsaw, beating the Warsaw Spire at 220 metres by seventeen metres.

Out of interest, you might like to know the heights of the various tall buildings you can see on the Warsaw skyline, so here they are:

Building	Location	Metres
Palace of Culture and Science	Centrum	237
Warsaw Spire	Plac Europejski	220
Warsaw Trade Tower	Chłodna/ Towarowa	208
Q22 (Deloittes)	Rondo ONZ	195
Złota 44 (The Walkie Talkie)	Złota	192
Rondo 1	Rondo ONZ	192

Building	Location	Metres
Hotel Mariott	Centralna	170
Warsaw Financial Centre	Emilii Plater	165
Intercontinental	Emilii Plater	164
Cosmopolitan Twarda	Twarda 2/4	160
Oxford Tower	Chałubinski 8	150
Intraco 1	Stawki/ Dworzec Gdansk	138
Spektrum Tower	Twarda 14/16	128
Biękitny Wiezowie	Plac Bankowy	120

One way to see these buildings is to visit the Viewing Gallery of PkiN on the thirty first floor. Prior to visiting with my daughter and with friend Max, It had been some time since I was up there and many of the tallest skyscrapers were not built then. The more recent visits have allowed me to compare the photos I took on the first visit with those of the subsequent visits.

The gallery extends to all four sides of the building, so every part of Warsaw is visible.

There may be an exhibition in the entrance hall, as there was when I was there for the first time. It was an exhibition about Leonardo da Vinci and the most memorable exhibit was a reconstruction of his helicopter. I think I must have been in information overload mode because that is all I remember about that exhibition.

Outside there was a book fair. All the books were in Polish, although some had English translations as well. One that took my eye was a book of photographs showing artistic depictions of various places in Poland. I still have it.

PkiN had an air of Communist Warsaw about it then, which was not very inviting, so I did not stay long, but moved on to my next port of call.

PkiN is located in its own grounds. To the south there is Plac Defilad, or Parade Square, which has gardens that form a short cut for pedestrians. Most of the square is a car park, which is unsurprising. What else do you do with the second largest square in the EU?

To the north of the building is Holy Cross Gardens.

On the western edge, going north-south, is Emilii Plater.

This road has always fascinated me, initially because of the two i's at the end of Emilii. Now I know that in Polish, all the letters are pronounced and that the last 'I' indicates the genitive case, but who was Emilia Plater?

She was a noblewoman in the Polish-Lithuanian Commonwealth who fought in the November 1830 uprising against Russia. This came about because the Russians increasingly ignored the agreements made in the Congress of Vienna in 1815. This had effectively sealed the long term partition of Poland. However, Poland (or rather, the Congress Kingdom) had a fair amount of autonomy. That was until, in 1819 the Tzar Alexander I introduced censorship of the Press and in 1825 he abolished freemasonry. Things became so bad that after 1825, Sejm (Parliament) sessions were held in secret. In 1829, Tzar Nicholas I crowned himself King of Poland. Things only got worse as Poles were replaced by Russians in key administrative positions.

On 29th November 1830, a young army cadet, Piotr Wysocki led a group of conspirators against the Belweder Palace, which was the seat of the Grand Duke. The final spark that ignited this revolution was the Russian plan to use the Polish army to quell the French Revolution, which was against the Polish Constitution. Unpopular ministers were removed and their places taken by people such as Prince Adam Czartoryski, Julian Niemcewicz and Jósef Chłopicki. Prince Czartoryski tried to negotiate with Grand Duke Constantine. He managed to negotiate the forgiving of the uprisers and get an agreement that the issue would be amicably settled, but a number of radicals, led by Maurycy Mochnacki objected.

What followed came from obstinacy on both sides. On the Polish side, there was a demand for complete freedom for Poland. On the Russian side demands that the Poles subjugate themselves to the Emperor.

On 4th February 1831 a 115,000 strong Russian army crossed into Poland. The first battle took place on 14th February close to the village of Stoczek, where the Poles defeated a Russian division.

The Russians advanced on Warsaw, where a few bloody skirmishes took place.

It was in Lithuania that twenty five year old Countess Emilia Plater formed a small unit of some 280 soldiers and 60 cavalry plus a few hundred peasants. She was one of twenty eight women who fought and by far the most famous. She was regarded as a sort of Polish Joan of Arc, so there was as much legend about her as fact. Probably more so.

It appears that after the death of her mother, her father disowned her, which may be why she turned to revolution.

Although she rose in rank, it appears that she fought in few battles and that her followers tried to keep her out of battles after one in which she fainted. This was a drag on her own side, who had to protect her while they got her off the field of battle.

The might of the Russians was always going to win and the Poles dispersed. Emilia was reduced to a small band of followers and in the cold of December 1831, she became ill and died.

She was a woman, a patriot and a revolutionary.

But most of all, a legend, with Mickiewicz writing poems about her, extolling her fictional exploits. She could do no wrong!

If you look at a map of Warsaw, you will see that several streets run from east to west across Plac Defiliad, or would do, were it not there. Chmielna and Złota are two. This shows that the present from Stalin was dumped on Warsaw, cutting streets in two. This is compounded by Jan Pawla II cutting north-south, with no crossing point between Rondo ONZ and Aleja Jerozolimskie.

I rented a flat on the eastern part of Cmielna one year and found that every journey seemed to involve a trip via the subway at Centrum. The only exception was when I went north on Marszałkowska. I suspect that the advent of the car in numbers on the streets of Warsaw has made pedestrian travel a bit more difficult. It is not possible anywhere in the centre to cross the roads on the surface, so getting lost underground is a common event. As a consequence, one gets fit going up and down stairs in abortive attempts to find the exit you want.

Now if I was to ask you to tell me who he Marshal was referred to in Marszałkowska, you would probably immediately think of Piłsudski. But this is not the case. The Marshal referred to is Grand Marshal of the Crown Franciszek Bieliński.

Never heard of him! You say. So who was he to have such a main street named after him?

Although he was a member of the rarefied aristocracy, he did a lot for Warsaw.

Born in 1683 to a Grand Marshal of the Crown, Kazimierz Ludwig Bieliński, he showed skill as an administrator and supported the right families to ensure his advancement. In 1732 he became Grand Marshal of Poland in his own right.

In 1740 he created the Cobblestone Commission, which was charged with paving the streets of Warsaw and setting up a sewerage system. Over the next twenty ears, 222 streets of Warsaw were paved. This would have been in the area that is now centred on the Old Town and New Town.

In 1752 he permitted the first professional fire brigade in Warsaw.

Five years later, in 1757, he created a *jurydyka* in the area that is now the city centre. This was a tactic used by the Roman Catholic Church and the nobility to get around some of the limitations imposed by municipalities. They were legal entities, so they could make their own laws, which, for example, removed some of the restrictions imposed by craft guilds. They could be profitable for their owners, which is presumably why they were set up.

Bieliński died in 1766 at the age of 83 and, in 1770, had Marszałkowska named after him. In those days it was shorter, running from the Saxon Gardens to what is now Centrum.

The Jewish Quarter

To the north-west of the Central Railway Station is what was once the Jewish Quarter of Warsaw. This was where most of the 30% of Warsaw's population who were Jews, lived. In the inter-war period some 80% of all the Jews in the world lived in Poland. Some lived in villages and others lived in towns.,

Like any numerous minority, they congregated together. They spoke their own language. They had their own economy. They interacted with the ethnic Poles, but they were also comfortable with their own people.

Eighty-eight percent of the population of the district of Muranów were Jewish according to the 1931 census. Large populations were also found in Wola to the west and Old Praga over the river to the east. A total of 332,938 people. However, emigration due to the Great Depression left an estimated total of 270,000 Jews by 1938. The Catholic (ethnic Polish) population tended to live out of the town centre.

I went to a concert one evening at the new Jewish Museum. It was a collection of songs, poetry and dance celebrating the people who lived in Ulica Zamenhofa in the 1930's. It was a most enjoyable evening.

It was only later that I found that the street was named after the inventor of Esperanto – Ludwig Lejzer Zamenhof (1859-1917). This is why there is a main north-south road at the edge of the old Jewish Quarter that is named after the language. His youngest daughter, Lidia (1904-1942) died at Treblinka.

Many street names give an indication of the trades and products.

Sienna	Hay
Twarda	Hard
Chmielna	Hops
Chłodna	Cool
Złota	Gold
Srebna	Silver
Platyna	Platinum
Miedziana	Copper
Żelazna	Iron
Towarowa	Goods
Grzybowska	Mushrooms
Wronia	Crow
Ciepła	Warm
Krochmalna	Starch

But the Warsaw Jewish Quarter is not remembered for its mundane everyday life events: it is remembered as a ghetto. So much so, that there is a perception that it was always a ghetto, that is, a place where people were forced to live against their will. Not so. Jews lived there because it suited them. So did twelve percent of the Quarter's population who were not Jewish.

So how did it get from being a place where people wanted to live to being a place where people were forced to live?

You will have heard of Auschwitz, persecution of the Jews by the Nazis, death camps and so on, but maybe have no idea of the build-up. Hopefully, what follows will acquaint you with the gruesome events that unfolded in this part of Warsaw.

In order to conquer Warsaw, the Nazis had to bomb and shell it. Although they invaded Poland on 1st September 1939, they did not take Warsaw until 29th September. This caused a death toll of 30,000 and the destruction of 10% of the city.

Once they had subdued the Poles, and agreed the Ribbentrop-Molotov line with the Russians, the Nazis divided the country into three.

Land on the west, which had been partitioned to Germany in 1795, was absorbed into Germany.

Lands on the east, which were occupied by the Russians were of no concern.

All the rest was the General Government run by the SS.

The Nazis wanted Polish land for Germans. This was not a new policy – it had been started at the start of the twentieth century, and even had a name - *lebensraum*– but now a measure of ruthlessness could be brought to bear as Hitler was a passionate disciple of this policy. The *untermenchen*(sub-humans) who currently occupied the land, were to be liquidated. Both the ethnic Poles and the Jews were classified as *untermenchen*. The Polish leaders and intellectuals could not remain in place, for they would only rebel against the Nazis taking their homes, businesses and farms, so they had to go, which is another way of saying 'murdered'. The rest of the Poles would be serfs in the new Deutschland. Within a couple of generations they would be wiped out. In the meantime they would serve the Nazi state.

The Jews were different. They would have their own Final Solution, because Hitler hated Jews more than he did the Poles.

On October 7th, the Judenrat was formed to run the Jewish community in Warsaw according to Nazi orders. Twenty four elder statesmen of the Jewish community in Warsaw were appointed by the Nazis. They were to be led by Adam Czerniaków – a senator and a municipal engineer of some standing. Their job would be to ensure that Nazi orders were followed.

On 26th October the Jews were conscripted into clearing bomb damage

On November 20th Jewish bank accounts valued at over 2,000 zloty were frozen.

On November 23rd, all Jewish businesses had to display a Jewish Star on doors and windows.

On December 1st, all Jews over the age of ten had to display a white armband with Jewish Star.

On December 11th, Jews were forbidden to use public transport.

From January 6th 1940, Jews were banned from holding communal prayers. The considerate Nazis said that this might encourage the spread of disease with so many people in close proximity to each other. What other reason could there be?

In spite of all of this, and also because the Nazis were persecuting Jews living in villages around

Warsaw, the Jewish population in Warsaw rose to some 360,000 souls.

April 1st 1940 saw the start of the construction of the Ghetto Wall. 113,000 Gentile Poles were expelled and 138,000 Jews from the Warsaw suburbs were imported. The Ghetto Wall was officially finished on October 16th 1940. Its area was 3.07 square kilometres and its population density was nine per room.

The ghetto wall averaged three metres high, surmounted by barbed wire. It was closed on November 15th and anybody escaping would be shot on sight.

The exact location of the wall is marked in many places today by bronze markers in the ground at places around the city. These are not continuous, but they are frequent so that you can get an idea of the size of the ghetto. It extended from Złota in the south (there is a fragment you can see today at 62 Złota) to Stawki in the north and from the Jewish Cemetery near Okopowa in the west to Jan Pawla II in the east, plus a bit to the north of the New Town. As the ghetto was reduced in size over time, these plaques show the date at which the location's wall was built.

Ulica Chłodna was an important east-west route in 1940, so the Nazis made a small ghetto to the south and a larger ghetto to the north. This left the east-west transport for gentile Poles unaffected. Initially there was a gate system to allow passage from south Chłodna to north Chłodna, but this was replaced by a bridge, although not until January 1942. If you have seen Roman Polanski's *The Pianist* then you will have seen it. There is only one view which is as it was in 1940, which is from the south-west corner of Chłodna/Żelazna towards the diagonally opposite corner. This was the angle Polanski used.

There are now alternating shades of pavement at the side of Chłodna to represent the stairs of the bridge. There are two towers with wires between them, showing the height of the bridge.

Although Chłodna no longer has trams, the old tramlines are still there in the road.

Nearby, on the southern side of the street, there

is an information point that is worth reading.

Throughout Warsaw's old Ghetto area there are inlaid bronze plaques in the ground to show where the ghetto wall was on the date indicated. But then it had to be big, because 400,000 people had to be accommodated. Think of the population of Bristol or two Milton Keynes.

It was cramped.

With the closure of the wall, food could be rationed. In 1941 the average daily ration for Jews was 184 calories. (For ethnic Poles it was 699 and for Germans it was 2,613.) Today, it is recommended that women consume 2,000 calories and men 2,500 per day – more if exercising.

The food arrival was tightly controlled by the Nazis. The only way of surviving was to have smuggled food. It is estimated that some 80% of food in the ghetto was smuggled at great personal risk, because any Jew found outside the ghetto would be shot on sight.

Some of the food was bought with money earned from producing goods in private workshops in the ghetto. Some was donated by Gentile Poles, who would throw food packets over the wall, or give food to the children who were used to squeeze through small holes in the wall. This was an act of generosity, considering that the ethnic Poles were on starvation rations.

With such a large pool of labour available, it was not long before Nazi profiteers arranged for them to manufacture supplies for the German army. The Jews who were 'fortunate' enough to work for these exploiters of labour were safe from the deportations that started in the summer of 1942 in what was known as *Grossaktion Warschau.* By then, it is estimated that 100,000 ghetto inmates had died of hunger-related diseases and starvation.

In *Grossaktion Warschau,* The deportees were rounded up, street by street and told that they were to be 'resettled'. On learning that they were actually being sent to their deaths, the leader of the Judenrat, Adam Cherniaków, committed suicide with a cyanide capsule. Today, he is commemorated by having a suburb in south-east Warsaw named after him, and a road leading to it from Solec.

Jews to be deported were taken to *Umschlagerplaz* at the western end of Stawki. Today there stands a memorial in the form of a walled in area the exact size of one of the cattle-wagons used to transport Jews to Treblinka – the death camp located some fifty miles north-east of Warsaw.

At that time, there were sidings of the Gdansk

railway station (so named because that was the line to Gdansk).

The memorial contains the four hundred most popular Jewish forenames, each commemorating a thousand people killed in the Warsaw ghetto.

Between July 23rd and September 21st 1942, at least 240,000 Jews were taken to Treblinka, although some estimated 300,000. This was a period of 62 days.

When I examined the reports of numbers, they seemed somewhat at odds with other numbers. This does not mean that those numbers are necessarily wrong, but they can give a misleading impression.

For example, the trains were said to be capable of carrying 7,000 people. At 100 people per wagon, this would give a train of 70 wagons. This seems a bit long for ease of loading and unloading.

There were two journeys per day - one in the early morning, for which deportees would be rounded up the night before, and one in the afternoon. Assuming the larger number of 300,000 people transported to Treblinka, this gives an average figure of just under 5,000 or so per day, or 2,500 per trip. This would mean an average of 25 wagons per train. This would be more manageable for loading and unloading.

It may be that there were longer trains to make up for earlier shortfalls, as the 25 wagon figure is an average. It may be that one of the trains had 70 wagons, but by no means every one.

The Nazis budgeted for between 6,000 and 10,000 per day, but the total figure for exterminations over the summer of 1942 shows that they thankfully fell short.

Whatever the real figure, it is a horrendous number and one which required a high level of organisation to carry out.

For comparison, the highest number of people killed in one day, November 3rd 1943, at Majdanek was 18,400, mainly by firing squad, as part of "Operation Harvest Festival".

There are only three recorded survivors from Treblinka out of some third of a million transported there. Unlike Auschwitz and Majdanek, Treblinka was a pure death camp, designed from the outset to kill people. Not only Jews, but intellectuals, gypsies, homosexuals and anybody else the Nazis did not like. It is often overlooked, but Poland lost one sixth of its population in WW2. Between 2.35 and 2.9 million were Polish Jews, out of a total estimated between 5.6 and 5.8 million Poles of all ethnicities, meaning that around half the Poles killed by the Nazis were Jewish and half not Jewish. A further 150,000 were killed by the Russians.

Some one and a half million people live within the boundaries of the City of Warsaw in the early twenty-first century, just to give some comparison. Killing one person a second would take ten weeks to kill six million people. Ten weeks with no stopping or slowing down. Two and a half months. Over the entire six years of the war, this means a Pole dying every thirty seconds. Day and night. However you look at it, it is horrible.

The new Jewish Museum – POLIN – is located on Anielewicza, named after Mordechai Anielewicz, a Polish Jew.

He was born in 1919 and at the outbreak of war fled east, but returned to Warsaw in January 1940 to set up a resistance group.

It was not until the end of 1941 that news spread of the mass murder of Jews. Anielewicz immediately organised resistance, but unsuccessfully. Maybe this twenty-two-year-old had little authority.

Anielewicz managed to escape the ghetto in April 1942 and travel to south-west Poland to organise resistance. It was a good time to leave, because at this time the Nazis started to organise the deportation of Jews to the labour and extermination camps.

By September 12th 300,000 had been deported, leaving some 55-60,000 in the ghetto.

Between September 1942 and January 1943 the Nazis left the ghetto alone, while they turned their attention to killing people from other parts of their Reich, which gave remaining Jews time to build some 600 fortified positions within the ghetto and the Polish Home Army managed to smuggle a small amount of guns, ammunition and explosives into the ghetto.

On January 18th 1943, the Nazis entered the ghetto with the intention of rounding up more Jews for deportation.

In the process, 600 Jews were shot and five thousand expelled from their homes. But this was brought to a halt by the appearance of hundreds of insurgents armed with handguns and Molotov cocktails. The Nazis were thwarted.

Emboldened by their success, the Jews executed a number of collaborators from an organisation known as Zagiew – a collaborationist fifth column who tried to infiltrate Jewish resistance organisations and Polish organisations helping Jews.

Peace reigned in the ghetto until April 21st, when several thousand Nazi troops entered the ghetto and systematically went trough it, burning and demolishing every building, murdering anybody they found.

Most resistance stopped on April 28th. On May 16th the Nazis marked the end of the operation by demolishing the Great Synagogue of Warsaw, which was located where the Biękitny Wieżowiec building now stands at Ratusz Arsenał.

By May 8th, the Jewish resistance was confined to a bunker, where three hundred people were hiding. Those that could get out had already gone: eighty had fought their way out and more had tried the sewer route.

There is a remembrance on the website of the water and sewerage authority that commemorates the departure of many insurgents on the night of May 8th 1943, guided by two employees of the authority: Wacław Śledziewski and Czesław Wojciechowski. After a few hours, they reached a manhole under Ul. Prosta, where, some accounts say, they waited 48 hours until it was safe to emerge.

There is a monument to this event at 51 Prosta.

Mordechai Anielewicz and his girlfriend, were either gassed or committed suicide in the bunker at 18 Miła, where a monument stands today.

According to the Nazis, the army disposed of 56,065 Jews; killed 7,000; transported 7,000 to Treblinka and deported the remaining 42,000 to other death camps.

A number of Jews escaped from the ghetto and lived to fight the Nazis with guerilla warfare. Some survived long enough to take part in the Warsaw Uprising of August 1944.

Mordechai Anielewicz has been remembered as a brave Jewish fighter. The road bearing his name passes by the new Jewish Museum, outside which is a memorial to the Ghetto Fighters.

Nearby is a pleasant square named after Mieczysław Apfelbaum – another leader in the ghetto Uprising, but also an officer in the Polish Army. The only problem is that there is no authenticated evidence that he ever lived. It would seem that the Warsaw Jews wanted a king Arthur figure to be a legend.

On the orders of Hitler, the Warsaw Ghetto was completely levelled after all the Jews had been removed, so there is nothing to see of the prewar Jewish area. There is a classic photo of the ghetto after it was destroyed that shows rubble everywhere. In the distance is a church. This is Saint Augustine's church on Nowolipkie, near Jan Pawla. This had been used as a storage warehouse, so was spared.

After the war, the Polish government needed to rebuild, so the rubble was bulldozed off the streets, compacted and built on. This is why, when you walk around the old ghetto area you see apartment blocks with steps leading up from the road to the entrance doors.

Two bits of the ghetto that did survive are fragments of the wall. These can be seen at 56 Sienna and 62 Złota. They are not easy to find, but worth the effort.

Military Museum and Zloty Teras

I should have know it would be a different day in May 2018. I had woken in the morning and started the day, only to realise that it was only 6:30 and I really hadn't had enough sleep. So back to bed and a crash out until gone eight, when I still felt tired. So dozed for another hour before getting up.
The night before I had sunk around 60ml of blueberry vodka (delicious) and this might have contributed to the lethargy.

Still no washing powder for the washing machine and I was soon going to smell too natural for comfort, so I dashed off a second text to the agents and groggily went about getting ready for an exciting day at the National Military Museum. This is situated next to the National Museum, which I had frequented in previous visits and found it to be a worthy museum – the sort I remember from my youth.

It was not the fault of the museum. They had to stock it with whatever they could recover from the material that had been confiscated by Goering and others. The country was too poor to outbid other museums for great works, but it was good for modern Polish artists, of whom there are many.

Anyway, this time I was going to see fighting stuff.

Both museums are effectively in the same very large building, but with different entrances. The large building is shaped like the letter E, with the prongs pointing towards the road. The top two prongs contain the National Museum and the bottom prong contains the military museum. The Military Museum is entered through a gate next to the Poniatowski Bridge. So all I had to do was to alight the tram after Nowy Swiat. This is the advantage of having been somewhere before – you know what to do. So I anticipated the stop after we left Nowy Swiat and the amazing palm tree at the Charles de Gaulle roundabout, and looked to alight opposite the museum.

Now there is a bus stop outside the museum, but not a tram stop. The next tram stop I knew of was on the other side of Poniatowski. So much for knowing Warsaw!

OK. It's a nice day and it will only cost ten minutes, so I'll catch one back and walk back from Nowy Swiat, now that I know better.

Out at the next stop, Rondo Waszingtona, and down the underpass to the other side of the tram lines.

It could have been the shapely figure of the young lady in front of me, or it could have been my poor eyesight, but when I went up the stairs to the platform, I saw that there were another two tramlines in front of me, with another stop beyond.

I rationalised the way you do in these situations, that I must be on the right platform. This was confirmed when I looked at the terminal destinations shown on the electronic departures board. Annapolis was, I knew, somewhere near Zoliborg, and Zoliborg was on the Warsaw side of the river.

But the arrival of the next tram from the Centre to my platform told me I was wrong. And yes, Annapolis is near Zoliborg, but somewhat east and over the river in the Praga side.

Down the stairs and up the stairs and on to the next platform and next tram

It had gone about half way across the bridge when I heard the announcement (in Polish of course) "Next Stop National Museum". So I got off. In the middle of the bridge. With no convenient path on either side to the National Museum. Or anywhere that was not off the bridge.

So it was down the steps to a choice of left or right.

As no tourist would ever dream of being here, there were no signs. Museum is on the left, so take the left, was my thought in response to the dilemma. This took me under the tramlines.

Then a choice of up or down. Up would go to the opposite platform (I climbed them just to be sure), so it was down. Down through a maze of steps that would not have been out of place in the nether reaches of the Paris Opera at the time of the Phantom. Down and down. Left and right branches. Always down.

To the road. And a sign that said Solec. That sign gave me A Quantum of Solace. There was a road sign that said "3 Maja" - Third of May – Constitution of 1791.

The bridge was now way above me. There was no choice. If I had been deranged, I might have climbed back, singing excerpts from the *Phantom* as I climbed the scaffold stairs again, but as men never ask for directions, I ploughed on along 3rd May hoping it would get to the 4th May. And ploughed on. Until what can only be described as a castle wall obstructing my way. A bit like an Escher drawing. And soon I could see Escher men (and women) ascending and descending hidden stairs.

It was too good not to photograph, as I hoped I would never come this way again.

It was then that I saw someone else with the same idea. He was probably in his early thirties with what can only be described as a continental beard. One that tames itself and is very black.

We got talking about the best place for a picture, during which process it rapidly became apparent that neither of us was Polish. He was Alex from Spain. He was here because there was no work in Spain. Nor was there any work for a non-Polish speaking Spaniard in Poland.

Now it has always bemused me why anybody other than those with Polish ancestry would want to be in Poland and Alex looked more Moor than Slavic. So why spend money he did not have to come to a country where nobody but Poles spoke the language?

The answer was obviously a woman. He had come with his girlfriend and she had dumped him. Probably because of his epilepsy. Added to which he suffered from Seasonal Affective Disorder in the crap Polish winter.

As his tale of woe continued, it encompassed the Poles who had no tolerance for people who did not speak Polish, unless they were spending money. I suspect that the Poles are equally as bad in this as every other nation on earth. Nobody likes a winger. Anywhere.

That set him off about the crap health service you could get for free in Poland and how you had to be rich to go private to get a proper service.

This then led onto the average wage of the lowest paid (somewhere between 100 and 400 'euros a month according to him.). According to figures I had seen, the average pay in Poland was around £1,000 per month, but I was not going to push it. And he was talking about the lower paid and not the average which was skewed by the rich middle and upper classes.

I can only hope he finds his way back to Spain, where at least he will get better light and will be able to speak to the crappy doctors in the crappy free health service in Spain, which he cannot do to the crappy doctors in the crappy free Polish health system.

Having successfully avoided having a fight, it was time to see what happens when diplomacy fails and look at some armaments.

I became one of Escher's figures and climbed to the top of the castle wall. I must admit to feeling rather proud of myself at having made it, as it was some climb and I am no mountain goat.

There it was. A crocodile of children, led by a

teacher, were snaking in through the gates of the military museum.

Muzeum Wojska Polskiego.

The museum has two parts: the outside part, which is free and the inside part which is not free.

In the outside part there are things that are too big to go into the inside part. Like the transport plane.

There were lots of planes and all seemed to be of a vintage pre-1990. There were a couple of what looked like MIGs, which looked like poor copies of the F1. One plane had painted flames coming from the front of the plane, from where the air intake sat. Whether this was bravado, showing what happened when the Polish pilots gave it some wellie, or whether it was a decoy to convince western pilots that the plane was going to crash anyway, so leave it be, I'll never know. It seemed rather an odd thing to paint on the plane.

There was a more modern fighter jet, looking a bit like a Typhoon or Tornado (my knowledge of military planes needs improving). It looked old, like all the other exhibits, rusting gently away.

The planes all seemed to come from the Polish Air force. The insignia of the Polish Air force is stylish: a square with alternating red and white quadrants, each outlined with a set-square line of the other colour.

It was not only planes that were outside. There were guns. Big guns, little guns; old guns, newer guns.

Guns that were mounted on ships and guns that were mounted on aircraft. There were missiles and their launchers and shells so big you would not be able to close your arms around their girth.

It was pleasant strolling round the exhibits in the sunshine, listening to the teachers describing the main exhibits and their importance to history. For many of the young girls this was boring and the odd one or two preferred picking daisies.

After some time of enjoying myself, it was time to stop. A rain cloud came over and started to accelerate the rusting process on the planes by watering the exhibits and me. It was time to see the paid part of the show.

At the cash desk (pointed to by a sign that also showed the way to the toilets) I was asked *normalny albo oglowy*? Normal or discount? Bless her. She should have seen that I was oglowy, so I told her and got a reduced price ticket for 8zl. I was gesticulated at to leave my rucksack at the cloakroom and not to use flash with the camera she could see dangling from my neck.

Rucksack deposited, I made my way to the entrance, where I was greeted by a lady. She was not a welcoming party, but there to see my ticket, off which she tore the stub and then welcomed me with a smile and a warning not to use flash.

So in I went.

The first room seemed to have maps on the wall showing the movement of somebody into Poland from the south west and another map showing people entering Poland from the north east and east. I could see nothing in English to tell me more, but presumably it was some time ago, because the next room was full of knights' armour. I spent some time trying to work out what I should be looking at in the detail, because to me all suits of armour look a bit the same, although on closer examination, each owner had put his own personality on it. Unsurprising, given what they must have cost to make.

One poor chap had a few dents in the breastplate . I was wondering whether the museum had acquired it from the owner's ancestry or from the victor's ancestry.

Then there were the pikes and blades with curves, with serrations, narrow and broad and with a Turkish influence, reminding me that this part of the world saw the Ottoman Empire as a real threat.

And so, gradually, we came to the first World War, with many uniforms and weapons. There were scenes of cabins in the trenches, although there were not many trenches in the East as the lines of battle were very fluid, unlike in the West. However, in the Polish-Ukrainian war which followed WW1, the battle did get bogged down in trench warfare.

It was fascinating to see the different weapons displays and uniforms. All rather well laid out. I could have done with more English descriptions, but then I suppose most visitors are Polish schoolchildren, judging by the number I saw.

After the best part of an afternoon looking at ways to kill people, I decided to take a random bus ride, which involves getting on a bus, getting off and onto another until the stops are all shuffled and then trying to get back to somewhere civilised. In doing this, I happened to end up by the Central Railway Station, which I knew was near Zloty Teras, which contained the Thai fast food place on the top floor.

This I must describe.

Zloty Teras

Zloty Teras is a modern building that houses a shopping mall and restaurants. It is approached from the Emilii Plater side via what looks like bubbles coming out of a large pipe, but in reality is a complex structure of glass triangles. Inside it has a number of elevators to take you to any of the three floors.

The top floor is fast food. All the usual American chains are there, plus some Polish ones. There is North Fish, which does unusual and tasty fish recipes and a Thai restaurant, which is my favourite.

The chef is a tiny, skinny Oriental who seems to be the hardest working person there. I have never seen him except when he is rushing around. The servers are all Polish women, who serve what you want from the canteens of different foods behind the glass front. Rice comes from a cauldron. Service is fast and efficient.

There are tables and chairs everywhere on the patio area that surrounds the food outlets, where one can eat and drink. At peak times it can be difficult to get a table, but there is high turnover, so something is usually available.

It was to this Thai restaurant that I went and ordered spicy beef and rice, with an orange juice drink to temper the flames.

So there I was with my spicy beef stew on rice and no empty table to sit at. I had seen the odd empty table outside the next restaurant, but now I wanted to sit, there were no free spaces. Except at a table for four occupied by an attractive young lady.

Now my food was cooling and I didn't really want to be thought of as a pervert (as anybody over the age of fifty is if they even look at a woman of any age). But my desire for food overcame any imaginings of perversification. So I asked in my best Polish whether a seat was free (which was so bad that it obviously came from a pervert who was English, and we all know what they got up to in their boarding schools and the way they could speak no other language than their own). So I avoided eye contact and tackled the delicious spiced beef stew as though we were the only things in the world.

She finished her meal, got up, looked me in the eye and beamed *"Smacznego"* which roughly translates to "enjoy your meal". She was lovely and normal and we had missed out on the opportunity for nice conversation.

So I continued eating my spiced beef as though we were the only things in the world when I was removed from my reveries by a gorgeous young lady of about twenty, who asked if she could share my table. Talk about living dangerously. Didn't she know that I could have been a pervert from an English boarding school?

This time I decided to behave like a normal human being and struck up a conversation with her. "Do you speak English?" I asked.

What followed was the most delightful hour for both of us as we smattered our way through in a combination of English and Polish.

She had the advantage of learning English for eleven years at school, but the disadvantage of not having the oral practise. But as she became accustomed to speaking her English, she became rapidly more fluent, unlike me.

She was in Warsaw from her home town of Kielice, where she was at university for the next five years. She was in Warsaw so that she could audition to become the Voice of Poland on the TV reality show. She was a singer.

Well, if I had not finished my spicy beef, I could have been wearing it at this news. And she was so modest. This did not come about until later in the conversation when we got to the "and what brings you to Warsaw" part of any strangers' conversation.

She would have my vote. She was delightful, pretty (in the pretty girl-next-door kind of way), caring, intelligent and without a trace of arrogance. I gave her my email address with a request to let me know the outcome.

It was during the later part of the conversation that she learned two new English phrases: bragging rights (as in what I would have at every opportunity until I die, as I dined out on the story of having shared a table with the Voice of Poland) and "it won't make any difference" (as in how I would feel about her whether she won or lost.

We walked to the railway station together and I learned the direct way from Zloty Teras to the railway station, whereas I would have taken her on a fifteen minute walk that would have involved Jana Pawel II and Jerozolymskie (and possibly Marszałsowska if we had got lost).

We parted and I can only hope that I hear from her. However, we lived in the moment for around an hour. It was delightful, but it was a memory.

My only regret was that I did not create an opportunity for such a conversation with the *Smacznego* girl. But then that conversation might have occupied the chair of the Voice of Poland girl.

Whatever, it shows that you get nowhere by not interacting in a human way.

As a postscript, many months later, I went onto the internet and searched on Voice of Poland and found my young lady. She had not won the competition, but had reached the finals. For the first time, I could hear and see her singing. She was delightful.

Ulica Szucha

Ul. Jana Chrystiana Szucha is a pretty street near to the Botanic Gardens. It runs from the southern end of Marszałkowska at Plac Unii Lubielskiej to Plac Na Rozdrożu. It is named after a German, Johann Christian Szuch, who was appointed by King Sobieski III to redesign, with a couple of others, Łazienki Park. For this, the king gave him a large estate, complete with serfs, in this area. Not a bad reward for doing a Capability Brown.

Szuch was born in Dresden in 1752 to a father who was a court gardener to a ducal dynasty. He would therefore have been well off, which he would need to be to attend the Dresden academy of Fine Arts, where he studied painting and civil engineering. To improve his knowledge, he travelled to the best gardens in Europe, including Kew, Grand Trianon and Schönbrunn Palace.

In 1775, he came to Poland and worked for the aristocracy until, in 1781, he became superintendent of royal gardens at the court of King Stanisław August Poniatowski. It was about this time that, with a couple of talented architects, he designed Łazienki Park.

Szuch never went back to Germany, continuing to design palaces and gardens for the rich aristocrats after the partition of Poland in 1795.

At the northern end of Szucha is number 25, where is located the Ministry of National Education, It is also the home of a smaller ministry – the Ministry of Struggle and Martyrdom, just inside the main door, on the left, which is where I went one sunny day in 2014.

In WW2, this building was home to the Sicherheitsdienst, or the SS to you and me. (We briefly mentioned this building in the description of the Royal Route.) You will not be surprised to learn that the whole road was closed to Poles, except for those specially invited, always with a Nazi or two to accompany them, should they get lost.

The entrance is down some stairs to the basement, where the accommodation for the Poles was located.

This area is now a museum, where the original construction has been preserved so that you can appreciate it as it was in WW2.

To help you appreciate what it would have been like there, there are recordings of what you would have heard had you been a guest . The sound of jackboots walking on the pavement outside and in the corridor, off which were the cells. The clink of manacles. The occasional scream.

And then there were the shadowy figures projected onto screens. You cannot make out exactly what is being done to them, but you can get a good idea.

It is perhaps the most chilling place I have visited and could only thank my luck that I was born in a different time to the people who passed into here, some of whom made it outside, but most of whom ended their lives here, or in the Pawiak Prison, which was a sister location.

Many of those who did not make it out of here were killed and burned, either here or in neighbouring buildings. After the war, the *weight* of human *ashes* found was 5,578.5 kilos and later buried at the Warsaw Insurgents' Cemetery. That is upward of five and a half tonnes of ashes.

After the war the site was designated as a site of martyrdom – a testament to the suffering and heroism of the many Poles who were tortured and died there. The jail would remain untouched. Hallways, four group cells and ten solitary cells were preserved. The Gestapo officer's room was recreated on the basis of recollections of those who survived.

The museum was opened in April 1952.

One sixth of the Polish population was killed in WW2 – some 6.5 million people, half of whom were Jewish.

The death of so many people is a statistic. The death of an individual is a tragedy.

People like Radomiła Zofia Piątkowska, née Śląska, born in 1920 and killed in 1942. She was a graduate of Warsaw University's History Faculty and the College of Journalism. She taught at an underground secondary school and co-operated with the Resistance by providing intelligence. She graduated to sabotage. She was interrogated and tortured at Szucha and hanged by the deputy prison governor, F. Burkl, at Pawiak Prison.

People like Jan Piekałkiewicz, who was a statistician. Born in 1892 in Kursk, he attended St. Petersburg University, after which he worked for three years until 1918 for the Russian Statistical Service. In 1918 he returned to Poland and settled in the family manor house near Biała. In 1924 he gained his PhD and became Chair of Statistics at the School of Political Science in Warsaw. He became a member of the Supreme Council of the People's Movement. He was isolated at Szucha for two and a half months, where he underwent severe interrogation and torture. He died of his wounds in 1943, aged 51.

During the war, some half million Warsawians were murdered, some 350,000 being Jewish. It started with the intelligentsia being murdered secretly in places like Kabaty forest and the parliament gardens. Later in the war, the executions became public and random as a means of instilling terror into the population.

In Szucha, the tortures could only be heard by other inmates, who could let their imaginations tell them what it would be like when it was their turn. Some of the cells of the museum let my imagination wander, ably assisted by those sounds.

The cell with the rod and shackle bolted into the floor. With a pointed spike next to it. The spike had a rubber ball at one end, presumably to protect the delicate hand of the Nazi who was using it on some poor soul.

The cell with the bookcase, devoid of books, but resplendent with rods and shackles of several varieties. How were they used?

I didn't really want to know, because I knew it would be something awful. Those screams did not come form somebody biting their cheek when eating a biscuit.

There was the infamous "Tramline" cell, where there were rows of seats facing the far wall. Single chairs on the left; double benches on the right. Inmates were told to keep quiet while waiting. Perhaps the scream I heard while looking at this cell came from someone who spoke to his neighbour? Waiting. Sometimes for days. Presumably they wet themselves, or worse. That would not make them popular with the fragrant Nazis.

As it became more difficult to conceal the deaths, so executions in public increased. I recalled the scene in *The Pianist*, where one of the characters was randomly selected, along with six others. The Nazi officer started at the other end, one shot to each forehead of the kneeling people, followed by collapse forward. Until the last one, because all the rounds in the pistol had been discharged. Surely the last person would be absolved? No. We waited an eternity for a new magazine to be loaded. Then the shot, followed by the collapse to the ground.

In the museum there is a map showing how prisoners were transported between Szucha and Pawiak, along with countless maps showing how many killings took place each year in each location of Warsaw, but by this time, it was too much for me. I wanted to go out into the sunshine. To go and get the bus by Aleija Armii Ludowi, briefly renamed after Lech Kaczynski. Lech Aleksander Kaczyński was the twin brother of Jarosław Kaczyński. They were respectively the President of Poland and the Prime

Minister. Lech died at Smolensk North Airport in Ukraine while he and ninety-two other Polish dignitaries went to commemorate those killed at Katyn. Naturally, conspiracy theories abound as to whether it was an accident or not. It did not help that he was an active anti-communist since the 1970's and prominently against corruption. As Lech was also a former Mayor of Warsaw, he is commemorated widely throughout the city and having a major road named in his honour was only one manifestation of that. However, it must have been a renaming too far, because it has now reverted to its former name - Al. Armii Ludowej – People's Army road.

Katyn

For the Poles, there is probably no more evocative word than 'Katyn'. A forest outside of Smolensk in Russia.

The story is interesting as well as macabre.

We have already come across the Soviet-German Non-aggression Pact of August 1939 and the subsequent invasion of Poland from the East by the Russians on 17th September 1939. It was during this invasion that the Russians captured many Polish soldiers and officers as well as civilians. I remember my father telling me of how he had to argue with his officer friend, Olek, to get out of his officer's uniform and put on a lowly soldier's uniform. Olek had apparently believed that the Russians would treat the officers well, but my father knew different. Following my father's advice was probably the best decision that Olek ever made. He survived the war as a result.

When the Nazis invaded the Soviet Union in June 1941, the Poles became allies of the Russians, so in forming his army, General Anders asked Stalin for the officers that had gone missing. "They've escaped and went to Manchuria," was the response. This was the first Russian lie about what happened to those officers.

So Anders was left with an army without officers.

The Nazi advance east in 1942 reached the area

of Smolensk. Captured Polish railroad workers heard from the locals of mass graves of Polish officers in the area. The information was passed to the Polish Underground State (basically, the Resistance), but they thought nothing of it, believing that there were few corpses.

It was not until April 1943 that the Germans announced that they had found the remains of 4,443 Polish officers, who had been interned at a prisoner-of-war camp nearby, until May 1940.

Goebels saw this as a propaganda coup to drive a wedge between the Poles, the Russians and the Allies.

The Russians denied this, saying that the officers had been on a construction project in 1941 and had been over-run by the Nazis when they took the area at that time. So they hadn't escaped to Manchuria! (They also had not been engaged on a construction project.)

The Nazis called in the German Red Cross and the International Red Cross, both of whom confirmed that each body had been shot in the back of the head between March and May 1940 – a time when the Russians controlled the area.

The date of May 1940 was the date that the Polish government-in-exile insisted was the date of the massacre. The Russians broke off diplomatic relations with the Polish government-in-exile and formed its own Polish Government composed of Polish communists.

The lie was promulgated for decades.

One attempt at obfuscation was to conflate Nazi massacres in Belorussia with the massacre of the officers and intellectuals. Coincidentally, there was a village in Belorussia called Khatyn, where, indisputably, there had been massacres by the Nazis of civilians. The Russians built a memorial at the village to the officers and those civilians killed by the Nazis.

But the Poles wanted the truth to come out.

The Poles in England were denied a memorial to the massacre while they insisted on including the date of May 1940. They could have a memorial, but not with the date. Opposition came from the British Government, under pressure from the Soviet Union. I remember my parents talking about this. On 18th September 1976 in Gunnersbury Cemetery, London, the first Katyn memorial in the world was unveiled. Designed by Louis Fitzgibbon and Count Stefan Zamoyski, it consisted of a black obelisk mounted on a plinth. Under a plaque is some soil taken from the mass grave at Katyn.

On the obelisk is the word 'Katyn' with the date '1940' underneath. There is no mistaking the message., which is probably why no British official attended the opening ceremony in official capacity, although several did unofficially. The wording on the plinth reads: *The conscience of the world calls for the truth. In remembrance of 14,500 Polish prisoners-of-war who disappeared in 1940 from camps at Kozielsk, Starobielsk and Ostazkow of whom 4,500 were later identified in mass graves at Katyn near Smolensk.* No punches pulled there then.

The wording on the plaque is equally

unforgiving: *This casket contains soil from their grave. Murdered by the Soviet secret police on Stalin's orders1940. The soil hereunder came from their graveyard 1990. As finally admitted in April 1990, by the USSR after 50 years shameful denial of the truth.* Gorbachev was the President who admitted that the NKVD had been responsible.

The leaders of the Polish government in Poland for 50 years refused to acknowledge the massacre, but then they were subservient to the Russians.

Following the formation of a non-communist government in the late 1980's, this Polish government shifted the blame from the Germans to the NKVD. In 1992 the Russians released documents that showed that the Politburo and NKVD had been responsible for some 20,000 deaths.

There are still other mass graves to be discovered, but it is likely that their contents would have been well and truly destroyed to save the Russian government any more embarrassment from the pesky Poles.

The reason for the massacre was simple: Stalin was looking to the post-war period and did not want a Poland run by intellectuals. It was not only officers that were murdered, it was policemen, professors and others of talent.

When in Krakow in 2005, I saw a procession commemorating Katyn and followed it to a simple memorial of a cross with 'Katyn' in metal letters and '1940' underneath. There was no mistaking the message.

In 2007 a film was released, called simply, 'Katyn' and directed by Andrzej Wajda, it was a dramatic telling of what happened.

According to declassified Russian documents released in 1990, 21,857 Polish internees and prisoners were executed after April 3rd 1940.

Of these, 14,552 were prisoners of war from three camps: Kozielsk (4,421); Starobielsk(3,820) and Ostaszkow (6,311).The other 7,305 were from Ukrainian and Belarusian prisons.

The BBC produced a very informative six-episode documentary called *Behind Closed Doors*, which covered the dealings between the three Allied leaders during the war. The fate of the Polish officers was raised several times in those meetings, without Stalin providing satisfactory answers. The documentary series can be obtained as a DVD box set and is worth watching.

In doing my research, I came across an interesting revelation in the documents released by the Russians: the guns used to shoot the Poles were originally Russian, but later were switched to German. Not so that the Germans could be blamed, but because their guns had less recoil and this was kinder to Russian wrists. One NKDV officer personally shot 7,000 Poles in the back of he head, so he would have had a case for getting time off work had it not been for a change in hand gun.

You should be able to pick up a copy of *Katyn* from any Empik store. It is worth watching.

Long Night of the Museums

This was the main reason for my visit in May 2018.

Every year, towards the end of May, Warsaw museums open their doors between seven in the evening and one the following morning. Entrance is free, so you can imagine that the event is well-attended.

Special buses are laid on that pass by many of the museums in the scheme and the route that takes in the tram depots in Wola is serviced by buses dating from the communist era. These buses are in demand just for the experience of riding a piece of history.

Now the reason that I wanted to partake in this night was to see a piece of Victorian engineering designed and managed by an Englishman – William Lindley. This was the water treatment works called Filtry. The clue is in the title – it filters the water from the Vistula so that it is potable.

Unlike most filtration systems, this is not placed by the river, but occupies some valuable land near the centre of the city – at the Ochota end of Al. Jerozolimskie to be precise.

I had seen this from the outside in previous visits to Warsaw and was intrigued by it. It looked solid and designed to last, but it did not have any Russianness about it. This had elegance and no sign of being finished to a deadline (although I am sure that there would have been one).

It was only when researching it one day that I found that it was open on the Long Night of the Museums and on International Water Day, which happened in March. It seemed sensible to book my next trip to include Museum Night.

But this isn't all that my research revealed. The history of the site and the project was also very interesting.

It seems hard to believe, but there was actually opposition to its construction in the late 19th century. There was opposition to the fact that it was being promoted by the President of Warsaw (1875 to 1892), a Russian general who had been appointed to the position. Secondly, the engineer appointed to design the works was English, and not Polish. In fact neither the president nor the engineer could speak any Polish. This was obviously a useful attribute when the objections were raised, because neither man would be able to understand that there were objections and so proceeded on with the task.

The project was designed for a city of half a million people, even though the size of the city at the time was only some 300,000.

In 1876, the contract for the design of the works was signed. I don't know whether this was signed in English or in Polish or both, but Lindley started work on it and a couple of years later presented the final designs to the council. The advantage of the design was that it could easily be extended as the city grew in size.

By 1881, the first phase had been developed. As William Lindley had retired in 1879, the work was completed by his son William Heerlein Lindley.

The works would be completed in 1886.

Warsaw joined an exclusive club of six cities in Europe which had a sewage system, although by 1888 only 55 houses had been connected to the sewage system. By 1900, the year in which William Lindley senior died, the sewage system was 234 km long.

The cost was enormous. The city's annual budget was in the region of 2.5 million roubles, and the cost of the sewage system was about 17 million roubles.

A by-product of the sewage system was construction of maps to show where pipes were. They were drawn up between 1883 and 1950 and are among the most outstanding works of cartography in the world and are still in use today.

Public donations enabled the bust of President Starynkiewicz to be erected in 1907. Even though all traces of Russian domination were removed from the city after 1918, the bust of Sokrates Starynkiewicz was left unharmed until the Nazis destroyed it.

There is a statue to William Lindley Junior in the Castle Gardens. The nearest statue of his father is in Hamburg, where it was erected in 2008. Perhaps it is time for another public subscription.

The plant still operates today in its original design form.

Before we go on to think about the water filtration plant, it is worthwhile taking a small diversion to learn a bit about Sokrates Starynkiewicz, for he is a remarkable man.

Sokrates Starynkiewicz

He was born in 1820 and served a career in the Russian army. In 1875 he was appointed the 19th president of Warsaw. He rapidly showed that he was a great organiser and engineer. His achievements while in this office were remarkable.

He created the horse-drawn tramway net, the first telephone lines, and a cemetery in Brodno. He paved many streets and squares and parks and in 1896 created the new Ujazdowski Park.

He introduced modern street gas lighting and built a modern marketplace at Halle Mirowska. He also started paving the streets of Warsaw and ordered the 1882 and 1892 censuses.

He must have been pleased with what he had achieved because after his retirement in 1892 he decided to stay on in Warsaw until his death in 1902. His funeral was watched by hundreds of thousands of Warszawians. He is buried in the Orthodox cemetery in the borough of Wola.

When I told friends and neighbours that I was going to Poland to see a water treatment plant, they looked pityingly on me. But even more pityingly on Lin, who had to live with this deranged man.

Even telling them about the English provenance of this undertaking did not much ameliorate their feelings.

Even knowing that a road in Warsaw, near the filtration system, was named after Lindley, did nothing. They all thought I was mad. I did not tell them about Lindley's design of the pre-stressed concrete bridge in Ujazdowski Park that I mentioned to you earlier. That would have really got them going!

The arrangement on the Long Night of the Museums was that two groups of twenty five would be given a half hour tour each half hour. That was one hundred people an hour.

I decided to get there for six, which should see me at the front of the queue, so I set off in good time and got to the end of the queue around six fifteen as the traffic had been heavy.

There was a steady stream of people arriving at the queue, both from the direction I had come and the other direction.

A tall, slim, early twenties woman joined behind me, followed by a group of Oriental/Polish, who seemed to be work colleagues, all talking loudly in English. The girl and I exchanged a few glances at this raucousness and then started a conversation. She seemed reluctant to speak to a pervert from an English boarding school, but, realising that this was going to be a long night, we started a stilted conversation.

She was an engineer by training and worked for Samsung.

She was joined by a colleague – a slightly shorter,

but still slim and attractive twenty-something who turned out to be a work colleague from IT. She also attended the Polish-Japanese University of Computing, which happened to have its buildings on the opposite side of the road to where we were standing.

Apparently, Japanese youngsters learn Polish because it is a difficult language, which then shows how clever the student is. (No doubt they will already have learned English.). As Michael Caine might have said "Not many people know that."

Some while later, a third slim, twenty-something joined. She was another work colleague and also, as I later found out, Ukrainian.

I was beginning to wonder if this queue joining was going on further up the line. We were still not making much progress, with the occasional shuffle of a few yard advancement every now and then.

Somehow, one of the Chinese behind us seemed to become one of our little group. One of his first questions was to ask whether any of us spoke Chinese. Surprisingly, the engineer said that she had been learning Chinese. "Have you been to China?"

"No."

"You must come. Speak Chinese. Only nine hour direct flight to Beijing from Warsaw."

"Nine hours seems a long time."

"No. Ver' quick."

"You been to China?" he asked me.

"No."

"Why not? You like big cities – Shanghai, Peking,

Hong Kong."

"I have no reason to go. There are plenty of places to see in Europe."

"You speak Polish?"

"A little."

"I been here one year. Polish difficult."

"Yes, but Chinese is more difficult."

"Yes."

"All those characters."

"Yes. Ver' difficult, even for Chinese."

He continued. "I be here one year. Still cannot pwonownce Polish words and street name. Even street here difficult"

I realised that he was not referring to Lindleya, where we were, but to the nearby main east-west road in Warsaw. "You mean like Jerozolymskie," I said with a certain amount of pride. I had practised this some time ago because it was an important one to get right.

"You say OK, but difficult for me." He reverted back to the difficulties of Chinese and by way of encouragement, he turned to the engineer and said, "If you learn for ten years, you will not know Chinese characters."

The engineer was now looking a bit pissed off. If this was the quality of conversation she could look forward to when fluent, she might change her mind about studying it further.

"Warsaw cheap." A new tack had begun. The engineer looked, and I felt, a bit hacked off by this.

"To buy flat ver' cheap. You buy flat?" This was directed at the pissed-off engineer.

"No."

"Why not? Get mortgage from Bank Pekao. Buy flat for ten year."

"I don't know where I will be in ten years."

"I buy you flat. Ver' cheap. You choose flat. I buy. Charge low rent. You sign ten year lease."

"So you buy the flat with the rent and have the flat at the end of the term," I said, hoping to make this man's intentions clear.

"You four," he said to the three women and one male work colleague, who had somehow joined them, "You four should buy flat, then buy another. One. Two three four." He flicked a finger up for each number to emphasise the point.

He may as well have been explaining this through Chinese pictograms for all the sense he was making to these women, who were probably struggling, even though they were of above average incomes (I assumed).

"Do you know what a mortgage is?" I asked the engineer.

"Not really."

I then made the mistake of trying to explain what a mortgage was to someone who didn't want one.

Fortunately the subject changed to the queue. The IT girl had gone off to the front of the queue and returned with the news that there were to be 300 lucky people to go on a tour of the works, but that we were somewhere over that number in the queue.

We debated this. We had been in the queue for

two hours and gained little ground.

I went to have a look for myself. The queue beat all my expectations. This must be the most popular event in Warsaw. People must have been queuing since four o'clock or earlier. And they were probably place-markers for friends to join them, judging by our lack of progress.

I returned. The group of four had decided that there was no chance of getting to be one of the three hundred, so were going to go to the Warsaw Spire – the second tallest building in Warsaw, where the 41st floor viewing gallery was to be opened to the public tonight. Even though they all worked in the building, they had never been to the 41st floor. They left, but I decided to wait for Chinaman, who had gone to see the situation for himself. He came back a few minutes later and confirmed that he would go, but not now. I bade my farewell and left. There was no pleasure in waiting four hours making conversation with a Chinaman, only to find out that you were number 301.

I filmed the queue before I left. We had no chance where we were, but we were only half way down the queue from what I could see. Those behind us must soon realise that they had no chance of getting a trip round the works.

I walked to Plac Zawiszczy to where the railway museum was. I had intended this to be my second museum in this long night, when I thought that I would actually see Filtry at a reasonable hour.

On entering the museum, my heart fell. There

was a large room full of people and model trains on tables. Not what I wanted. But I followed the flow of people and the source of cool air and found myself outside with real trains and slightly fewer people. This was more like it.

The first train I encountered was not a train, but a carriage with seated people inside it and standing people outside in a small queue. I joined the queue and could see through the window that there was a man explaining the variations in the cross-head rivets in the seat backs. (Or something like that.) He seemed to be in full flow, so, having had enough of queuing for one night, I proceeded down the platform to the next piece of ironmongery. It was a gun wagon. A swivelling armoured pair of guns of some 50mm calibre. There were a couple of these gun carriages, painted in camouflage khaki.

You don't get many of those in England!

On then to a communist era carriage with no queue, so I entered and saw the slatted seats of a bygone era. But there was more space than on a modern train.

And so it went on, one carriage after another down the platform.

At the end, I turned round and walked back, to see, with delight, that all was not over. A short distance away was a stylish looking green engine. A cross between the old Coronation class and the A4 Class back in England. (The A4 class being the class of engine that included the Mallard, just in case you were wondering.)

There were two tracks of these engines, all of different types. All steam, except for a few diesel.

There were enough engines there in fairly poor condition to keep all the volunteers on all the heritage sites in Britain happy for years.

For a brief few minutes I was behind an English enthusiast and his girlfriend. He was pointing out to her some of the interesting features of the various valve arrangements and how they used the steam. He sounded quite couth and educated, so perhaps they are still together as a couple.

And so I walked on, happily taking photos of all the engines, just because I could and so I could get something from this night of the Long Queues.

I was now feeling hungry not having eaten for longer than I could remember, so I made my way back the Defilad Square – the hub of the evening – and looked for some of the street food.

The last time I had done this evening, there were many different vans serving a wide variety of food.

Tonight there was one van selling Tibetan food to a long queue. No thanks. So I bought a large ice-cream - one of those spirals of ice-cream atop a cone, where on one side there is chocolate and the other is vanilla. It's really clever how they do that.

And so I found an information person in high-viz jacket.

"Do you speak English?" I asked her.

"Leetle."

"Gzie są stare autobusie?" I asked and was surprised at her Polish response of "go straight on then turn right then go straight on and you will see the queue."

I was amazed because I understood, so I repeated it back to her and she repeated it back to me.

I was delighted that I could get by in Polish and no doubt she was delighted that she did not have to do it in English.

So I joined the queue, finished my ice-cream and took some photos to pass the time.

The Palace of Culture and Science looked very nice, being floodlit in different colours under a new moon.

Eventually I reached the head of the queue. Literally. The last bus could not even take one more, so I was first for the next, which was an early version of a bendy bus.

However, three youths raced past me and dived for the back part. I entered the front of the bus and sat on the left, where there were single seats. (The ones on the right being double seats.)

The idling engine made me wonder whether we would get round or not, it was misfiring a bit. My fears increased when we started off. There was the terrible sound of gear teeth grinding as the driver tried to mesh them into first gear. It was a sound that I had not heard for decades.

They must have been made of strong stuff, because we did get round.

One of the things about having visited Warsaw a few times is that you get an idea of where you are, so I could see that we were heading for Wola at the west of the city centre. We passed other old buses returning, so part of the journey was an out and back.

We passed many new apartment blocks. One was memorable because it had a blue and a yellow light outside each apartment. This made it look like a large chequer board, with only the blue lights on. The lights then changed from blue to yellow, starting at the lower left and working diagonally upwards until all the lights were yellow. Then they moved into other moving patterns.

There was another apartment block where the outside of the apartments, including balcony area, were outlined in strings of LED lights. This said "opulence – would you not like to live here?"

And so it continued, sometimes through really crappy areas, that were presumably ready for redevelopment, sometimes through rich. I wondered what the engineer would choose for the Chinaman to buy for her.

We made a couple of stops outside the tram depots in Wola, letting off a few people each time and taking on many more, who now had to stand on the way back.

We made our way back more or less the way we had come and reached the square in good order, ready for those at the head of the long queue to take our places.

I was tired by now as it was approaching midnight, so decided to take one more bus ride. I chose route F, because this one went past Filtry and I wanted to see if there was still a queue.

Of course there was, but by now it was about a hundred metres long – still opportunities for disappointing many people. I stayed on the bus as we moved towards Daszynskiego, where the Warsaw Spire stood. On impulse, I decided to alight and see what it was like at the top of the Spire.

Well, if I could have found the start or end of the queue I might have done, but the whole foyer area was stuffed with people.

I could see many people leaning over the reception desks that were in the middle of the foyer area, but could see no way of getting there.

I left and went for the next Line F bus, which arrived soon after.

We then went round what would have been the old Jewish Quarter, passing POLIN, the new Jewish museum, along the way, before returning down Marszalkowska to Defilad.

At that point, enough was enough and It was time for bed (said Zeberdee.)

Some people never learn, and it would appear that I am one of them, for when Max came with me the following year, I suggested that we visit the Kopernik Experience on the Long Night of the Museums.

Fortunately, I had assumed that the Experience would open at seven, so we arrive around 6:15pm and followed the signs for the queue. It did not seem that long, so we started our queueing.

I had done a good selling job on this to Max, because he happily stuck with the queueing, even though I was having my doubts. Then we learned that the opening time was 8pm. We would be queuing for an hour and a half. No matter. We wanted to see this place and this was the only time we had to do it.

Eventually the queue started to move and we were allowed admission and given a white piece of plastic, like a blank credit card. We would give this up on exit so that another person could take our place. It appeared that there was a finite number allowed in – I think I heard the number 'one thousand' mentioned.

By the time that we entered, all the nearby experiments were occupied, so we watched people doing them. One I remember was of the famous Michaelangelo man with arms stretched to the sides and legs apart with feet resting on a circle. There was a movable marker to measure the height of the person in the contraption. This seemed to adjust the markers for the arms so that one could see that arm span is approximately the same as height. Very simple and very effective.

Max was taken by the pendulum. This is described in the chapter on the Kopernik Experience, but he kept returning to it.

For my part, I looked out for the memorable things I had seen on my first visit, much to my disappointment. I will tell you about these in the chapter on the Experience, rather than bore you twice.

We had a couple of hours of fun visiting as many exhibits as possible, until, after a couple of hours we decided that we had seen all that we wanted to and it was time to let some other people in.

When we were outside, we saw that the queue had now reached an impossible length. It had snaked past where we had started, until it was around four times as long as it had been when we started. It was now 10pm and there could be no chance for those towards the end of the queue.

But that was not our concern. We were off to get the metro to the apartment, where there was beer, crisps and vodka to enjoy while we had a seat. It and been a good evening.

The Kopernik Experience

This is a science museum like no other. It has hundreds of interactive exhibits that enable you to discover scientific laws for yourself. A big and little kids' playground.

It is located on the banks of the Vistula, not far from the Swiętokrzyski bridge. There is now a metro station on Line 2 called Centrum Nauki Kopernik.

I first went there on an early visit to Warsaw. It was a weekday. No chance of getting in because it was chokker with school children.

On a later visit I went in on a Saturday, thinking that I would have had to book a slot on another day, and found that I could get immediate access, so I went in.

My third visit was in 2019 with my friend Max, when we visited it on a Long Night of Museums evening, described earlier.

The idea for this centre came from the Mayor of Warsaw in early 2004, one Lech Kaczyński (he who died in the Smolensk plane crash in 2005). The first part was opened in November 2010 and throughout 2011 all the other parts were opened.

The first thing that struck me when I entered was the Foucault Pendulum.

This consisted of a very large metal ball suspended by cord from the top of the building. Near the extremity of the swing were hinged vertical rods set in a circle. Some of the rods were horizontal when I arrived.

The Foucault Pendulum, which was invented in 1851 by Leon Foucault, demonstrates the rotation of the earth and there was a small model to explain this nearby. This model seems to have disappeared, because I could not find it in 2019.

The pendulum swings in the same absolute direction relative to the Universe and the Earth rotates around it. This gives the appearance that the pendulum is not retracing the same path as it swings back and forth, but is moving ever so slightly to one side. After a while it will have moved sufficiently to one side to knock over a hinged rod

If such a pendulum is located at one of the Poles (North or South), then the time taken to precess to the starting point is one day. At other latitudes the rate of rotation can be determined by a formula.

Foucault erected a pendulum in the dome of the Pantheon in Paris (where the Curies are buried). He used a 67 metre long wire from the top of the dome.

The Pantheon is 48 degrees 51 minutes North and the full precess cycle takes just under 32 hours. As the speed of precession is proportional to the sine of the latitude, the pendulum in the Copernicus museum at some 52 degrees North will precess a little faster than the one in Paris.

A pendulum at the Equator, at zero degrees North, will not precess and will continue to swing in the same direction relative to Earth.

So much for the science. The visual impression

was fantastic. Max was fascinated by this pendulum more than any other exhibit and he kept returning to it to see what was happening.

I will not describe everything there was, for you will want to go and see for yourself and my descriptions will only bore you. However, there was a lot of fun to be had there.

Little models showing how efficient different methods of raising water were.

Illustration of conic sections.

How an object could apparently roll uphill.

There was one demonstration that, in hindsight, was significant for me. It was a "test your grip strength" machine.

On my second visit I happened to arrive at the test-your-grip experiment about the same time as a small family. (Mother and father in their early forties and son some ten years old. Very middle-class.) They had just started to try this out and I watched, interested. The father was fit. He gripped something like 40 Kg. Mother was next at something like 30Kg. Finally, son gripped at something like 15 Kg.

They politely indicated for me to have a go. To my shame I gripped something like 20Kg.

I must look fitter than I really am, for the expression of pity on the father's face was obvious. As though to say "I know I am fit and young, but surely you could do better than that? Not even able to grip as well as my wife."

It was the early summer of 2014. By the end of the year I was diagnosed with Parkinson's Disease.

One of the effects affects muscular strength.

Undeterred, I continued round the two floors of the museum, playing with as many objects as I could.

After many hours, during which I never once thought about food or drink, I became aware that I was getting tired and hungry, so went to the cafe for literal refreshment, after which I was ready to go again.

The cafe offered a range of foodstuffs and drinks, all of which looked appetising. I cannot remember what I chose, but it was sugary and full of carbohydrates to give me an energy boost, yet not interfere with the dinner I planned to have that evening.

Even for a revived senior citizen (or *emerytura* as the Poles would say), I only had so much stamina left. Exhausted, I reluctantly left the building while the sun still had some strength in it and made my way back to my apartment, stopping at a cafe near to it to swallow a large beer before flaking out on my bed.

It had been a wonderful, if unexpected, day.

Pole Mokatowskie

I decided to have a go on the Metro. Warsaw has had two of these since 2016. The first, established in the 1990's, runs north to south, from Młociny to Kabaty. The crossover is at Swiętokrzyska, not far from the University.

Between the World Wars there had been an aircraft works and an airfield at Mokatow on this open ground to the south of the city centre. I had never seen it, so thought that this was an opportune moment on this sunny morning.

The Polish aircraft industry was one of those 'might-have-been' stories. And it was all down to one man: Zygmunt Puławski.

He was born in Lublin on October 24th 1901 in the Russian partition of Poland.

At the age of 18 in the summer of 1920, when Poland was at war with Russia, he volunteered for the Boy Scout Battalion before starting his advanced studies in engineering at Warsaw University of Technology, from which he graduated as a professional engineer in 1925.

Whilst at university, he had joined the Students' Mechanical Club in the Aviation section.

To gain experience, he went to France and worked at the Baguette Aviation company. (One has visions of flying bread sticks!) When he returned he had to do national service, which he did, completing national aviation school in Bydgoszcz in 1927.

He then moved to the State Aviation Works in Warsaw, which was then located at ul. Słupecka in Ochota. He was a main designer and designed a new aircraft, the P1, to meet the requirements of the Polish Military. For this aircraft he designed the gull wing, which gave the pilot an excellent all-round view. This had an in-line engine. The later P6 was similar to the P1, but with a radial engine. The P6 was voted the best fighter in the world in some of the Press.

He was not only a designer of aircraft, but also a pilot, and it was in a prototype of his latest design, an amphibious lying boat, the P12, that a strong wind at take-off caused him to crash and lose his life. Another project he was working on, the P11, was completed and became the main fighter aircraft at the outbreak of WW2.

Unfortunately, without Puławski, the fighters were not developed further and the P11 was obsolete by the outbreak of war.

It just goes to show how fast aircraft development was in the early 1930's – somewhat similar to our own day, with the development of mobile computing.

There is a major road in Warsaw named after him. It runs from near where I came out of the metro station to the Botanical Gardens.

I took the metro from Centrum a couple of stops south to Pole Mokatowskie, one stop south of the Technical college at Polytechnika.

On emerging up the stairs to street level, I looked around to get my bearings. From the map I knew that the green space was north of the metro station, so with the sun as my guide, I headed into my shadow.

The first green space was a large car park, set in trees. I walked through it to a fence some distance away. Fortunately, there was a gap and I could enter a small woodland that looked a bit unkempt. A sign was trying to tell me something, but there were too many zeds to let me understand, so I went ahead anyway.

It was uninspiring, but birds were singing, competing against the sound of traffic from the main road. It was also not an airfield as it was big enough only to launch a model plane.

My path led me to a housing estate of apartment blocks, so I aimed north and hoped for something better. Soon I was on the east-west main road through Mokatow – ul. Batorego. Crossing this gave me access to Pole Mokatowskie proper.

Stefan Batory (1533-1586) was the third elected king of Poland. In those turbulent times, he had to establish power, because he was challenged by Maximilian II, Holy Roman Emperor. He had a victory against the Russians in the campaign in Livonia and signed a peace agreement (Peace of Jam Zapolski).

On looking around, the park looked like your average park – a mixture of trees and grassed areas. Along the paths that fanned out from the corner, where I was standing, were benches, where people were sitting, enjoying the sunshine.

I chose a path at random and walked along it, getting further from the traffic. Eventually I came across a pond beneath some trees. There was an empty bench nearby, so I took the opportunity to do as the other people in the park were doing – I sat and enjoyed the sound of the parkland birds in the sunshine until the bench became too uncomfortable to sit on any longer.

As I walked, I came across a main path running from right to left. As I looked, a girl with flaming hair was moving rapidly in her in-line skates. I wondered what she would do with her skates when she reached her destination, for she was not wearing a rucksack. A few minutes later, when I reached the path, I saw her coming back in the opposite direction. This was her morning exercise. Soon she was back again. After a while, we developed a relationship good enough to smile as she went by. By the time I had reached the end of the path, she had finished her exercise and I never saw her again.

Along the path I came across a large lake with fountains playing in the distance. I sat on a nearby bench and enjoyed the scene for a while. A dog was having fun in the shallow water of the pond by walking around with deliberate splashing. I swear he had a smile on his face.

As I continued along the path, I noticed a stretch of open field that could have been an airstrip, so took a photo. There was a bank at the end, behind which was the lake. Maybe this was the first ski jump runway?

I continued and came across the bronze statue of a dog. This was erected in 2004 and appears to commemorate nothing. It is a delightful, very happy dog and was worth a photo. It was well-loved, because its head and shoulders were polished by thousands of hands over time.

    As I was getting towards the exit of the park, a crowd of teenagers in wheelchairs, accompanied by a walking teacher, came my way. They all appeared happy and with no sign of infirmity. My thought was that these children were being allowed to feel what it was like to move around by wheelchair.

    Some years earlier, I had seen a simple exhibit at the Kopernikus Experience, where one could sit in a wheelchair and go through a door. The door only opened one way, as most doors do, so the experience covered going both way through the door. Not easy when the door opened towards you.

    Warsaw is getting better for wheelchair access, but still has a massive way to go, because it seems that you cannot go far before the way is blocked by stairs. It is getting better. There are now lifts at subways, but not everywhere.

    If it was a teaching exercise, it was a good one and the children seemed to be enjoying it. But then if it was easy for in-line skates, presumably it was easy for wheelchairs. Unless the teacher had a surprise!

    As I left the park heading towards the main road, I espied a bus stop. I walked to it, interested in seeing what buses went this way. Imagine my surprise to find that my old friend the airport bus, the 175, would take me back to Centrum. Its mate the 128 also came this way. As it happened, the 128 came first, so I got onto a fairly full bus.

A short time later I heard the announcement that the next stop would be for Pomnik Lotnitsko, or airman's column. I had heard it called many times on my way to the airport and only glimpsed it once or twice before, so this seemed a good opportunity to see it properly, so I got off the bus and looked around for something resembling a column with an airman on top. Eventually I spotted it and crossed a couple of roads to get to it

It was a monument to all Polish airmen (and presumably women) and was erected near to Mokotow airfield some time before WW2. It was destroyed in the war after the Warsaw Rising and resurrected in 1967.

Having seen it and taken a photo to remind me, I went back to the bus stop and caught the next bus into town.

One thing I wanted to do following the Sunday Chopin Concert was to get a CD of Joanna Różewska., so I called into Empik – the place in Poland for all books, CDs and stationery. There was one convenient to the apartment, so I went there, but could not find one.

When I got back, I looked for one online. It was as though she never existed. Even when I went to her website, there was no way of ordering the CD that was described so well. I will need to contact her and have stiff words with her! Katarzyna Kraszewska had brought some CDs to sell after her 2014 performance and she had autographed one for me. I have enjoyed it many times since.

I was hot and tired, so had a small kip in the afternoon before making a journey to Witolin.

Why Witolin? Because I had never been there and I could come back a different way to Warsaw West railway station, which happened to be by the long-distance bus station.

The journey to Witolin was easy, as the bus went through Centrum every fifteen minutes or so. The journey was uneventful, passing through some poor places and some nice ones. I have concluded that the nice apartments are built in localities where there is a lot of greenery.

At Witolin I was dropped at the last bus stop and I assumed the other bus would be nearby, as this was a terminus. It was, only I couldn't see it as the little bus station was round the corner. However, luck was in and I got on a bus with a few seconds to spare. From what I could see of Witolin, there was not a lot of reasons for me to delay departure while I looked at (or for) the sights.

The first part of the journey retraced the outward one before veering off into the rush hour traffic and on to the railway station.

I got out at the railway station and made my way towards the bus station to see how much it had changed since I was last there.

My last visit was in 2012, when I had arranged to go to Lublin for a few days. I had planned to go by rail, but my enquiries at the rail station elicited the fact that it would take five hours and the train was not going for another five hours. You can imagine my amazement at hearing this news. Lublin is a pretty sizeable city and you would think that there would be a reasonable rail service. But then when I got to Lublin I realised that it was not a place you would rush to see.

A kind man overheard my problem and directed me to a bus that would take me to the bus station.

When I arrived the first time I could see that nothing had been done to it since the communist era. It must have been tacky even when new, but now that the concrete was chipped and paint flaked, it was a real down-at-heel place.

Coupled with the unhelpfulness of the staff and my lack of knowledge of any significant Polish, it was a wonder that I caught the bus. But three and a half hours later, I was in Lublin, Which was before the train would have left Warsaw on its five hour journey.

I was pleased to see in 2018 that some money had been spent on the bus station. There were signs on each of the platforms and there were indicator boards telling from which bay the bus would depart. I had just missed the bus to Tarnopol (which is in part of Ukraine which had been Polish between the wars). I used the excuse that I had not got my suitcase with me. It was interesting that the place had been called Tarnopol, the Polish spelling, not Tarnopil, the Ukrainian spelling. This was the nearest city to where my father had lived between the wars, which is why it held an attraction for me.

There were a lot of notices in Russian (or maybe

Ukrainian, as they use the Cyrillic alphabet.)

I noticed a bus operated by the coach operator "Kresy" standing at one of the bays. The part of Poland that was lost after WW2 to Ukraine was called Kresy, so presumably that operator went between present day Poland and what used to be Poland, just to rub Ukrainian noses in it.

After extracting all the pleasure I could from a bus station, I wanted to go to the adjacent railway station, but could not see an entrance. However, there was a hole in the ground with steps leading downwards. By now I was getting used to the idea that my way forward was usually preceded by my way down.

And so it was this time. Down the steps and along a subway to Platform One for the train to Śródmieście. A wait of ten minutes for a crowded train full of office workers from somewhere upstream of Warsaw. I got on and had an uneventful journey to the centre.

Time was now getting on and I had a concert to go to at Frederick Chopin University School of Music. I had around forty five minutes to start moving in that direction, so I went straight for food rather that go to the flat.

I went to a restaurant I had been to earlier in the visit and stood looking lost in order to be directed to a table. A fresh-faced youth, who had served me last time, sat me at a crap table in the middle of the others. I sat down and waited for my order to be taken.

Two men finished their meal and went. Theirs

was a nicer table, adjacent to the edge of the outdoor area, so I moved there, from where I could see my waiter standing at the bar. He saw me and continued bonding with his fellow waiters. I decided that I would never get served, so left.

I don't think that the waiter realised that to get tipped you have to serve food and drink. To get tipped well, you have to look after the customer.

I left and went to a bar that served food and Polish Craft beer. At least they recognised that I was part of their livelihood.

And I got away in time to get to the concert.

Polish Air Force

We have already learned about the Polish fighter aircraft of the 1920's and would assume there was an air force to fly them. The Polish air Force came into being after the end of WW1, using planes from the Prussian and Austrian empires following their collapse.

After the Polish-Russian war of 1920-21, the air force was equipped with French planes. The first Polish-designed planes were not introduced until 1930, when the PWS-10 came into being. From 1933 the PZL-P7a, designed by Puławski, was used. Fighter design was fast-moving in those days and the P7a was succeeded by the PZ11a and PZ-11c. The final version, the PZL-24, was not the best and was built for export only. There is no doubt that Puławski's death was a blow to Polish aircraft design.

When the Nazis invaded Poland on September 1st 1939, defence rested on the out-dated P11. In spite of this, the Polish Air Force shot down 170 Nazi aircraft.

Inevitably, the superior aircraft of the Nazis and the invasion of the Russians on 17th September 1939, meant that the Polish Air Force was defeated, but its pilots and others managed to escape to France, where they became part of the French Air Force.

However, the French did not equip them with aircraft until May 1940. Can you believe it? You are given a load of battle-experienced pilots and what do you do with them? You give them a vacation while your own pilots get shot down. Then, when your stupidity is obvious, you allow the unit to be equipped with the massively inferior Chaudron C714. These were so bad that after a mere 23 sorties, they were ordered to be withdrawn on May 25th – one week after they were deployed. But, having nothing else offered, the Poles continued using this aircraft against the mighty Messerschmidt 109e, succeeding in shooting down 12 enemy aircraft.

There were other Polish units who were equipped with somewhat better aircraft, but still massively inferior.

In the whole of the Battle of France, the Poles flew 714 sorties and shot down some 57 Nazi aircraft.

With the fall of France, most of the pilots and support escaped to England, where the British were unwilling to accept the independence of the Polish Air Force. However, the British government told General Sikorski that Poland would be charged with all costs associated with maintaining Polish forces in Britain.

The battle-hardened pilots were not allowed to join the RAF, but only the RAF Volunteer Reserve in the lowest rank of Pilot Officer. This was at a time when the RAF was suffering heavy losses due to the lack of experienced pilots. It was only because the attrition rate of British pilots reached 25%, which resulted in a shortage of pilots, that the Poles were allowed to fly.

Still the intransigence lived on. Instead of letting

the Poles form their own squadrons, they were integrated into the RAF, with all the language problems and different command structures. Every Polish officer had to have a British counterpart. So while British pilots were being shot down, the Polish pilots were at training school. Presumably learning how to shoot down enemy aircraft the British way.

After a preliminary agreement was signed between the Polish and British governments on June 11th 1940, the Poles were given two bomber squadrons (300 and 301) and two fighter squadrons (302 and 303). The fighter squadrons were equipped with Hurricanes and would become the most efficient RAF fighter unit in the Battle of Britain, having the most kills to losses. 145 Polish fighter pilots took part in the Battle of Britain. They consistently had the highest number of kills and it is fair to say that, without them, it is quite likely that Britain would have been invaded.

By the end of the war, some 19,400 Poles were serving in the Polish Air Force in Great Britain.

There is a monument to the fallen Polish Airmen in Pole Mokotowskie in Warsaw. It represents the trails of fighter aircraft involved in an air battle. There is also a wall with 1,879 names of pilots killed in the war. It was erected in 2003,a after the Russian domination of Poland ended.

On April 6th 1944, the Polish Air Force came under the direct command of the Polish Government-in-Exile and no longer under the control of the RAF. At the end of the war, all assets of the Polish Air Force were returned to the British, presumably so that they would not incur a cost for them.

I don't know if the cost of the Polish Air Force was passed to the Polish government in Poland after the war, but I can imagine that the response to such a request would contain many deleted expletives.

Most of the assets in the form of personnel remained in Britain after the war. The few who returned home, if not shot, were treated very badly. Thank goodness that my father did not go back to his homeland.

At Northolt Airport in London, there is the memorial to Polish Airmen killed while on service with the RAF. It was unveiled on 2nd November 1948. Known as the Polish War Memorial, it originally contains the names of 1,243 names, but following refurbishment in the 1990's a further 659 names were added. The memorial was refurbished again in 2010, in time for the 70th anniversary of the Battle of Britain. Five years later a garden was opened behind the memorial in time for the 75th anniversary of the Battle of Britain.

There are many other memorials to Polish airmen throughout Britain, the most notable being at St. Clement Danes, the RAF church in London, and between terminals 2 and 3 at Manchester International airport, which used to be RAF Ringway.

Two Polish presidents, most notably Lech Wałęsa in 1991, have visited the memorial. The other was Aleksander Kwasniewski in 2004.

Zoliborz

Zoliborz is a district directly due north of Warsaw Centre. Its name is a Polonisation of the French Joli Bord, or Beautiful Embankment. It also has a citadel, which I thought would be worth a visit.

Not being entirely sure how I could get into the citadel, I got off the bus at Plac Inwalidów and made my way towards what I hoped was the citadel direction.

Totally unexpectedly, I came across a monument. (No! Really? A monument in Warsaw! How rare! I hear you say.)

Hear me out for a moment.

It was unexpected in that it was unusual,

The monument is impressive, being a tall column surmounted by the scary headdress of ancient cavalry and with a representation of a magnificent Polish eagle partway down the column. Actually, to call it a scary headdress is misleading. It was a hoop with feathers attached that was attached to the shoulders. This would give the horseman height in olden days. It is appropriate for this monument to the 1st Tank Division, whose logo incorporates a stylised version of the headdress.

It was paid for by forty cities in Belgium, Holland, France and Scotland. The contributing cities are listed on two faces of the pedestal. This alone makes the monument intriguing. Why should Scotland pay for a Polish monument?

On a third face of the pedestal is a moving inscription "A soldier of Poland fights on all fronts for all nations, but he only gives his life for Poland."

The fourth face of the pedestal shows a map of western Europe to show the movement of the Division from August 1944 to the end of the war. This was from Caen on the 1st August to Wilhelmshaven by 5th May 1945, with many battles fought along the way.

The sculptor was Jerzy Sikorski and the architect was Andrzej Kicinski.

It made me realise more than ever that the Poles had lost their country and were fighting in foreign parts for allies who would not give them back their country when the war was over. This was the selfishness of war. Every country is preoccupied with its own problems and only acts for other countries when there is some benefit for their own.

In 1939, Britain had promised to go to war if Poland was invaded. A fat lot of good it could do against the war machines of Germany and Russia, but, technically, it did go to war, although it was inevitable, Polish invasion or not, that Britain would go to war against Germany sooner rather than later.

Fortunately, Britain could count on the help from Empire nations and escapees from Nazi-conquered European countries. One can speculate on the outcome of the war in the air had it not been for the battle-hardened pilots of Slovakia, Slovenia and Poland

This monument was erected in 1995. After the fall of the Communist masters of Poland in 1990.

Seeing this monument was an emotional experience, so I did some research. What I found was a sad story.

The Polish First Armoured division was founded at Duns in Scotland in 1942 under the command of General Stanisław Maczek, a veteran tank soldier of the First World War. At its peak it had 16,000 soldiers.

So who was Stanisław Maczek?

Stanisław Maczek

Think Montgomery for a comparison with a known western commander.

Maczek was born in March 1892 in what is now Ukraine and went on to study Polish philology at the University of Lwów, which was then part of Russia. Not the sort of subject a soldier might choose. But then the outbreak of WWI encouraged him to sign up, hopefully to join one of Piłsudski's Legions, but instead into the Austro-Hungarian army. His first assignment was to go to the Italian front in the Tyrol. He was the only Polish battalion commander in the Austrian alpine regiments, when he was promoted to lieutenant in 1918.

When the Armistice was declared, he returned to Poland and became involved in the Polish-

Ukrainian war, which developed into trench warfare over the winter of 1918/19. Perhaps it was this static warfare that led him to develop the idea of a motorised unit that could quickly be deployed to areas needing support.

By the end of fighting in summer 1919, he was promoted to the rank of major.

His division fought well in the Jarosław and Zamość areas during the Polish-Bolshevik war.

The inter-war years saw him remain in the army, rising up the ranks, until in 1938 he was given command of the Polish 10th motorised Cavalry Brigade, the first motorised formation in the Polish Army.

When the Nazis attacked Poland on September 1st 1939, Maczek was in the south-west of the country, where he succeeded in slowing the Nazi advance to a crawl, in spite of overwhelming odds.

He was moved to defend Lwów, so that the Polish Army could escape via the part of Poland that is now Ukraine. This was known as the Romanian Bridgehead, but when Russia invaded Poland on 17th September 1939, this bridgehead was in danger. Maczek was ordered to leave, with as many of his army as possible before it was closed. This he did and made his way over to France.

Maczek joined the free Polish army and was promoted to brigadier.

The French wanted to incorporate his men into the French army, but this would have meant wasting their knowledge of motorised warfare, so Maczek refused. Instead, he set up the 10th Armoured Cavalry Brigade, but received almost no equipment and what he did get in March 1940 was obsolete.

Until, in Spring, the Germans bypassed the Maginot Line and conquered France. Then Maczek could take his pick of equipment. However, it was not enough: the soldiers were not trained to use the new equipment and there was not enough time to train them. All the French units were either in retreat or routed, so even when Maczek managed to surprise the Nazis at Montbard, over the Burgundy Canal, there were no troops available to capitalise on this victory.

Maczek was surrounded on 18th June. He decided to scrap all of his equipment and escape on foot in small groups that could pass through the Nazi lines. A lot of them made their way to Britain via Vichy France, Spain and Portugal.

The situation in Britain was that the government wanted to use the Poles as defenders of the Scottish coastline between Aberdeen and Edinburgh, but when Maczek arrived with his men, the plan changed and the 1st Polish Armoured Division was created in February 1942. They were equipped with state-of-the-art tanks in the M4 Sherman and Churchill tanks and given two years' training in preparation for the D-Day landings.

The Division landed in France at the end of July 1944 and saw action from 8th August, when they were instrumental in closing the pocket round Chambois, capturing a large number of Nazi soldiers at the end of what was known as the Battle of Falaise.

Maczek then proceeded up the French and Dutch coasts, where battles were fought and won against the retreating Nazis.

In one battle, Maczek outflanked the Dutch town of Breda, where fighting was hard, but not one resident of the town was lost. After the war, Maczek was made an honorary Dutch citizen.

Greater success was to follow when Maczek accepted the surrender of Wilhelmshaven with the entire garrison and 200 ships.

Maczek was promoted to major-general and went on to be the commanding officer of all Polish troops until they were demobilised in 1947.

Maczek left the army in September 1948.

Now one would think that this war hero would have been given a pension by the British government when he retired to Britain. The communist government of Poland stripped him of his citizenship, so he had nowhere else to go, having returned to Scotland after the war. But for some reason, probably because they did not want to upset their communist friends, the Labour government refused to give him one.

He worked as a barman in an Edinburgh hotel until the 1960's.

However, in 1950, the mayor of Breda in Holland became worried when he heard that Maczek was in dire financial straits, partly because he had to pay for the medical care of his daughter. The Mayor persuaded the Dutch government to help the man who had liberated the Netherlands and, through a secret fund, the Dutch paid him an annual amount.

The Dutch population, unaware of this payment, raised a petition to pay this hero of theirs so that his daughter could receive the medical care she needed in Spain.

In 1989, with the fall of communism imminent, the last communist Polish Prime Minister – Mieczisław Rakowski – issued a public apology to the General and in 1994 he was presented with Poland's highest honour, the Order of the White Eagle.

He died on 11 December 1994 at the age of 102 and was buried, as he requested, in the cemetery at Breda among his soldiers.

Contrast the treatment of this hero with that of Wellington and one has to wonder what it is the British seem not to like about the Poles. Enigma, Battle of Britain, Monte Casino and the liberation of Europe all seem to be ignored.

I am extremely thankful that my Wanderings in Warsaw had stumbled across this monument and its history, although I did not realise it at the time.

I ploughed on towards the Citadel

On the way, I passed a plaque to Krzysztof Komeda Trzcinski on a small apartment block. The inscription informed me that he lived there from 1961 to 1969. The musical staves were a dead giveaway that he was a musician and the inscription also mentioned that he was a composer and jazz musician.

Krzysztof Komeda Trzcinski

Subsequent research revealed that he wrote the film scores for four Roman Polanski films, including *Rosemary's Baby* in 1968.

He was born in April 1931 and died after a tragic accident in April 1969. In those 38 years he was not only a writer of many film scores, but also instrumental in moving jazz away from the American influence towards a distinctly European aesthetic, with his album *Astigmatic* being regarded as one of the most important European jazz albums.

Originally from Częstochowa, where he was born Krzysztof Trzcinski, he studied medicine in Poznan and became an otlaryngologist.

He took the stage name Komeda so that he could separate the two parts of his life – the medical and the music. He had had a strong interest in music from an early age, which obviously became more important as he grew older, judging by the amount of composing, playing, recording and travelling he did in the 1960's.

In 1968, he went over to Los Angeles to be with Polanski while he composed the score for *Rosemary's Baby*. While there, at a drinking party in December 1968, during which there was a bit of friendly rough and tumble, he was pushed off an escarpment and suffered a haematoma of the brain. He was treated in an American hospital, but did not save his life. He remained in a coma and was transported to Poland, where he died in April 1969.

I marched on, still unsure of direction, but full of hope I walked along the Polish Army avenue and came to a rather lovely children's playground, alongside of which was a pathway, which I went down. Eventually I could see the red brickwork of an old wall, but could see no entrance.

I walked along the pleasant paved pathway that ran some distance away, and parallel to, the wall. Eventually I stumbled across an entrance gateway and entered the Citadel.

Citadel

The citadel was constructed by order of Tsar Nicholas 1st between May 1832 and 4th May 1834 following the November 1830 Uprising. It is roughly pentagon shaped and was modelled on the citadel in Antwerp, which was destroyed before the Polish one was completed. (Although the completion date is said to be in 1832, it was actually under construction until 1874.)

It was a symbol of Russian presence in Warsaw and, to add insult to injury, the Russians made the City of Warsaw pay for it. In peacetime it held approximately 5,000 soldiers, but after the January 1863 Uprising there were 16,000 soldiers with 555 pieces of artillery that could shell the centre of Warsaw.

It will not surprise you to learn that prison cells were built within the citadel to house mainly political prisoners. The list of Prisoners reads like a Who's

Who of Polish politics: Piłsudski; his rival Dmowski; the father of Joseph Conrad, Apollo Korzeniowski; Romuald Traugutt, leader of the January 1863 Uprising; Jarosław Dąbrowski, leader of the 1871 Paris Commune; Feliks Dzierżynski, a leader of the 1917 Russian Revolution and founder of the Chekka, or Secret Police. Eligliusz Niewiadomski was executed by firing squad in the citadel.

On December 9th 1922, Gabriel Narutowicz was elected as the first President of the new Poland. On December 16th he attended an art exhibition at the Zachęta Art Gallery at Plac Stanisław Malachowskiego, just off Krolewska near Plac Piłsudskiego, to which Niewiadomski was also invited. Niewiadomski shot the President and was arrested on December 30th. He was found guilty and executed by firing squad at the Citadel on January 31st 1923.

There is an interesting story behind these bare facts.

Niewiadomski was educated as an artist in St. Petersburg and Paris and taught drawing at the Warsaw Polytechnic.

He was also a nationalist, which did not go down well with the Russians, especially when he smuggled nationalist literature from Galicia into the Russian area of Poland. For several months he was a guest at the Pawiak Prison and, when released, lost his job at the Polytechnic. To stay solvent, he taught art at a number of schools. Eventually he joined the new Poland's Ministry of Culture.

He took part in the Polish-Russian War in the

Fifth Legion and rejoined the Ministry of Culture in 1921. He took umbrage when the government refused to give his department more money and resigned, after which he survived on producing book illustrations.

It must have been the vote by the National Assembly to vote Narutowicz as the first President that really annoyed the right-wing Niewiadomski. Narutowicz gained 289 votes, whereas the right-wing Maurycy Zamoyski only got 227. However, Narutowicz had 113 votes from minority national MPs, which Niewiadomski did not consider to be Polish.

It's a good job that things seem to have calmed a little, otherwise we would be missing quite a few politicians in today's political climate!

Having made it to the Citadel, I wandered around in the sunshine and admired the cannons and other bits that were there. I now read that there is a museum there, but not when I went some years ago. There is a bit more to see now. There is Pavilion X and the Katyn Museum for starters. These will be on my list of places to see on my next visit.

Anyway, I had a pleasant time there and then found a way out that took me to the pretty embankment, where there was a bus stop. The only problem was that I had no idea which bus to take me to somewhere I knew, so I got on the first.

Mistake! I realised this when the bus veered right over the river and not left towards the centre of Zoliborz. I got off as soon as I could at a place called Zeheran: a massive road junction with flyovers and stairs to different levels.

I had to go up and down most of these stairs before I could find a stop with buses which went to Marymont – a place I knew would have a good selection of buses, trams and the M1 underground (which at that time was simply "the Metro" as the M2 had not been built.)

When I arrived at Marymont, I found the metro station and decided to take a break and travel to other far end to see what was there at Kabaty.

Kabaty

Kabaty seemed to be a prosperous suburb. As I exited the subway station, I was presented with wide avenues and smart flats. I had also seen from the ZTM map that there was a Tesco superstore, which, being hungry, was a magnet.

The store was visible from the metro station, so I made my way there, going in through a narrow pedestrian gate and across the car park. Tesco Poland had the same idea as Tesco England – nobody would be expected to shop on foot, because the weekly shop would need a car boot.

They did not reckon on my 25 litre rucksack.

I made my way to the large Tesco sign over the entrance and entered.

I then looked for Tesco.

That's right. Tesco could not be seen. It had disappeared and in its place there was a mass of small shops and trading stalls. I began to panic a bit. Had Tesco reverted to the original Marks and Spencer, where they started with a barrow and a notice that said "Don't ask the price – it's a penny."

It was not to be. The Tesco entrance was round a corner, so I entered.

Now my Polish in those days was not as good as it is now (which is far from good), so I could not understand much. Fruit and veg were all right, but branded goods were difficult, as many of the brands were peculiar to Poland.

Still, it was fun wandering around the store. I bought some Danish bun sort of things and some croissants for tomorrow's breakfast, some pierogi that looked as though they could be cooked by boiling the packet in boiling water and some oranges to be healthy.

I then found the hooch area and picked up a bottle of coffee vodka and a bottle of toffee vodka as they looked interesting.

I could have bought a bicycle or a hi-fi system, but decided against. But I did get a couple of cans of beer as the spirits were only half litres.

I could not find anything that was like a Ginster's Slice, which was the sort of food I fancied as a mid-afternoon lunch.

Outside the store was an ice cream cabin, so lunch was a large ice cream cornet.

Time to venture back, slowly so that I could finish my ice cream before getting to the Metro.
One event sticks in my mind from that journey back to my flat.

A few stops into the journey a couple a teenage girls got on via the door near where I was sitting. One had an iced lolly, which she was eating quickly before it melted. It was not very big by this stage and she was having a job to keep the drips from falling off the stick and onto the floor.
Alas! She failed to keep up with the melting lolly while trying to talk to her friend and the remaining coloured ice slid off the stick and landed on the floor.

A most amazing thing then happened. The girl reached into her handbag, extracted a tissue, bent down and picked up the ice and wiped the floor before disposing of the tissue and its contents into the waste bin.

I was amazed to see such consideration for public property. Having travelled on public transport in England and seen the way that our youth have little respect for our communal property, this one act said all there was to say about the differences between our two cultures.

In England, our youth regard it as completely normal to put their feet on the seat opposite and to discard snack packets and cans wherever they happen to be when they have emptied them. There is no doubt that litter is a blight in England.

When I was in the Boy Scouts and we were about to go abroad, it was made very clear to us that we were ambassadors for Britain and that everything we did would be a reflection on our country. It was important that we behaved with courtesy and consideration. The youngsters of Poland, in my experience, behave very well indeed.

I went to Lublin one year and wanted to take a bus journey to Zamość. The only problem was that, having reached a main road near the area I could not see where I had to go. At a nearby bus stop there was a group of people, so I approached an extremely attractive and well-dressed woman who looked to be in her late twenties and asked her if she spoke English. She said she did, looking at me a bit suspiciously, as well she might, for she was VERY attractive. I explained my problem and asked if she could give me directions to the bus.

She started to explain, then must have realised that I was probably thick, so she told me to follow her and she set off at a cracking pace in her high heels and tight skirt. I had a job keeping up with her, but she went up a small road and around a few corners to the minibus station. She walked up to a bus stand where there was a white minibus. "That's the one you want."

I thanked her profusely, or rather, I thanked her back profusely, for she was already hot-footing it to her own bus stop.

How nice was that?

I would have loved to see her again to treat her to a coffee and cake as recompense for her kindness, but I would only have dribbled.

I never did see the extensive rail depots that are located at Kabaty, nor did I see the Kabaty forest, which is a favoured recreation area for Warszawians at the weekend. And during the week.

It was on one journey back from Tesco's on the Metro that three women of a certain age were on the train. They did not look like Tesco shoppers, unless Tesco Poland had started selling used walking boots and Nordic Poles.(Perhaps I should have written 'Nordic poles to make it clear that I am not talking about Poles from the Nordic countries, but sticks from Nordic countries.) My! They looked as though they could crack chestnuts between their knees and acorns with their little fingers.

They must have wondered why I was wearing Regatta Adventure trousers with lots of pockets, when I had obviously been to Tesco's. Perhaps the chink of vodka bottles in my little rucksacks gave me away.

It was probably the same trip when I had encountered the stall selling cherries just outside the Tesco car park.

I like cherries and these looked delicious, so I bought a kilo for something like forty pence. They lasted me two days and were absolutely delicious.

There is a road that goes due south from the edge of the nearby Ursynów urbanisation into the Kabaty forest. This goes to the weather forecasting station in the forest, at which there is a commemorative plaque to the three mathematicians who unravelled the Enigma secrets. Probably not worth a visit if there are other more pressing things to see, but interesting nonetheless.

Praga

On the east of the River Visła is the former city of Praga, now a suburb of Warsaw. It is worth a visit.

The most striking thing about Praga is the cathedral – Cathedral of St. Michael the Archangel and St. Florian the Martyr. It is a prominent brick-built structure with a pair of tall spire towers.

It is easy to get across to as it is adjacent to Al. Solidarność, where there are plenty of trams and buses from Ratusz Arsenał and the Old Town. Alight at Park Praski.

As you stand before the front of the cathedral and rick your neck looking up at the twin towers, you will ask yourself "Who was Father Ignaci Jan Skorupki?" You cannot miss his memorial statue.

So let me put you out of your misery.

Father Ignacy Skorupka (1893-1930) was a Polish priest and chaplain to the Polish Army in the 1920 Battle of Warsaw. His fame seems to be literally legendary.

He was pretty unremarkable in his early life. He studied at a seminary in St. Petersburg (remember that before 1918, Warsaw was part of Russia.) He took Holy Orders in 1916 and became a parish priest somewhere within the Russian empire.

In 1918, during the Polish-Russian war he became a leader in the Kresy borderlands, although what he did, we don't know.

From late 1918 to late 1919 he practised his religious profession in Łódż, before moving back to Warsaw, where we know that he gave several sermons in St. John's Cathedral.

In 1920 he became a military chaplain in the Polish Army and was killed on 14th August at the Battle of Ossów. It was here that his career really took off.

Accounts of his death vary markedly.

In one account he was leading the service of the anointing of the sick for a fatally wounded soldier when he was killed by a bullet.

In another, he was killed while encouraging soldiers to advance, cross in hand. This was the official army version.

The next day his body was transported to an army garrison church in Warsaw and then buried in the prestigious Powązki Cemetery in Wola, where he was given a state funeral and posthumous honours were bestowed on him.

His death was used by opponents of Josef Piłsudski to attribute his victory as The Miracle of the Vistula, rather than the genius of Piłsudski's strategy.

Whatever the truth, he has a magnificent statue in front of Praga's Cathedral.

Go down the road, Florianska, to the left of the cathedral as far as Kłopotowskiego. On the corner is a five piece, cloth capped, busking musical band made in bronze by Andrzej Renes. It is the iconic piece of Praga and is a must-see. Not because it is brilliant, or better than any other statue, but nobody will believe you have been to Praga if you say you never saw it.

On the opposite side of the road there is the tax office. Why a tax office has to have a rainbow coloured building is beyond me, but when you have seen it, you will not forget it.

Turn left as you come out of Florianska and go a few yards to Jagiellonska. This is the oldest undamaged road in Warsaw, mainly because it was in Russian hands when the Nazis were demolishing the rest of Warsaw. It is pretty unremarkable, but the cinema on the corner is notable as it has reliefs of a number of famous Poles from the world of cinema. The side of the building you want is on Ul. Księdza Ignacego Kłopotowskiego.

By now you will be recognising streets named after people and will be wondering who this street was named after.

Księdza Ignacego Kłopotowskiego is named after the Blessed Ignacy Kłopotowski (1866-1931). He is famed for doing good works, following a long period of study in Lublin, with graduation in St. Petersburg.

In 1892 he became vicar of Lublin cathedral and went on to found a school for children as well as an employment centre. He went on to found a number of orphanages and houses for the elderly, as well as place for girls to escape from prostitution.

He also founded a number of rural schools for children, but fell foul of the Russian authorities at the time. So he went and started a newspaper. What was he thinking? This was 1905, when there was a bit of turmoil; in Russia. This probably saved him. We don't know whether Tsar Nicholas II mellowed, whether he read the newspaper – The Polish Catholic, by the way – or whether he didn't want to upset the population unnecessarily, but he gave it approval.

So in 1908 Kłopotowski moved to Warsaw. Where, we don't know, but by 1919 he was pastor of the parish of our Lady of Loreto based at St. Florian's church, Praga.

On 31st July 1920, he established his own congregation – the Sisters of the Blessed Virgin Mary of Loreto

In 1931 he died.

The beatification process was under way in 1988 and by December 2004 he was named Venerable after Pope John Paul II confirmed that he had lived a life of virtue.

So there you have it. Lead a virtuous life and you get beatified and have a road named after you near a prominent cathedral.

Continue east along Kłopotowskiego and cross the two main north-south roads to the buildings on the far side. Going south a short distance brings you to the Bazar Różyckiego. This is part of Warsaw's past and definitely not its future.

At one time, under communist rule, it was an important place for obtaining black market goods. These were the items that, under an economy controlled by the people, you had to go to an economy controlled by other people, to obtain goods that the people could not provide, but which other people could provide.

A little further down the road is the museum of Praga. This is a nice little museum showing history that is not focused around the world wars.

I once had a very pleasant couple of hours with the curator of the museum, while researching material for a screenplay idea that required me to get an understanding of life in Poland before WW1. As part of this visit, he showed me around part of the museum which, although small, is interesting.

I had made contact with the curator of the Warsaw Museum, located at the north side of the Old Town Square and, although she did not feel confident in her command of English, she put me in touch with key people at POLIN (the new Jewish Museum) and the Rising Museum, as well as the Praga Museum. All the people I met were utterly charming and helpful, as well as having a good competence with Polish history and English.

From near the Praga Museum, one can take the number 6 tram north to Plac Hallera. I mention this for two reasons. The first is to make you aware of old tram cars still in use, because the number 6 tram is almost always an old tram, only one step away from being in a museum. The second reason is that it gives me an excuse to explain who Haller was and why he has a square named after him.

Josef Haller

Josef Haller von Hallenburg (1873-1960), to give

him his full title, was a supporter of Polish independence.

He was born into the Austrian part of partitioned Poland in a village not far from Krakow. He attended the Vienna Military Academy and fought with the Austrians, where he reached the rank of Captain.

At the beginning of WW1, in the Austrian part of partitioned Poland – Galicia – Polish Legions were formed to fight against the Russians. Although not surviving long, the legions became the start of the path to Polish independence.

Two legions were founded at the start of WW1: the Eastern and Western legions. The Eastern Legion did not last long after being defeated by the Russians at the Battle of Galicia and subsequently refusing to fight further against the Russians.

The Western Legion was reformed into three brigades. The First Brigade was led by Josef Piłsudski and the Second Brigade was led by Josef Haller.

In 1918, Haller broke through the Russian front to Ukraine, where he teamed up with Polish detachments which had left the Russian army. In March 1918, the Germans signed the Peace of Brest-Litowsk with the Russians and declared the presence of Polish soldiers in Ukraine as illegal. This came to a head in May 1918, when the Poles fought the Germans at the Battle of Kaniów and lost. Haller escaped and went to France via Moscow and Murmansk, where he founded his Blue Army (named after the colour of the French uniforms they wore), This army was composed of Polish volunteers, many from America. They fought on the western front until the armistice, whereupon they moved to Poland to fight against the Russians in the Polish Russian War of 1920.

After all the fighting, Haller fell into disfavour with fellow Polish politicians. He objected to the election of President Gabriel Narutowicz, first President of Poland. (He has a square named after him in Ochota.) Narutowicz was assassinated a few days after his inauguration.

From 1920 to 1923, Haller was President of the Polish Scout and Guiding Association.

He objected to Piłsudski's coup d'etat of May 1926, which did not endear him to the great man and he was retired, after which he went to live in relative obscurity for a while.

By 1937 he was leader of one of the opposition parties.

After the start of WWII, he made his way to France via Romania and joined Sikorski's government in exile and set about recruiting Poles in America for the Polish Army in France.

With the fall of France, Haller made his way to England via Spain and Portugal. He lived the rest of his life in England.

So there we have him. Nationalistic, patriotic, courageous but perhaps not a politician. But definitely a large part in the creation of the Polish Second Republic.

I always associate Praga with Russia, probably

because the Russians sat here offering no help to the 1944 Rising, which was taking place over the river. Retracing one's steps back to Al. Solidarność and turning left, brings one to an unmistakably Russian Orthodox Church. It is a sort of mini-St. Basil's of Kremlin fame.

I went in on one of my visits and found it to be very ornate and in good condition.

Except for some rusty old bells outside. This got me thinking about the noise that such bells would make. Not the rich sounds of English bronze bells, but more of the tinny sounds of eastern bells. The pieces of bell that I saw had long given up making a sound of any kind.

Retracing steps back towards the Old Town brings one to the bear pit, a reminder that the zoo is not far away.

Whenever I have seen the bears, they look bored, with no amount of gurning on my part able to evoke any reaction from them. Perhaps I don"t gurn in Polish.

I had not realised the impact my tales of these bears would have on my daughter. When she came to Warsaw with me in late 2018, this was one of the places she wanted to see.

It was with great sadness that we arrived at the bear pit to find no sign of bears. We even walked into the park at the rear of the pit to see I they were hiding in the trees, but they weren't.

So great was her desire to see the bears that we returned the next day. And still no bears.

She was only cheered up when I sent my half dozen pictures that I had taken on earlier visits.

It is rumoured that this pit is soon to close, and may already have been closed when we visited in late September 2018. If so, it will be a shame, for there have been bears here since 1949.

I can now report that the bears were back in May 2019, but still looked very bored and stressed, endlessly pacing the same route. They did not look in a good state, so perhaps they will be moved to a better place.

Going a little way further, crossing Ul. Walerian Łuckasińskiego, brings one to Park Praski.

Before we get there, a word about poor old Walerian. He lived from 1786 to 1868. He was a political activist sentenced by the Russian Imperial authorities to 14 years of solitary confinement. He died after 46 years of solitary confinement. Over half of his life spent alone. For that he deserves a road named after him.

Heading back up the road towards Wilenski underground station, head for the number 25 tram to go south to Rondo Waszingtona. This roundabout lies between two objects at extreme ends of the spectrum.

On the left is the National Stadium. Started in 2008 and completed in 2011, it was the venue for many of the 2012 UEFA football matches and is still used mainly for football matches, where it can hold up to 58,145 seats. For concerts it can hold up to 72,000.

The pitch is heated. This is covered by special panels for concerts, but these panels have to be removed within five days of being laid, otherwise the grass is harmed.

It has a retractable roof, a volume of more than a million cubic metres, a training pitch, underground parking for 1765 cars, the largest conference centre in Warsaw, with a capacity for 1600 people and 25,000 square metres of office space, restaurants, a fitness club, pub and many other delights.

The facade is striking, with red and white panels emulating the Polish flag.

During my visit with Max, we saw many people wearing Polska scarves. We later found out that they were all going to the Formula One Speedway Championships. As a fan from Belle Vue, Manchester said, "Seventy miles an hour with no brakes, what's not to like? You should get tickets and come." Unfortunately, it was the Long Night of the Museums and we had a queue of an hour and a half to have, in sight and sound of the National Stadium, where the motorcycles were racing. It was a close call as to whether we made the right decision or not.

There is a great view of the stadium from the Old Town, as we saw in an earlier chapter. Max and I had a great view of it from our flat as well.

To the east and south of the stadium is Skaryszewski Park, a monumental park designed and created by Franciszek Szanior in 1905. Its name derives from the village of Skaryszew, which used to own the fields and meadows in the 17th and 18th centuries.

This is the park that one weekend in 2017 had

an "Art in the Park" event. This was very enjoyable. For some reason there was a snack buffet with fruit juice, wine and breads just outside the park, where one could sit at long tables set up for the purpose. An ideal start to a wander round the park and its lakes.

Although there were many samples of art, the ones that remain in my memory are the members of the Warsaw Philharmonic orchestra dotted around the park, each playing one or two notes on their different instruments, separated by long pauses. Ever since the days of the Polish Modern Jazz Quartet in the 1960's I have regarded the Poles as very advanced in art. By "advanced" I mean "I don't understand it". So the orchestra's performance was in keeping with my idea of "advanced". I met a couple of the players and managed an exchange of smiles with them during one of their long pauses. It was all very friendly.

Another advanced musical event was set up by the side of the lake. There were deck chairs to sit in and headphones to put on. It seemed that the headphone cables went into the lake. When put on, the sounds seemed to be the sounds that mermaids might make while they sang to lure sailors to the rocks. Or something like that – it was too advanced for me to understand. It sounded pleasant and I didn't fall asleep, so it must have been good.

Then there was the tree wired up with tiny loudspeakers, each of which played a different birdsong. This seemed to be art imitating life. Very clever, but the lack of birds in the area seemed to indicate that either it was not real enough, or else the language used by the recorded birds was offensive to the genteel birds of this lovely park.

Whatever the art, the day was sunny and warm and the park very pleasant to stroll in.

I was pleasantly surprised to see that a statue to Edward M. House, a close advisor to President Woodrow Wilson, and advocate for Poland's independence after WW1, had been reconstructed by a Polish sculptor named Marian Konieczny (1930 - 2017). Sadly, I don't think he is any relation. However, he did design my second favourite statue in Warsaw – Nike. More of which later. I also saw his name on the Grunwald Monument in Krakow, where he was responsible for reconstructing that in 1976 after the Nazis had destroyed it in WW2. As the destruction was comprehensive, he had to remake it from sketches that had survived the war. The monument had originally been built in 1910 with money provided by Paderewski, as you will no doubt recall from an earlier chapter.

Saska Kępę

South of Rondo Waszyngtona is the area named after countries. It is the district of Saska Kępę.

Going roughly south of Waszyngtona is Francuska. Every year, on what seems to be the last Saturday of May, the community around this area organises an event. I don't know what else to call it. A carnival implies a procession of some note. The first time that I saw a procession, it was a fairly sad affair, but in 2019 I saw a procession of youngsters doing a very effective carnival dance with synchronised movements. It was very jolly and the participants were having a great time.

I stumbled across this event around 2015. I forget how, but my Polish visits have been designed to coincide with it whenever possible. The information office rarely has information on it until it is almost happening. I put this down to a lack of publicity by the organisers, because I know that our modest Village Fete takes six months to organise and the date is settled before the organisation starts. In this case, some notice must be given, because the whole street is closed off to traffic.

There are stalls on both sides of the street, interspersed with sound stages on which locals perform. And what performances!

One year there was a fabulous group of man and young woman – he playing guitar and she singing Polish blues to die for. I only caught the end of their slot, but recorded some of it. It is so good that it does not age.

Another year there was the male violinist in his twenties who played (I think) Monti's Czardas with a backing of strings and guitars. He made this complex, fast piece look easy. He looked as though he was having the best fun, relishing the attention of the crowd and teasing us by varying the pace at which he played. He was very accomplished.

Then there were the schoolchildren. Talented singers. One teenage girl sang a Parisian song in

French. I was transported to a bar in Paris, she was so good. Everything about her was French. The bright red lipstick. The white blouse and black pencil skirt. The hairstyle. She was brilliant.

Then there was the young couple doing a jive. I can remember nothing about him, but lots about her. She had an amazing figure with little of it covered. What coverage there was was a front panel with lots of tassels and sequins and a low-cut rear. She was stunning. And she could dance the jive - perhaps my favourite dance. I just hope that my drooling was not too obvious. Hopefully people would think I was just an old man dribbling. However, for a moment, I was back in my teens, although unfortunately I never danced with a girl dressed like that.

If they were devils, then the angels had to be the born-again Christian group who sang modern Christian music to the accompaniment of guitars and tambourines. If it were a competition, then the devil would have won hands down. (This is evidenced by the fact that the Christian choir has not been seen at the fete for at least a couple of years.)

In 2019 I saw another quartet of talented musicians on violin, double bass, guitar and sax (alto and bass). The lady violinist also sang classic jazz pieces in a Polish accent that was exceedingly endearing, especially the way she pronounced the word 'love' – a sort of cross between 'loff' and 'love'. She was also an exceptionally good violinist, making it look so effortless.

The stalls were of every kind. From hand-made

ice cream to a hand-made shaving brush made from real badger bristles. I coveted this brush in 2018 and regretted not buying it. Fortunately, it was still available in 2019, so I bought it.

It is a very pleasant way of spending a few hours.

Philharmonic

After visiting the fete in May 2019, I had thought of going to the Philharmonic that evening to hear the Warsaw Philharmonic Orchestra play a couple of Tchaikovsky pieces, one of which was the Manfred symphony. This is not played that often and is a favourite of mine since university days. I had also wanted to see the Philharmonic Hall, which was near the Warsaw Uprising Square, close to where I was staying.

It was just as well that I had deferred booking until that morning, because the programme had changed and was now Shostakovich's 10th Symphony. Not much difference! I felt sorry for those who had booked and found themselves not getting what they had paid for, but happy at my fortune for having left booking to the last minute.

Monuments

One of the nice things about Warsaw is the number of monuments it possesses. I have already described a number of them, but some of them don't seem to fit into descriptions of places. One of these is my second favourite monument, Warsaw Nike, or, to give it its proper title, The Monument to the Heroes of Warsaw.

Monument to the Heroes of Warsaw (Nike)

This was designed by my namesake, Marian Konieczny, but it was not because of this that I like it so much. It is because it is powerful.

As you travel from Ratusz Arsenał to the Old town, just before the underpass under the Old Town, there is a small park on a slope on the right. There you will see a pedestal with a statue on top. That is Nike, goddess of Victory, which is a strange choice given that it commemorates so many hundreds of thousands of Warszawians who died.

The idea was to erect a monument to those who died in Warsaw in WW2, including those who died in the defence of Warsaw in 1939, the Warsaw Ghetto Uprising in 1943 and the Warsaw Rising of 1944 as well as the many who died at the hands of the Nazi thugs for being Polish during the period of the General Government.

The decision to commission such a monument was made on July 30th 1956 by the Metropolitan Council of Warsaw. By February 1957 some 196 entries had been received from home and abroad, but they were not happy, so did what all councils do when difficult decisions are to be made – they sat on it and did nothing until January 1959, when they announced a second competition. Naturally, they included the likely winners from the first competition and ended up with 106 entries. Marian Konieczny won, along with his architects, Zagremma Konieczna and Adam Konieczny. Presumably these were relatives, but their expertise would have been needed, because the monument is massive. Her sword alone weighs around a metric tonne and can deflect 15cm in strong winds.

The whole sculpture, without pedestal, weighs in at ten tonnes.

I seem to remember a reference to the model being a young seventeen year old girl guide who died on the third day of the Warsaw Rising, but another account said that it was the sculptor's adolescent daughter. Given that Konieczny was 26 when he entered the first competition and 29 for the second, a girl with the womanly attributes of the statue would have had to be at least sixteen, giving Konieczny a daughter at the age of thirteen at the latest. Highly unlikely. I prefer the idea of a girl guide model. However, she would have been killed in 1944 when Konieczny was fourteen, so at best he could only have modelled the face on a photograph of the girl guide, for it is almost certain that the photograph did not depict her as bare-breasted, as the model. We will probably never know.

Many descriptions of the statue say that she is reclining, which implies lying on her side or on her back. She is actually flying, supported on a cloud, with both legs behind her. Her left hand is extended in front of her, seemingly grasping for an enemy, while the sword is held behind her, ready to slay whoever she holds.

The statue was made in Silesia and shipped in two parts on a special rail carriage to Warsaw Gdansk station.

It was unveiled on July 20th 1964 in Theatre Square, where it stood until November 14th 1995, when it was taken down to allow for the redevelopment of the theatre area.

Marian Konieczny, by now a famous sculptor, was consulted about the new position. He saw Nike floating above the clouds and wanted a plinth some twenty metres high. The authorities disagreed, presumably thinking of the cost and proposed six metres. Eventually the compromise of 14 metres was chosen.

The new base was designed by Marta Pinkiewicz-Woźniakowska. It is made from reinforced concrete, made to look like stone. The base had to be a serious one, because it is placed on a slope made of rubble under the grassy exterior.

The relocated statue was unveiled in its new location on December 15th 1997.

Although impressive on its tall column, it is difficult to get into a position to see the detail of the statue. Viewed from Ul. Miodowa, you get the distant back view. From the park you get a wide variety of views, but always from below. Perhaps it is an application for a camera drone.

AK Monument

I had come across references to the Monument to the Armie Krajowe, who had put up such resistance in the Warsaw Rising, but had never seen it. I had read that it was on one of four mounds created in the city after the war in order to store the rubble from the destroyed city. Every time I read something about the reconstruction I am filled with more awe for those dedicated people who planned and worked for the re-creation of the city.

After I had taken Max to the airport for his flight home, I returned to the flat with the intention of doing no more than sink a couple of cans of Żywiec and flaking out, but after half an hour of not doing very much, and aware that I had to make the most of my remaining days in Warsaw, I looked on Jak do Jade for the details of how to get there. It seemed simple enough – catch a bus like the 116, 222 or 180 to the far end of Ujazdowski Park and hang a left Clyde for a few stops on the 167 to a stop named Budexpo, that I had earlier determined seemed to be the nearest place to the monument.

The first part of the plan went without a hitch. I

got to the far end of Ujazdowski. I knew where I was, because this was the stop before the one I use when going to the Chopin concerts. But I had never asked myself where the 167 bus stop was. This lack of knowledge was now becoming important.

There were some stairs going down under the road junction. Perhaps they would go down as far as the road below.

No chance. It went down, along and then back up.

I surfaced and decided to make for the pelican crossing that seemed to be on a route towards another set of stairs that looked more likely to lead to a stop that would get me the 167 to Budexpo.

As luck would have it, I got stranded half way over. There was one lifebelt in my situation in the form of a young lady, who was also stranded halfway over the road, so I metaphorically grabbed her with both hands. Actually the conversation went something like:

"Przepraszam. Mowisz po angielsku?" (*Excuse me, do you speak English?*)

"A little".

"Do you know where I can get a 167 bus?"

The clouds came over her face. She was going to join the vast army of people who knew everything about this spot, other than where to find a 167.

The pelican lights changed and the warning beeper emphatically told us to get a move on.

"I'm sorry. I am keeping you."

"Hush. I am thinking."

"Sorry."

The beeping stopped and the traffic roared. She turned to me and said, "You can go down that road over there. Go past the Indian embassy and there is a bus stop soon after. Catch the 108, which will take you to Budexpo."

"Thank you so much."

The beeping resumed and I crossed just behind her so that she could get away from this irritating foreign idiot.

She turned round. "There's the road. Go down there."

"Thank you very much".

Then I don't know why, but I blurted out, "I want to see the AK monument."

"It isn't in a nice area", she replied. "I don't think that we Poles are proud of it."

She was now walking with me and we were turning into the road I had been advised to take. I later found out that this was Ul. Agricola.

"I hope I am not taking you out of your way."

"I go home this way."

She seemed to be less frosty now. It is understandable that a young lady would be cautious about engaging with a stranger, but by now we had the measure of each other, so we talked of many things until we had passed the Indian Embassy and the statue of King Sobieski III that I mentioned in the chapter on Łazienki Park.

And so we came to the bus stop.

"Thirteen minutes for the next bus. It is a five

minute walk. Do you want to walk?"

We walked and we talked and we came to the spot where we would have to part company.

She held out her hand. We shook hands. It was a long handshake, more like a holding of hands. It was a case of parting is such sweet sorrow. Sweet, because we had just spent half an hour or so in each others' company and both did not want it to end. There was no sex or emotion in our conversation. It was just pure enjoyment.

"What is your name?" she asked.

"Tony. And yours?"

"Magda."

"Nice name".

We clumsily said our goodbyes and I turned and went for the hill. I did not dare turn round. I don't cry these days, but I think that was a time I might have.

Magda. If you read this book, this chapter is dedicated to you.

The entrance to the monument is part way between the Budexpo and Bartycka, although nearer to Budexpo.

On later examination, it would appear that I should have stayed on the 180 until the stop after Łazienki. On such trivial errors do we change the course of our lives.

So through the gap by the tatty car park and up an endless flight of steps to the top where was the AK monument.

As I climbed the shallow steps I noticed the wooden crosses at the sides of the path. They were simple, each with a diagonal of white and red ribbon. There were not that many, but when clustered they conveyed a powerful message.

This hill was formed of rubble from the demolished city. There was a lot of rubble.

I continued walking up the endless stone steps, along the path named after 'W Hour', when the order was given to start the Rising, until I could see the first signs of the monument.

It was impressive and there was a view over part of Warsaw. The monument did not need an explanation. The main inscription just said '1944' and the AK symbol would be familiar to all Poles.

The AK symbol is the letter P with the bottom of the vertical splayed into what looks like an anchor. The top part of the P looks as though it could be the handle of a sword. It is a very distinctive and impressive symbol. Even more impressive when built to the size it was at the top of the hill of rubble.

I took photos and came down again.

I also took some photos of the crappy area at the bottom, where I turned right, went over the zebra crossing and continued to Budexpo.

There were a lot of people at the bus stop, so a bus was probably imminent. I had time to read the route of the 108, and saw that I could go to Pole Mokotowska, where I could catch the underground. The bus that arrived was the 167 and I had not a clue where to go, until I saw on the indicator board that had Plac Trzech Krzyży at the end.

"Home and dry," I thought and settled down to

enjoy the journey through parts of Warsaw that were new to me.

At last we arrived at the terminus. But before we did, the indicator board had been reset and Plac Trzech Krzyży disappeared as a stop.

But all was well. The bus stopped and I tried to work out where I was and in which direction I should walk.

Off I set and saw a bus that would get me home. Someone ran for it and I followed suit, diving on just before the doors closed.

"Funny. Nowy Swiat doesn't normally look this green."

We were only going back towards Ujazdowski Park!

Off the bus. Across the zebra. Under the underpass and wait with the small crowd for my homeward bus.

I did get home and I did get that beer, but not until long after it had been planned for.

I later found out that, on every August 1st at 9pm, a fire is lit at the monument, started by a flame carried from the Tomb of the Unknown Soldier in Plac Piłsudskiego by a 'Relay of the Generations', comprised of soldiers, scouts and ordinary citizens. This fire lasts for 63 days, to commemorate the length of time that the 1944 Rising lasted.

Monument to the Polish Underground State and the Home Army

A bit of a mouthful, this title, but it's what it says on the tin.

The Polish Government escaped from Poland, so it never surrendered, but became the Polish Government in Exile, for most of the war in London. The Home (or Underground) Army reported to the government-in-exile.

I came across this monument one day when returning from an afternoon concert in the park. I foolishly took a bus other than the 116 or 180 and found myself veering off from a known route at Plac Trzech Krzyży. I found myself in the parliament area and stumbled across this monument.

It looks impressive, although, from a distance, it is not clear what it represents. Only on closer approach does the wording indicate that it is something to do with the AK. In fact, it has the names of the president and prime ministers the government in exile and the names of the supreme commanders of the AK.

On a low wall are the names of the towns and cities where there were outposts of the AK.

The material used in its construction is Polish granite, except for the top of the 32 metre high obelisk, which is made from Italian granite.

It was unveiled on June 10th 1999 and dedicated by the Pope on June 11th.

It is located at the corner of Matejki and Wiejska.

It is only my opinion, but I think that the AK

monument near Budexpo is far more impressive.

The Warsaw Rising

Whole books have been written on this topic, which relates to the period 1st August 1944 -4th October 1944, events leading up to it and what followed. I can only hope to give a brief description of what it was and where it is commemorated in Warsaw today.

To put it into perspective, the London Blitz lasted longer (7th September 1940 to 11 May 1941) but resulted in fewer casualties as there was air defence and no enemy soldiers on the ground.

In June 1944, the Allies in the west landed in Normandy and made their way south to Paris. At the same time, Russia launched an offensive from the east, using troops made up of those Poles who had not joined Anders' army. They were commanded by two Polish generals -Bering and Rokosovsky – although all the officers were Russian – just to ensure that the Poles did not get the idea of working against the Russians. (Bear in mind that they had all come from the Gulag and were not favourably disposed towards their former captors.).

The idea was to weaken the Nazi counter-offensive in the west by getting them to fight on two fronts.

A couple of days before the Allies were due to arrive in Paris, the French Resistance rose up and took control of the city. In the same way, the arrival of the

Russians in the east was the trigger for the Polish Home Army (Armia Krajowa, or AK) to rise up and throw out the Nazis from their city.

The only problem was that the Russians stopped on the right bank of the Vistula in Praga. There are many theories as to why they did this, but the most likely is that Stalin hated the Poles from the time he had been a general in the 1920 Polish-Russian War and had been routed. There was also the fact that most Poles were averse to communism.

There is much debate about whether the AK should have risen when they did, but there were signs that the time was right.

A few Russian T-34 tanks had managed to get into Warsaw on a reconnaissance mission on July 31st.

Radio Moscow had broadcast an appeal to the Warsaw citizens to assist in the impending liberation.

On July 30th a Polish language broadcast from the Russian-controlled radio station had issued an emotional appeal for the population to rise as the Russians were about to drive the Nazis out of Praga.

It was feared that the Nazis were about to reinforce defences on the west of the Vistula, so there was an incentive to stop them from doing this.

General Bór-Komorowski was given the authority by the Government in Exile in London to decide when, and if, to start the Rising.

Bór-Komorowski

Tadeusz Komorowski (1895-1966) was born in

the Austro-Hungarian part of partitioned Poland and fought for the Austrians in the first World War, but joined the Polish army once there was peace.

He rose to command an army cavalry school and was a member of the Polish equestrian team in the 1924 Summer Olympics.

When WW2 broke out, he fought against the Nazis, but, on the over-run of Poland, he helped organise the AK in the Krakow area. He was given the code name Bór (forest). By 1943 he was commander of the AK.

On 4th October 1944 he surrendered the AK to the Nazis and was interned in Germany until the end of the war, when he moved to England.

From 1947-49 he became Prime minister of the Polish Government-in-exile, although hardly any country recognised this government.

He became an upholsterer.

When he died aged 71, he was buried in Gunnersbury Cemetery, but his ashed were transferred to the Powązki cemetery on 30th July 1994.

There is a road in the Warsaw suburb of Gocław named in his honour.

It was a difficult decision, but the factors in favour of starting the Rising outweighed procrastination.

So at 5pm on August 1st 1944 (W Hour), the Rising began. It was expected to last a few days until the Nazis retreated from an advancing Russian army.

But the Russians stayed put in Praga.

The excuse was that the army needed to rest after its push from the east.

The Poles therefore found themselves between a rock and a hard place. The Rising would have to last for more than a few days.

When the Poles asked for help from the Russians, none was forthcoming.

The call went out to the west for provisions.

When the Allies asked the Russians for permission to use landing strips in the areas they controlled, access was denied. This was crucial for replenishing food and arms in Warsaw by planes sent from Brindisi in Italy. Without the ability to land, planes could only carry about one ton of provisions. Even worse, they had to fly a direct route to minimise fuel consumption. The Nazi anti-aircraft divisions were not slow in making use of this fact. Losses were high.

Only ten percent of supplies dropped reached the AK: the other ninety percent was a present to the Nazis.

For the first few days the AK put up a good show and took control of much of the city.

However, the Nazis controlled the air and the Stuka dive bombers were effective in bombing targets while the Wermacht was organising itself.

The Wermacht entered Warsaw via Wola, west of the centre. In three days they murdered everybody they came across. Estimates are that around fifty thousand civilians died in three days. There are many harrowing accounts of Nazi brutality that went along with the burning of people within buildings and the executions by firing squad. It was all consistent with the Nazi view of the Poles being *untermenschen* and therefore did not count as being part of the human race.

The AK still fought on with weapons made in little factories and arms captured from the Nazi oppressors.

They survived shelling, the use of anti-aircraft guns at close range, flame-throwers and a particularly nasty invention, Goliath.

This was a cable-controlled armoured mobile mine that made a frightening sound as it progressed. It could cause tremendous damage when it exploded. The only way it could be stopped was to cut the cable, either by shooting it or for a soldier to axe it. This latter option was extremely dangerous.

The terror of these things was illustrated in a 2016 film *Miasto '44* – a love story set during the Rising.

The use of anti-aircraft guns against buildings is also horrendous. These use shells designed to explode somewhere near an aeroplane and to release a cloud of shrapnel in the hope that enough of it will hit the aircraft and bring it down. When fired into buildings it kills and maims and brings down walls and ceilings.

Andrzej Wajda, the talented Polish film director, made a trilogy of films in the 1950's about this time.

One of the trilogy was called *Kanal*. It focused on the movement of people between AK controlled parts of the city using the sewers. Fortunately in the AK there was the Chief Sanitation Engineer of the City of Warsaw and he knew his way round the sewers and could guide them and draw maps.

Even so, thousands died in the sewers. They succumbed to disease, drowned and were blown up by the grenades that the Nazis dropped down the manholes into the sewers.

There is the monument in Plac Krasinskich that depicts soldiers emerging from a sewer.

Nearby is the Brutalist monument, erected in the time of Poland's membership of the Warsaw Pact, that showed a fictional view of soldiers charging the enemy.

One of the first museums created after the fall of communism in 1990 was the Rising Museum, or Muzeum Powstania Warszawskiego, about 350 metres north of Rondo Daszynskiego at Ul Grzybowska. 79.

When you go there you will see why it was not built under communist rule, although the idea was mooted in 1983. It does not show the Russians in a kindly light. It was opened on July 31st 2004 to mark the sixtieth anniversary of the start of the Rising.

It is one of the places to see in Warsaw. Allow the best part of a day to make full use of it.

Its website indicates its importance – www.1944.pl

The Rising caused the death of about 16,000 insurgents, with another 6,000 badly wounded. Some 150,000 – 200,000 civilians were killed, mostly from mass executions. More fighters would have been killed had not General Bor-Komorowski negotiated with the Nazis for the resistance fighters to be treated as soldiers, and not as terrorists, after the surrender.

Although they were soldiers, those who made it to England after the war were not given pensions, as other Polish soldiers were. As Norman Davies said in his book *Rising '44*, "It seems that the only people who did not regard the AK as soldiers were Russia and the UK Ministry of Pensions.

8,000 Nazis were killed and a further 9,000 badly wounded during the 63 days of the Rising.

During the fighting, 25% of the city was destroyed. After the fighting, 35% of the city was systematically destroyed, using troops that could have been more valuable on the western front. After this, some 85% of the city was in ruins.

Were the deaths of all these people necessary?

Necessary? No. But perhaps more inevitable than we might like to think.

Hitler hated the Poles and the Russians as members of the Slavic race, and therefore, in his view, inferior to the Aryan race of the Germans. They needed to be eliminated. An example of what was in store in a Nazi controlled Poland occurred in the region of the city of Zamość in the south of Poland. Poles in some 300 villages were evicted to make way for Germans. Many of those evicted found themselves taken to the Rotunda in Zamość. This was an ammunition store in the days of the Tsar, but made by the Nazis into a local killing ground. For this it was ideally situated, being in an isolated part of the city close to a railway line. It was here, in the middle of a circular courtyard that the bodies were burned. After the war, archaeologists dug down into the earth below the cremation site and found human fat down to a depth of two metres. Ten thousand or so people were cremated there. There is no reason not to suppose that this kind of action would have been repeated throughout the whole of Poland once the 'Jewish problem' had been dealt with.

Meanwhile, in the east, the Russians hated the Polish intellectuals – a term that covers a large range of people. These people were to be eliminated, as was the case of those murdered at Katyn in 1940. Ordinary people were also killed, as in the case of those sent to the Gulags.

Stalin killed more people in the 1930's than Hitler ever did.

It was a bad time for Europe when these two monsters were alive.

Other Leaders in WW2

There needs to be mention of some leaders of Poland in the build-up to WW2, but where to put them is difficult to determine. Hence this separate chapter. You will come across their names and will only wonder who they were if I don't tell you, so here goes.

They were all associated with Piłsudski and give an insight into life at the top of politics.

Edward Rydz-Smigły

He was a contemporary of Piłsudski and Sikorski and has a sizeable park in Warsaw named after him.

Edward Rydz-Smigły lived between 1886 and December 1941. He attended the Jagiełłonian University in Krakow, where he completed his studies while drafted into the Austrian army. He became a professional soldier, fighting with distinction in the Polish Legions in WW1 and in the Polish-Russian war of 1920, where he annihilated the Russian 12th Army and stood firm as the central part of the Battle of Warsaw in 1920.

With his impeccable war record, he rose rapidly through the ranks and became a trusted deputy of Piłsudski.

After the death of Piłsudski in 1935, Rydz-Smigły took over the position of Commander in Chief of the Polish armed forces and became the official

'Second Man' after President Mościcki.

By March 1939, Hitler had occupied all the countries to the west of Poland and Rydz-Smigły could clearly see the impending danger posed by Germany. However, time was too short to create a new strategy.

In early August, the western powers tried to persuade Rydz-Smigły to allow the Russians to cross Poland to mobilise at the German border. How out of touch could you get? Rydz-Smigły responded by refusing, on the grounds, among others, that, once inside Poland, the Russians would never leave.

When the Nazis invaded Poland on 1st September, he was immediately made Commander-in-Chief. A week later he ordered the evacuation of Warsaw. The army then moved in and tried to defend the city. There was always an expectation that the British and French would come to the aid of Poland, but they didn't as they were expecting Poland to fall.

The final straw came with the Russian invasion on 17th September. He ordered Polish troops to make their way to Romania and avoid any contact with the Russians. (At this time, the Kresy region of eastern Poland had a border with Romania, which was not yet involved in the war.

By crossing into Romania, the government avoided surrender and allowed Polish troops to carry on fighting.

Like many of his troops, Rydz-Smigły made his way through Romania. But whereas his troops could make their way to France and then, when France fell, into Britain, Rydz-Smigły was interned in Romania, where he set about initiating the creation of an underground army in Poland.

In October, he relinquished control of the army: this passed to Władysław Sikorski in London.

Rydz-Smigły was hampered in setting up defences before the war started by the poverty of Poland. Remember that this was a new country and it did not have a lot of income. To build modest defences in the west would have cost around two years of the entire Polish budget, and there was a need for defences in the east as well. Poland never stood a chance when attacked on two fronts by two massive armies led by dictators who, for different reasons, wanted to annihilate the Poles.

Rydz-Smigły was moved from the internment camp to a villa once owned by a Prime Minister of Romania. He escaped from there in December 1940 and crossed into Hungary. This annoyed Sikorski, who had been an opponent of Rydz-Smigły ever since the May 1926 coup of Piłsudski. (Rydz-Smigły had supported Piłsudski, whereas Sikorski had opposed the coup.).

Sikorski made it clear to Marshal Grot-Rowecki, leader of the AK, that the appearance of Rydz-Smigły in Poland would be regarded as an act of sabotage.

Rydz-Smigły stayed in Hungary until late October 1941, when he entered Poland and made his way to Warsaw, where he took the pseudonym Adam Zawisza and enrolled in the AK as an ordinary soldier. It was as an ordinary soldier that he was buried in Powązki cemetery after he died in December 1941 of heart failure. In 1991 his real name was put on his tombstone and in 1994 the people of Warsaw provided a new tombstone for him.

He seemed to be quite brilliant, although he also appeared dictatorial. He was, perhaps unfairly, blamed for the defeat of Poland by the Nazis. But then he was also the hero of the Battle of Warsaw in 1920. You can't have it all.

Władysław Sikorski

Sikorski was a soldier and politician who became part of the Polish Government-in-exile. As far as I can tell, he was not related to Igor Sikorski, with whom he was contemporaneous. Igor went to America and founded the Sikorski aviation company, renowned for its helicopters.

Sikorski (1881 – 1943) was born and lived in various parts of Galicia (the Austro-Hungarian part of partitioned Poland). He went to school in Rzeszow and Lwów Polytechnic, where he gained a diploma in hydraulic engineering. While studying for his diploma, he became involved in an organisation that promoted literacy among the rural population.

He volunteered to join the Austro-Hungarian army, where he went to officer school and became a second lieutenant in the reserves.

In 1908, in Lwów, he joined the Union for Active Struggle with, among others, Josef Piłsudski. Its aim was to bring an uprising against the Russian Empire.

In 1910 he formed a chapter of the Riflemen's

Association. This was to train Poles in military skills. Many of the graduates of this programme were the founders of the Polish legions in WW1.

During the latter stages of WW1, Sikorski had disagreements with Piłsudski. Sikorski wanted to co-operate with the Austro-Hungarians, whereas Piłsudski did not. Indeed, Piłsudski was so opposed to co-operation that he refused to sign the oath which swore allegiance to the Austrian Emperor and he was interned in the fortress of Magdeburg for his pains.

The two did come together in 1918, with Sikorski coming over to Piłsudski's viewpoint and the two were interned together.

After the war ended, Sikorski fought in the Polish-Ukrainian war, where he secured and defended Przemyśl in October -November 1918.

He fought many battles and took control of the north sector in the Battle of Warsaw and held it while Piłsudski mounted the counter-offensive. He fought well in several battles that followed, until the Treaty of Riga in 1921.

He occupied several high offices, until, in 1922, after the assassination of Roland Gabriel Narutowicz, he became Poland's Prime minister, a post he held until May 26th 1923.

One of his achievements as prime minister was obtaining recognition of Poland's eastern borders from Britain, France and the USA, although, as we already know, a fat lot of good this did when the chips were down.

After being prime minister, he held several posts

of high office. From 1925-28 he was military corps commander in Lwów. This was at the time of Piłsudski's May 1926 coup. Sikorski refused to supply any troops to aid the coup, much to the annoyance of Piłsudski. After being relieved of his post, he spent much of his time writing, and lecturing at the Paris War College. He was also a member of the Sejm (parliament) in opposition to the Sanacja party of Piłsudski, along with, amongst others, Paderewski and Haller.

He was denied a military command after the invasion by Germany and escaped to France via the Romanian route. There, on 28th September 1939 he joined Stanisław Mikołajczyk and Władysław Raczkiewicz in a Polish government-in-exile, where he took command of the Polish Armed Forces in France.

Although recognised by the Allies as the official government, the Allies refused to see Russia as an aggressor, even though it had invaded Poland. Which just goes to show the verity of the expression *There is none so blind as those who will not see.* But maybe they realised their limitations.

The Polish navy had sailed for Britain shortly after the outbreak of war and thousands of troops had made it to France via the Romania route. There was also the large resistance movement. There were also 86 planes.

Marshal Petain proposed that the Poles surrendered to the Germans. (It gets more absurd the more I discover about what happened in this period of history!) The reply was short and everything Polish moved to Britain. It was just as well, because, in spite of reluctance on the part of Britain, Polish forces distinguished themselves at Narvik and also in the Battle of Britain, where the Polish (and Czech) 303 Squadron had more kills than any other squadron. It can be argued that, without the Poles, the Battle of Britain would have been lost. The Poles had actually fought in anger defending their homeland, so had experience. They had also seen Stuka dive bombers wreak havoc on Polish cities. Most pilots had lost family members in the year up to the Battle of Britain. They saw Luftwaffe pilots as 'Nazi bastards', not as players in a game.

After the Nazi invasion of Russia in 1941, Sikorski went with a diplomatic mission to Moscow, where he signed an agreement with the Soviet Union and got them to rescind the Molotow-Ribbentrop Agreement of 1939. Of most importance, he got the Russians to agree to the release of tens of thousands of Polish prisoners (among whom was my Dad).

In April 1943, the news of the finds at Katyn broke and Sikorski refused to accept the Russian explanation. Stalin then broke off diplomatic relations with the Polish government-in-exile.

Sikorski still believed in some form of normalisation of relations with Russia, whereas Anders, who had experienced Russian hospitality for two years in Moscow's Lubianka prison, did not believe that this was possible.

Sikorski spent some time in the summer of 1943 visiting troops in the Middle East to boost morale. but it was while he was returning from one of these visits via Gibraltar, that his Liberator plane crashed on take-of from Gibraltar, killing all on board, other than the pilot. There are many theories about that crash, but the official line was that some cargo had shifted during take-off and destabilised the plane. The plane had crashed 16 seconds after take-off.

Sikorski was buried in Newark, England, until 1993, when his remains were transferred to Wawel Castle.

He was without doubt the best representative that Poland could have had in London. He was respected by Churchill. No other Polish diplomat achieved the respect and outcomes that he had done. He was a massive loss to the Polish cause.

Stanisław Mikołajczyk

He was the Prime Minister of the Polish Government-in-Exile in London.

Born in 1901, he joined the Polish Army in 1920 and took part in the Polish-Soviet War being wounded in Warsaw. Discharged from the army, he returned to his home area of Posnan, where he inherited his father's farm.

He became active in politics, joining the Polish People's Party (PSL) then was elected to parliament in 1929. He rose to the position of President of the PSL in 1937.

He was a passionate opponent of the authoritarian regime established in Poland after the death of Piłsudski in 1935.

In September 1939 he was a private in the Polish army and took part in the defence of Warsaw, but then escaped to England via Hungary, Yugoslavia, Italy and France. He was immediately asked to join the Polish Government in Exile and rose to become Deputy Prime Minister in 1941. Following Sikorski's death in 1943, he became Prime Minister.

After the German announcement of the discovery of bodies at Katyn, he refused to accept the Russian explanation and, as a result, Stalin severed diplomatic relations.

He was opposed to totalitarian government, instead believing in the Four Freedoms: political, religious, personal and economic freedoms. Mikołajczyk and Stalin never agreed – the main differences were over Katyn, Poland's eastern borders and the imposition of a Communist government after the war.

Stalin conceded somewhat with the formation of a National Government of Unity for Poland, led by Edward Osóbka-Morawski as Prime Minister, Władysław Gomułka as one of the two Deputies. Mikołajczyk resigned from the Government-in-exile, against strong opposition, and became the second deputy prime minister.

Once in Poland, he set about re-establishing the PSL, which soon became the largest party. However, this was not what Stalin wanted, so he set about persecuting the democratic parties. 32,477 people were prosecuted for 'crimes against the state'. To ensure that the elections would give the right result, the security apparatus appointed 47% of the electoral committees as agents. Then the elections were held and the right result announced: 394 for the Communist Party and only 28 for the democratic parties. Mikołajczyk resigned and returned to London, where the Government-in-exile rejected him. He emigrated to the USA, where he died in 1966. In 2000 his remains were returned to Poland, where he was buried.

Władysław Raczkiewicz

President of the Polish Government-in-exile from 1939 to his death in 1947, aged 63.

Born in 1885 in Georgia to Polish parents, he followed his father, a judge, into Law. In WW1 he fought with the Russian Army, but after the Russian Revolution he worked for Polish independence. He served under Piłsudski for a time.

Between the wars he served as the head of a number of Polish provinces (voivodehips). Effectively this was the local government route.

When the Nazis invaded Poland, he managed to get himself to France, where he joined Sikorski and Mikołajczyk, but he did not approve of the Sikorski-Mayski Agreement, whereby Stalin revoked all previous Soviet-German agreements, declared an amnesty for the two million prisoners-of-war and the resumption of diplomatic relations between Russia and Poland. Presumably he did not like the idea of having the Russians as new friends. And this was before the disclosures of Katyn were released.

At Yalta, in February 1945, Churchill and Roosevelt swallowed the Soviet line that only a pro-Russian Communist government in Poland could guarantee the security of Russia, and so the Allies withdrew support for the Polish Government-in-exile.

Raczkiewicz died in 1947 in Ruthin, North Wales, and was buried in the cemetary at Newark-on-Trent, England.

He does not appear to have the charisma of the others described above, else he would have been transported to a grave in Poland after 1989. However, his name is on the Monument to the Polish Underground State and the Home Army.

Konstanty Rokossovski

Rokossovski was the Marshal of the Soviet Union who held his troops on the eastern bank of the Vistula while the Nazis killed Poles and destroyed Warsaw during the Rising.

Rokossovski came from an influential Polish family that had, by the time he was born on December 21st 1896, fallen on hard times. His grandfather had demonstrated his Polish credentials by taking part in the November Uprising of 1830. Orphaned at the age of 14, he took whatever work he could, including being a stone-mason, in which role he took part in the reconstruction of the Poniatowski Bridge.

He was drafted into the army as a consequence

of WW1 and survived, siding with the Bolsheviks in the 1917 October Revolution that took place in Russia. He became part of the Red Army and showed military talent in the inter-war years. He fought in Mongolia, where he prevented the Mongolian dictator of the time from severing off a part of Eastern Russia.

Very few escaped the Stalinist purges and in August 1937 he was accused of espionage for the Japanese and Poles. He was tortured and beaten up in an effort to extract a confession. (Nine front teeth knocked out, three ribs broken, toes broken with a hammer, one eye knocked out.)

He was held in Kresty prison, Leningrad from 17 August 1937 to March 22nd 1940. He was only saved by a former superior who had risen to be the Marshal of the Soviet Union – Timoshenko. He was sent to the Crimea to recuperate and then made a Major-General.

In 1936 he was sent to Spain to advise the communists in the civil war there.

He took major roles in the battles of Moscow, Stalingrad and Kursk.

He also directed Operation Bagration, which freed Belarus from Nazi occupation.

There is no doubt that he was a formidable commander, but his decision to hold his troops off from supporting the Warsaw Rising of 1944 is a matter for argument. He always claimed that it would have been disastrous for him to enter Warsaw, and that may have been true, but, combined with the refusal of Stalin to allow supply planes to use Russian airfields, one does begin to smell a rat.

Rokossovski became a Marshal of the Soviet Union and was one of the stars in the Moscow Victory Parade after the war ended.

For four years after the end of the war, Rokossovski remained in command of the Russian forces in Poland. Then, under the Beirut government in Poland, he became Minister of Defence and Marshal of Poland, on the direct orders of Stalin.

Although Polish by ancestry, he was truly Russian and he played a major role in the suppression of anti-Soviet activities on the part of the Poles.

He instigated the formation of labour battalions in the army, to which any 'undesirable' could be drafted. Some 20,000 Poles found their way there, including those who had fought with the AK. A thousand people died within a few days of joining the labour battalions and many others were crippled after working in mines (coal and uranium) and quarries.

In the Posnan protests of 1956, he sent in the military, with tanks, and killed 74 civilians.

Shortly after these protests, Rokossovski went to see Khrushchev in Moscow to persuade him to use force against the Polish State, but Khrushchev listened to Gomulka. As a result, it became impossible for him to remain in Poland, so he returned to Russia, where he became Deputy Minister of Defence and then Chief Inspector of the Ministry of Defence, until he retired in 1962. He died in Moscow in 1968, aged 71 and was buried in the Kremlin wall necropolis.

I cannot say that I warm to the man.

Dentist

There was one occasion when, just before a planned visit to Warsaw, I had some problems with my teeth. A tooth had cracked and a filling had partially come out of another tooth. Having heard about the professionalism of Polish dentists, I decided to book an appointment for while I was there. But who to book with?

I phoned my apartment supplier and asked his advice and he recommended a dentist based on the experience one of his staff had. He did not visit dentists, so could not give first-hand advice.

So I booked an appointment with a branch of this company. I won't give the name, because it's a bit like restaurants – you go to one, love it and tell your friends, only for them to go and find it was terrible because the chef had changed.

Anyway, the communication I had with them seemed to indicate that they would be OK, so I went at the appointed hour during my next visit to Warsaw.

It was an easy journey by tram and I actually found the place without too much trouble.

It was a functional, but spacious building with three receptionists at the desk inside the door. A few patients (or should I say 'clients') were waiting, some reading magazines. Professional-looking people were moving about dressed in white coats. It all looked professional and efficient.

I registered at the desk, using my poor Polish and the better English of one of the receptionists, and went to the waiting area.

A very short time afterwards, a lady in a white jacket came to me and checked that I was the right patient. (Although the other patients seemed to be dressed in Sunday finery, while I was in my Regatta Adventure trousers and probably looked like a fish out of water, but at least they checked, which was good. Although, with a name like 'Konieczny' they might have thought that I really was Polish.)

So far, so good. I followed the lady down a corridor and into a spacious room, where a lady in her thirties was waiting. She had a magnificently Russian name, but turned out to be very Polish with very good command of English. She greeted me warmly and checked that I was the right patient.

"What seems to be the problem?" she asked.

I should have realised that she was sceptical. Seems to be the problem. Not 'what is the problem'.

"I have a cracked tooth and a lost partial filling.

"Let's have a look then," she said.

I opened my mouth and she intoned the way dentists do. "Seven, six, five, Confusion, four, three, Obstruction, two one, demolition, one, two, missing, three, four, knock on the door, five, six, pick and mix, seven eight, eight, seven..." And so it went on until every tooth had been described.

"Your fillings are dreadful. Were they done on the National Health?"

"Most were."

"I can see, although you have a couple that are good, for some reason."

She obviously did not think much of our wonderful NHS.

"You know, the only two criteria for fillings on the NHS are One, that it should not hurt and Two, it should last twelve months. I could do fillings with bubble gum that will do that."

I was not sure whether she was just saying that out of real concern for my dental health, or whether she was on commission and wanted to get the maximum possible from my wallet. I decided it was the former, since she had acknowledged that two of the fillings were good. These had been done by a superb dentist I had once had. He had twice the number of patients as any other dentist, but did such a good job that his customers only needed to see him half as often (or less). Unfortunately he turned a part-time occupation into a full-time one. This was acting as an expert witness in court cases involving dentists. Presumably such dentists had either caused pain, or their bubble gum fillings did not last the full twelve months. With four girls at the most expensive school in Britain, presumably he needed the cash more than he needed us patients. He was a sad loss and I never did find a great dentist after that – at least not until after I had been to Warsaw on my dental visit.

So she whipped out my NHS fillings, tidied the cavities and filled with white compound that set rock hard. These fillings continue to serve me well.

She also suggested that I had an appointment

with they hygienist. As the price was reasonable and I wanted to get my mouth into the best possible state for once, I agreed.

A few days later, I was back at the dentist's to see the hygienist, who turned out to be a slim woman in her forties with no speak English. So we would rely on sign language and my poor command of Polish. It looked like a recipe for disaster, especially when you realise how difficult it is to communicate with anybody who is moving instruments around your mouth.

Fortunately, while learning Polish, I had come across the word *ból* (pain). She used it a lot, but only to check that I was not feeling undue *ból* while she was using an ultrasonic descaler, nasty pointed hook or other instrument which could so easily have belonged to the SS.

She was the utmost gentle person and I only felt minor *ból*.

The most *ból* was when I received the bill. I worked out afterwards that it was somewhere in the region of what my new UK dentist would charge, but, because he seems to be good value, less than your average UK dentist would charge. But I had got, in return, a perfect set of teeth that were devoid of anything growing on them. And I had got the latest technology at the time.

When I cracked a tooth just before another visit to Warsaw, I went to the same company, but different location, as my Russian-sounding Pole was on holiday. He spoke English, was professional and did a good job, but he was nowhere as charming as the two ladies. It's an example of what I was saying earlier about the recommendation of a restaurant – the chef had changed.

Hospital

I had to go to hospital to have a couple of stitches taken out of my leg. You probably deserve an explanation for this statement, so I will enlighten you.

I had been walking along the main road in our village a couple of days before setting out for Warsaw, when a lorry had zoomed past me. Now I was on the pavement and the lorry was on the road, but something on the lorry must have been overhanging the pavement, because I was hit on the leg. When I got home, Lin had a look at the damage and immediately insisted that we go to the hospital, where a nice nurse ordered an X-ray to make sure that there was no metal in the wound, before she closed the hole with a couple of stitches.

"Get these taken out in a week," she ordered.

"He's in Poland then," said Lin.

"How long for?" asked the nurse.

"Another week."

"Well it really can't stay in that long," said the nurse.

"It is a fairly civilised country and I will be in the capital," I said. "I'll sort it."

The day the stitches should have been taken out was the day that I had arranged to go on a tour of the Filtry water works.

I arrived at the waterworks early and waited for the tour to start. There was a group of men at the gatehouse. It transpired that they were contract workers about to start work that morning and they were waiting for the formalities to be completed. Meanwhile, I asked questions of them. The youngest of them said that he spoke some English. He was obviously very embarrassed to do so, but he had a passable grasp of the language – certainly more passable than my attempts at Polish. However, none of the men, nor their supervisor, could provide me with any information about the tour.

Eventually I was asked to speak into a telephone by the man in the office.

"Hello."

"Oh, hello," said this female voice at the other end. "What are you here for?"

This was not sounding good. I explained.

"I am sorry, but you made an on-line booking with our Customer Service department."

I was not seeing where this was leading, but it sounded as though my tour would not be taking place.

And so it turned out. But the lady at the other end would write to me by email to let me know when I could have a visit. Unfortunately it would not be this week, or next. And it turned out to be never.

There is no point getting annoyed. Polish bureaucracy, when it sets its mind to it, can grind you down, so you just have to go along with it.

There would be other visits to Warsaw. In the meantime there was the matter of the stitches.

I had found a hospital close to the waterworks before I had set out that morning and so I made my way there after the disappointing phone call. Surprisingly, I found it and went in.

Now I am old enough to remember the NHS in its early days and I suddenly had a sense of deja-vu. There was a long corridor with very high ceiling and on both sides there were people who looked like extras in a war movie: bandaged body parts galore; crutches; concerned relatives all in an endless queue. I despaired.

A lone woman leaned against a wall. "Mowisz po angielsku?" I rattled out my stock phrase. "Troche." It was enough to know that she admitted to a little.

"What do I have to do?"

"You need to register at one of the windows up there," she said, pointing towards the end of the corridor. "There are two windows, one is for children."

I thanked her and made my way to where she had pointed.

There were a few people in front of me in the adult queue that was being serviced by two ladies. Fortunately I saw the young lady. She spoke English and spoke it well.

"You need to see a surgeon. They are used to taking out stitches after operations. It is complicated. I will show you." Thankfully she was referring to the directions being complicated and not the removal of my stitches.

She came out from behind the window and suddenly looked much taller. We walked down the corridor of extras. I smiled at the lady who had explained the process to me. She had not moved. She might still be there.

Anyway, I was escorted to the front door.

"At the end of this street is Novogorodska. You turn right and look for Pavillion 11. It is 200 metres. Ask there."

"Thank you very much. You have been very kind."

She went back in, presumably to organise the extras.

I set off with a bit of a spring in my good leg and hoofed it to Novogorodska. Turned right and walked along by a long, high wall with no sign of a break. But eventually, there was and the address was 59. It was going to be more than the promised 200 metres.

A little distance after 59 was a road junction that never expected pedestrians to encounter it. I gave up and went back to look at 59 to see if the nice girl had got the address wrong.

Now it does not matter who gives directions, they always miss out a vital piece of information. In this case it was the address. Number 59. Because inside the break in the wall were buildings called pavilions and these were labelled 11A, 11B and 11C. I took the one straight ahead, 11B and found a security guard who spoke no English. The translator on my phone came to the fore. 'I need to have some stitches removed,' it translated. He beamed and pointed to the far side of the hallway that was stocked with extras for another film, or maybe just extra extras for the same film. I didn't care. I hot footed it to the pointed direction and to another reception area.

Translator out. Point to the translated sentence. Beam from the receptionist. She picked up a small square of paper and wrote '62 Novogorodoska, ATTIS' on it.

"Dzienkujem." I thanked her and retraced my steps to where I had noticed Number 62 while looking for Number 11.

There was a pharmacy on the corner of the building. I didn't know if this was ATTIS or not. After all, I could have been given misleading information again. ATTIS instead of Apteka.

But no, I was told by one of the staff that I needed the next door down. I felt as though I was making progress. Perhaps I could have been a detective after all. But perhaps not.

Luck was with me. Inside the building was a security guard who spoke no English, but the translator sorted things. He held up four fingers and indicated the fourth floor. This was becoming a game of travelling Charades. Hospital. Two words. First word: four.

I found the lift and went up the four floors to where there was another reception area, manned by a woman who spoke no English and obviously thought that, as I was in Poland, I should be able to speak fluent Polish. The translator failed to illuminate her, but fortunately a colleague was able to suss things out and gave me specific directions to go to room 203 on the second floor.

When I got there, I knocked and tentatively entered. The man inside (sporting a Lech moustache) spoke little English but looked as though the translator caused something to register. He indicated that I should wait outside.

During the wait there was the sound of big band music from inside the room, yet nobody entered or left. Being of a benevolent disposition, I concluded that he was developing a play list for a physiotherapy session.

Shortly after the big bands started, I was accompanied by a short, elderly gentleman, who said something to me in a husky voice. I smiled sweetly and explained that I was English. Presumably he thought that being English meant that one did not have to have manners and engage in pleasant small-talk with one's fellows. So we sat in amiable silence.

An elderly woman joined us. Asked a question to the world at large , to which the elderly gentleman responded. She shrugged her shoulders.

A rather plump woman, dressed as though going to church, next joined us,saying nothing and not being spoken to.

Eventually a woman who would not be out of place in an NHS Management meeting entered room 203. Perhaps she was the doctor's jive partner?

Soon after the woman entered she reappeared at the door and said something. The elderly gentleman stood up and started to walk to the door, but was soon put in his place by the NHS Manager. It was me they were after, so up I stood and entered the room.

The doctor had now put on a white coat. It was one of those tie-up-at-the-back white coats, except that it was the right size for him in his shirt sleeves, but he had not taken off his thick jacket, so the white coat barely covered his shoulder area. As he was not expecting a lot of blood spatter from removing two stitches, this was probably all that was needed to ensure that his 1940's jive outfit was not stained.

As he spoke no English, she did all the talking. She had put on a conventional white coat, but had not buttoned it up. Presumably she was going to hide behind the broad frame of the doctor when he did the procedure, so she would be in the blood shadow.

She told me to lie down on the couch. I figured that I would need to drop my trousers as this would be easier than trying to roll them up over the scar. She indicated her approval of this action, presumably because "Drop your trousers" was not part of any English language course she would have done. I now turned so that my wound was facing up and therefore easier for the doctor to perform his ministrations.

But no! The woman was taking charge and going to do the job.

It was a demonstration of faith in the hospital security that they would not let in any unqualified person to mess about with someone else's body.

She held up a spray bottle – the sort that I might use to spray the roses – and gave me a couple of squirts over the wounded area. I could not see what she used to cut the stitches, but my guess would be a tiny scalpel. Anyway, I felt a slight discomfort as she did it, stepped back to admire her work before spraying my aphids. After a few seconds she dried the area and applied a plaster.

"You must leave this plaster on until tomorrow and then take it off."

"Thank you. I will do that,"

"Did you register?"

"No. Nobody asked me to."

Her eyes rolled upwards, but as she was not really an NHS Manager, she did not relish the thought of taking me through that business, especially as there would be a High Court inquest in why the figures for removing stitches were down this month.

I thanked them both for their ministrations, but was not convinced about the doctor, who was a dead ringer for a mad doctor out of a Boris Karloff movie.

I didn't notice any cameras, but if you ever watch a foreign-language movie on BBC Four on a Saturday evening and there is a scene where a man drops his Regatta Adventure trousers before getting on the couch, then you are probably looking at me. Especially if the film also features a lot of wounded extras.

Elecyjna

it seemed appropriate that a visit would be made to 'Elective' on the date of the election of European Members of Parliament. Actually, it is not the tram stop (10, 13, 26, 27, 28) that is of interest, but the Szymanskiego Park that I wanted to wander around.

The tram stops by a wide Pelican crossing.

I arrived to find plenty of people waiting to cross, while traffic seemed to be waiting for lights to change so it could start moving. It looked as though everybody was waiting for someone else. All of us pedestrians stared at the little red pictogram and presumably the drivers stared at their red traffic light.

We must have been the first to blink, because the traffic moved.

After a while it stopped again and I expected (literally) to be given the green light, but no such luck. I resolved to walk across the next time the traffic stopped. I did. I was the only one. The break in the traffic was short. I was two thirds over when the traffic made 'I am ready to move' noises. I ran the rest of the way and then walked nonchalantly into the park.

Edward Szymanskiego Park.

At the entrance was a memorial stone of the

type I had first seen at Wilanów. It was a Tchorek cross, named after the sculptor Karol Tchorek.

After the war, people placed makeshift markers at sites of killing. The communist authorities, surprisingly, agreed to organise a competition for a design of a common memorial. This competition was won in 1948 by the sculptor Karol Tchorek, who submitted a design of a Maltese Cross bas-relief on sandstone with text below describing the event being commemorated. Across the cross was written the inscription "This place is sanctified by the blood of Poles fighting for their freedom." This was subsequently changed by the authorities to "This place is sanctified by the blood of Poles fighting for the freedom of their homeland."

There were other linguistic considerations. Germans were not mentioned, being referred to as 'Hitlerites'.

The communist authorities also had some dilemmas to face, because many of the sites commemorated events associated with the Rising of 1944. These events were directed against AK soldiers and civilians, and the official line was that the AK soldiers were 'bandits'. Consequently, many of the plaques were not erected until after 1989.

Underneath the Maltese Cross is a description of the event being commemorated at that spot.

In the case of the one at Szymanskiego Park, it was to remember the killing of some 4,000 inhabitants of Wola in twelve apartment blocks nearby, who were executed in the yard in front of the forge at 122/124 Wolska Street on Black Saturday, August 5th 1944.

I have read some harrowing first person accounts of these killings in the area from the few who survived the searches made by the Nazis in the first couple of weeks of August 1944. These accounts turn statistics into tragedies. Four thousand people executed in one day is definitely a statistic, but the way they were rounded up and herded to a convenient execution wall gave a reality to the process. How those people must have felt, even after years of brutal murdering by the SS occupiers, can only be partially imagined.

There are many Tchorek plaques in Górczewska and Elecyjna streets nearby, as there were many witnessed atrocities in this area as the Nazi reinforcements rode in from the west.

Altogether in Warsaw there are some 180 of these plaques.

Walking on, I saw that the park had paths for cyclists and skaters, the latter's paths being marked with pictograms of in-line skating boots. Whenever I see such delightful paths, I have the urge to try skating. Perhaps next year?

Straight ahead was a fountain display, such as one sees at the Fountain Park, but this had no sound or lights.

It was ecologically sound, having 54 solar panels on nine solid supports providing the power. All around the fountain area were comfortable benches so that lots of people could enjoy the spectacle. I took a rest and watched the display for some time. It was very soothing

The park is named after Edward Szymański, poet born in 1907 and died in Auschwitz in 1943.

Tearing myself away from the fountain area, I continued along the path and came across, what I was to soon find out, was a series of interconnecting ponds, each with a fountain, presumably powered by the solar panels round the fountain area. It was delightful.

There were pleasing barriers of two heights close to the water's edge – orange for adults and lower, blue ones for children.

I could see no fish, but the waters were well-reeded, so I would expect an abundance of wildlife. There were certainly plenty of butterflies on the day I was there.

I continued my stroll up the waterway until I reached the end. The last pond was bigger than the others and boasted a powerful fountain that shot water high into the air.

It was a lovely park. Now it was time to visit the Eastern Orthodox cemetery.

I followed a footpath towards the main road, Ul. Elekcyjna and turned left, past the road named in honour of the Zoska battalion in the 1944 Rising, until I came to some open gates in the fencing that had been my companion. Now I have found all sorts of interesting things by following my nose, and this proved no exception, because I was entering the Park created in memory of Josef Sowinski.

Josef Sowinski Park

Very soon I came across a fairly dilapidated building. It had a sign in white writing on a red background – Wolski Centrum Kultury Amfiteatr. And sure enough, when I was past the building, I could see the tiered seating under a sail-like roof. A better view was to be had as I rounded the fencing and joined a paved path.

It all looked a bit tired, but still definitely functional.

So on down the path and behind the trees on the right there was a wall. By any guess, this was the wall to the cemetery.

There was still some way to go before I could get to the cemetery. In fact I would have to go back to Ul. Wolska and go in via the main entrance by the church.

But as I left the park, I turned round to look up the driveway behind me. There was a magnificent statue on a tall pedestal. I had to have a look.

On the way down the drive I passed a Tchorek memorial stone, recording the fact that Hitler had murdered 1,500 people in this park and burned the bodies of 6,000 people killed in homes in Wola.

The statue was for Josef Sowiński, a general in the November 1830 uprising.

Josef Sowinski.

He was born on the Ides of March 1777 and, after graduating from the Warsaw Corps of Cadets, at the age of 17 he was made a lieutenant in the Kościuszko uprising of 1794.

After the partition of 1795, Sowiński's regiment was made part of the Prussian army. He fought for the Prussians at the Battle of Eylau in 1807 and received the highest Prussian honour.

He returned to join the Polish army in 1811 after Napoleon Bonaparte declared the Duchy of Warsaw. He fought many battles on Napoleon's side until he lost a leg at the Battle of Mozhaysk during the invasion of Russia.

After the Congress of Vienna in 1815, he returned to Warsaw to command the Arsenal.

During the Russian assault on Warsaw on September 6th 1830, he personally commanded the defence of the western part of the capital in Wola, with 1,300 men against the overwhelming 11 Russian battalions.

After signing the surrender documents, Sowiński was bayoneted to death, although the Russians said that he had been killed at his post.

Orthodox Cemetery

I left the park and turned right to the cemetery, where the church stood at the entrance.

The church roof was undergoing restoration. Some new, white cobblestones had been laid round the church and now workmen were on the roof under the tarpaulins doing something at the end of the compressed air hose that swung from the compressor on the ground to the tarpaulins above.

A couple of men were sitting on a wall of a grave, smoking roll-ups. I looked at them with my 'Am I alright to go in here' face, but they ignored me, so I went in.

There were some pretty impressive graves with Russian inscriptions. Being close to the church, they must have been important people in their day, but now they were mainly forgotten. At least by me, although I could not have forgotten them, as I had never heard of them. It all amounts to the same thing.

I continued my walk, passing a pair of graves, where on the far side were grave candles and tributes to the departed. The nearest grave was devoid of decoration, so I could clearly see the headstone which had a name and one date: 1935-. Presumably this person was still extant and waiting to occupy the designated spot for all eternity.

Here there were two visitors sitting by a grave. Having looked at the cemetery, I realised that it was extensive and that I was not going to find the gave of Sokrates Starynkiewicz, who we heard of earlier – he being the Mayor of Warsaw at the time Filtry was commissioned. The visitors looked as though they might be mourning, so I looked at nearby graves, hoping to see someone from whom I could ask directions, but nobody appeared, so I went to the two mourners. They were happy to show me the way. I reproduce the directions here in case you ever want to retrace my steps.

From the entrance on Wolski, with the church on

your right, take the right hand path and follow it to the end of the church, whereupon take the next left main path. Walk some hundred metres and you will see a pinkish building, where the last word above the door is 'Gudzowatych'. Walk a few more yards and the large, black grave on the right of the path is that of Sokrates Starynkiewicz.

The man giving directions told me he was Swiss and did not speak much Polish. (We had been conducting our conversation in a sort of Polish until then.) So we switched to German while he asked me where I was from. We continued in English once he knew I was English. Perhaps he did not understand my German. He was bemused at the thought of an Englishman being in a Russian Orthodox cemetery in Warsaw, as this was definitely not on the tourist trail. He was even more flabbergasted when I told him I had come to see the grave of Sokrates Starynkiewicz. He gave me the directions, but I swear that he was shaking his head as I left him. Maybe he will buy a copy of this book and then he will understand a bit more about this atypical Englishman.

Having come to pay homage to this great man, I retraced my steps and looked for a tram to take me somewhere near the centre. As I passed the spot where I saw the Swiss man, I saw them walking off with a priest, not looking in my direction and being absorbed in conversation. I could not hear what language they were speaking. Probably Russian, just to add to the surreality of the situation.

Now, standing at the gates of the cemetery, it

was easy to see where the trams going out of the city would stop, but there was no sign of a tram station going the other way. To the right was a curve in the tracks that obliterated any sight of a station and to the left there was no sign either. I thought that I saw a tram slowing down and stopping towards the left, so I went there, only to find that it had slowed at a road junction. I walked back to Elekcyjna and caught a tram to Kino Femina, where I fancied a McDonalds.

Skaryszewski Park

A few days later I decided to bag some parks as it was a fine, sunny day, so I walked down Nowy Swiat, crossed to the tram stop for the Praga direction and caught a number 9 to Park Skaryszewski. I could also have caught the 24.

The tram stops at a dead straight road called Międzynarodowa, that leads off Aleja Waszyngtona. On the right of this road is Kamionkowskie Bionia Elekcyjne. I went for this one and found myself among trees and meadows abundant in wildlife (including one young couple who looked as though they might be 'doing it' in one of the meadows. I left them to it while I entered a wood.

Shortly after entering the park, I had come across a canal of sorts. Not the sort of canal with boats on it, but more like a thin lake. This blocked any route to the right, so I missed out on seeing the Wembly-sized football pitch. Actually, if I had known it was there, I don't think that I would have changed my walk.) It was a lovely walk through nature, with only the distant hum of traffic telling me that I was in a city. Too soon I was at a fence, beyond which was a car park. Fortunately the path kept away and I could veer into the park with no problem and I continued walking until I arrived at a road – Stanisława Augusta – presumably referring to the king of that name, whom we met earlier.

I was now at a junction and had to decide which way to go. Fortunately, a large group from the nearby Day Centre were embarking on a walk, so I let them have a head start and followed. They entered Park Skaryszewski where there was a lake. I immediately recognised this lake, because it was in this park some years earlier that I had attended an Art in the Park event that I described earlier. This time I could just enjoy the natural beauty of the place.

It was a pleasant stroll to the end of the lake, where, on the right, is the chocolate factory of E. Wedel.

As I exited the park, I saw a small concrete obelisk with writing on it. It was giving some information about the German-Polish garden that was near here. It was triangular in cross section, with one face written in German, one face written in Polish and one face with the logos and names of the companies who had donated to get the garden off the ground. It looked very much like an attempt by the Germans to dissociate themselves from their Nazi past. It has to be done and it will take a long time, given all the Tchorek plaques around the city. The Poles will not forget for a long time, but small joint projects might help both to recognise that times have moved on.

Not that I was moving on, situated on a main road (Zielemiecka) with few crossing places and no idea of where I could get a tram to Park Praski, which was to be my next stop. So I took a tram south for one stop, crossed the tracks to the platform the other side and took a tram north to Park Praski. I was glad that I had done this, because the stops at Zielemiecka were well spread out and I don't think that I would ever have found the stop I needed.

Park Praski

We touched on this park earlier, while rambling round Praga, but omitted any description of the park itself. This time I wanted to go to see if the bears really had gone. Thankfully, there were still a couple in the bear enclosure, but they were showing signs of stress, which was not good. Their surroundings were as good as could be made in a city, but it was no substitute for the bears' natural habitat.

On this occasion I did not walk round the park, as I had done so on a few other occasions.

It is not a special park. It has trees and grass and paths and a photogenic central lake. It is a nice place to be on a hot summer's day, but its proximity to the road and the National Stadium is never going to make it a haven of tranquillity.

On one of the occasions I visited the park, I spent some happy time experimenting with the different scene settings on my camera, which I had not long had. I got some nice moody pictures of the mallards on the lake, but not much else.

From Park Praski it is an easy step to the Old Town and thence to catch the 128 to Szczęśliwicki, where the bus terminates at a park.

Park Szczęśliwicki

What is there not to like about a place called Happiness in an area of the city called Clean? It was an obvious contender for a visit while I was bagging parks.

The park is very visible from the bus terminus and offers paved pathways into a natural environment. It also offers, reassuringly, a blue portable loo. Shortly after starting on the path, a lake came tantalisingly into view and remained that way while I completed the circuit.

There are many photogenic views along the way and I made the most of them with my new camera. At one point I came across a coot trying to install some discipline into her wayward brood and not succeeding. She called and shepherded, but there was always one that managed to go its own way as the urge to explore overcame the entreaties of Mum.

There were a few visitors while I was there. Dog-walkers and mums pushing prams being the most common sights, although retirees came shortly after, sitting on benches. Where the bench contained a couple of elderly men, there was a philosophical or political debate to be had. It was all good-natured.

Dotted along the path were picnic tables and seats: steel structures set into the ground. They looked artistic in a functional way, with the tables being square, with a seat on each side, also with square, wood-latticed seats on a concrete pillar support. These were sited so as to give three of the seaters a view of the lake. The fourth member would either have to turn their back on the company to enjoy the view, else converse, else find something interesting about the trees and the grass behind the table.

Part way round the circuit I came across a closed-up, outdoor swimming pool that looked very nice. However, the water would be cold, because there had not been enough time for the sun to heat it up this early in the year.

More walking and I came back to where I had entered. It had been a lovely experience. There was no need to report it to the Advertising Standards Authority, because it had made me happy and it had been clean.

Back to the centre for some refreshment.

POLIN

POLIN is the relatively new Jewish museum in Warsaw. I first visited it when it was newly built and had no exhibits, other than the structure of the wooden synagogue. Now it was time to give it a proper visit, so I took the 111 (or 180) from Nowy Swiat.

Now here is a cautionary tale.

If there is no bus of any description passing either way down a main street, then it is odds-on that something is amiss. I waited 20 minutes learning this, having just missed a 180.

There were some flashing blue lights on a police car at the junction of Świętokrzyska and Nowy Swiat that became significant. But still I waited with all the other people at the stop until it became obvious that nothing was going to stop at our stop. Yet in the back of my mind was the appearance of the 180 just before I could get to the stop. Anyway, it's not far to the University stop, so off I went. At the street corner there was a police car with lights flashing, blocking the lane that would let traffic into Nowy Swiat. Presumably there was the other car of the pair at the other end of Nowy Swiat.

That corner was chaotic as all the traffic was trying to go on the same three roads, some turning left, some right and some straight on. It was all good natured though.

Having seen buses at the junction, I felt happier

going to the next stop, where, after a few minutes' wait, I caught a bus to POLIN.

Now POLIN is Jewish and they are paranoid about security, so there are airport-style checking gates to go through.

First, I had to empty my pockets of anything metallic. This turned out to be everything I had in my Regatta Adventure trousers.

    Spectacle case and reading glasses
    Wallet;
    Parkinson's foil tablet packs (2);
    Apartment keys (2 sets);
    Camera;
    Mobile phone;
    Approximately 40zl in loose change.

Then there was the watch and belt. It filled the little tray.

As I had not had a large breakfast, my trousers were loose around the waist, so without the belt there was nothing to hold them up. I had to do a spread-legged walk through the gate in an attempt to keep them up. Fortunately, for two reasons, there was nobody behind me, waiting to enter. Firstly, they would have been pissed off in having to wait for me to retrieve enough artefacts to see me in comfort up the Orinoco and secondly, there was nobody to see my spread-legged lurching through the metal detector.

I went through the metal detecting scanner and it was silent. I had passed.

Not quite. I had to be swept all over with a wand of some sort. It was not a Harry Potter wand, so presumably they were not looking for Potions. And I had spent ages unloading all my heavy metal and been passed clean by the gate. Anyway, whatever they were looking for did not register on the wand. Perhaps its battery had run out? I am so used to detectors finding some metal about my person that I am almost paranoid about going through security.

Anyway, I was in.

Over to the ticket desk and a sweet young lady beckoned me over.

"How much is it?" I asked.

"15zl."

"Is that discounted?"

"Yes." She looked embarrassed. "I took a view before I gave you the price."

This was a change from the lady at the Castle, who wanted to see definite proof that I was not younger than needed to be to get a discount.

As an aside, some youngsters would give up their seat for me, while others would not. Presumably the ones who did not were relatives of the Castle lady.

Anyway, as I had sufficient in small change, I scooped it out of my pocket and she kindly took it all.

"Do you want me to change all of this into notes?"

"That's very kind of you."

"If you have the time."

Of course I had the time to get rid of a big weight.

It turned out that there was 41zl and a few groszy, so she gave me two twenties and a one zloty coin plus the shrapnel that amounted to less than a zloty. What service! And she had already taken out the 15zl entrance fee!

"The exhibition entrance is downstairs. Enjoy the visit."

And so I went off with a much lighter step to where a lady at the top of the stairs was checking tickets.

The first gallery told me that POLIN in the language of 960AD meant 'rest a while', which the first Jews did as they passed through the country on one of their trading routes. There are some who say that this is the origin of the word 'Poland'. I could believe that if they spoke with a Geordie accent.

The POLIN museum clearly says that it is the history of the Jews in Poland for a thousand years. All to often these days the combination of 'Jews' and 'Poland' in any sentence means 'Holocaust', but the museum celebrates a thousand years of Jews living in Poland and there are galleries devoted to each of the periods.

There was a lot of writing to read and multimedia shows that seemed to add little to the story, but not much in the way of artefacts.

I tagged on to an English-speaking guide leading a group of French and American women around so that I could give my eyes a rest from reading. She was interesting, but I kept looking at some of the cards as well.

I can understand that the religion has kept the widely-spread Jews within a single identity, but the

Irish seem to do it well without a religion of Ireland (unless you count drinking Guinness a religion). The Poles are also widely spread, but they tend to assimilate so that their Polishness dies out in a few generations. But then, does that matter? People fall in love across ethnic and religious barriers and raise children. As long as those children are brought up well, the religion should not matter, as all religions promote the idea of good behaviour. It is when the religion becomes the over-riding dogma that problems occur.

There was a story in POLIN about two merchants in the Middle Ages whose wagon broke a wheel. They repaired it, but they had lost time and it was a Friday. The Sabbath started at Friday sunset and lasted until Saturday sunset and they were not going to get to the safety of the city in time. Their religion banned travel on the Sabbath, so they had a dilemma: whether to obey the Sabbath rules and stay where they were until sunset the following day, when they could be the victims of robbers, or whether to break the Sabbath rules and head for the city, arriving after sunset. They chose to travel with the knowledge that they would be condemned by the religious elders.

This was a Jewish story told against their own elders.

At one point of the tour I found an interesting quote: "You should study the Talmud. "Whoever understands the Talmud understands everything". It was an eighteenth century quote, so they know less than we do, as we have had two centuries to learn more. So I know that the quote is wrong. The Talmud will not help me to fix my printer when it refuses to talk to my computer. If the quote was right, then there would be no need for NASA, because the Talmud would tell us about the composition of the atmosphere of Uranus, and other fascinating discoveries. So the word "everything" in the quote needs some extensive qualification, eg 'Everything about interacting with your fellow man'. But then there are probably sociological studies that have added to the contents of the Talmud in the last two hundred years.

    I came across a Hanukkah lamp and a pair of candlesticks in a display case. These were very pleasing to see and I admired the craftsmanship.

    Then I came to the reconstructed synagogue. When I had last seen it, it had been unfinished in its construction. Now it was complete and painted in all its colourful glory. It was good to know that there was still craftsmanship available today.

    An early dulcimer in a glass case intrigued me. There were six wires per note and ten sets of wires. Each set of wires went over three areas of the dulcimer, so that three different notes could be played per set of wires.

    The shape of the instrument differed from a modern instrument, in that it was rectangular, rather than the rhomboid shape of today.

    Interesting.

    Round more exhibits until I came to a model of the Great Synagogue. This was located near today's plac Bankowy and was destroyed by the Nazis in WW2. It was lovely to see in its three dimensions.

On to a multimedia representation of a street between the wars with film clips showing Nazi bombers destroying the city.

And that was about it.

It was a good attempt to give an appreciation of a thousand years of Jews in Poland. It seemed to me to be well-balanced and did not focus on the trials of WW2 or the problems of Jews after the war.

I went to the restaurant and had a very nice meal from a choice of foods offered. This made a fitting end to the tour.

Outside one can see how the building reflects the parting of the waves as Moses led his people to the Promised Land. Outside, on the opposite side of the square is the Memorial to the Heroes of the Ghetto.

This monument as unveiled in April 1948 and built partly from materials the Nazis had brought from Germany in order for them to make their commemorative works. It is located at the spot where the first shots of the Ghetto Rising took place.

The monument is 11 metres high and evokes not just the Warsaw Ghetto wall, but also the Great Wall in Jerusalem.

The wall facing the museum shows a group of insurgents, led by Mordechai Anielewicz, armed with guns and Molotov cocktails.

On the back wall is a depiction of the persecution of the Jews under the Nazis.

It was at this monument that Willi Brandt went

down on his knees in 1970 and stayed there for some time in silence. He had lain a wreath at the monument. His visit to Warsaw was to sign the Treaty of Warsaw, which defined the final border between Poland and Germany.

Cemeteries

Given the number of people living in Warsaw, and their inevitable fate that awaits all of us, there has to be somewhere to lay their earthly remains when they are gone. Hence the number of very large cemeteries in Warsaw.

The number and size of Jewish cemeteries is a relic of the time that 40% of the Warsaw population was Jewish. They are tucked away in Cmentarz Żydowski, of which there are several.

Powązki

I am a fan of green burials, so the Powązki cemetery was not my cup of tea when I visited it.

There were gravestones, statues, obelisks and every other type of masonry imaginable. There were lighted candles and flowers on many of the graves, showing that loved ones still lived. This may have been the smell I was getting. Or it might have been subterranean decaying bodies. Or the mature trees that made the cemetery dark and foreboding. Some of those trees had probably been planted in 1790 when the cemetery was created.

The site extends to 106 acres and holds an estimated one million bodies. With all those slabs of stone it will be difficult to recycle the land, so presumably more land will be needed.

I never found their graves, but Frederick Chopin's parents and sisters are buried in the cemetery. What I would have said had I seen the graves is pure speculation, but I have a feeling that I would just have said "Oh."

Jewish

The cemetery of the Jewish Ghetto is located to the west of Okopowa, to the south of Powązki. During the war, this used to be within the ghetto walls, presumably to keep Jews within the walls even after they had died.

I went there one day after noticing it as I went to Powązki cemetery one evening. Because it was evening, it did not stay open for very long after I arrived, so I had a short amount of time to look around. Apart from the proliferation of Hebrew script, there is little difference between the look of the two cemeteries.

At the entrance there is a grave finder list. Presumably this is for visiting Jews to help them find ancestors, as there will no doubt be lots of Jewish visitors in Warsaw. There was really no reason for me to be there, so after a quick mooch around, I left.

South of the Jewish cemetery is the one for, what appears to be, all other religions, except for Orthodox Christians. I did not visit.

Rising

The first cemetery I visited in Warsaw was the one dedicated to the fallen of the Warsaw Rising. This is to be found at the tram stop Sowinskiego on the Ul. Wolska. It is sandwiched between the orthodox Catholic cemetery and the Wolski cemetery.

Much of the cemetery is lovely parkland leading to a powerful sculpture of The Fallen Unconquerable, under which are the ashes of 50,000 victims of the uprising.

Some 200,000 citizens and 10,000 resistance fighters were killed in the 63 days of fighting. Approximately half, mainly unknown, are buried in this cemetery.

People were originally buried near wherever they fell in makeshift graves, but many were not buried.

This cemetery was opened in 1945 and the huge task of exhuming and reburying the bodies continued for a couple of years. It cannot have been a nice task, which is probably an understatement.

Other victims of the war are also buried here. These are mainly unknown victims of the 1939 Siege of Warsaw and those inhabitants murdered by the Nazis during the six years of the occupation.

One year I noticed a change. Along one of the walkways were numerous poles. Sleeved on each pole was a four-sided weatherproof sleeve listing names of the fallen in the Rising, in alphabetical order of surnames. There were a lot of names on each sleeve.

There were a lot of poles along the long walkway. There were a lot of Poles on all the sleeves on all the poles.

It is a place for reflection. A remnant of a horrid time. I walked around the cemetery, feeling very glad that I had not been in Warsaw during the war and sad for all those who had been.

I also reflected on the post war period, when Communist rule deprived Poles for forty five years of the freedom they had been fighting for. It put the minor irritations that one encounters today in true perspective.

Bródno/Targowek

Wherever there is a cemetery in Poland there are flower sellers. Nowhere more obvious that the phalanxes of them outside the cemetery on the Bródno/Targowek border. It is a huge cemetery of 1.3 square kilometres, including the small Jewish cemetery to the south.

I came across it while taking a visit to a district whose name translates to 'dirty'. I can't imagine advertising to all bureaucrats that I came from a dirty place in Warsaw, so I thought a ride on a tram might throw some light on it.

Having seen the place from the safety of a tram, I can only conclude that it must be a historical naming, for the bits that I saw looked quite pleasant in the sunshine.

Stefan Starzyński

On the way back I passed on the tram through Rondo Starzyńskiego and then went down Ul. Stefana Starzyńskiego. So who was Stefan Starzyński?

It turned out that he is the most popular and respected Warsaw resident.

Now you might think that we had already encountered the most popular President of Warsaw in the form of Sokrates Starynkiewicz, whom we encountered in the Long Night of the Museums, especially as it is easy to get the two surnames confused.

In the true character of a coward, I will not claim that one was better than the other. Both were great men for whom Warsawians should be grateful.

At a time when Warsaw and Poland were suffering in the Depression of the late nineteen twenties, Starzyński was a stand-out figure.

Stefan Bronisław Starzyński was born in Warsaw on August 19th 1893 and joined Piłsudski's Ist Brigade after war broke out in 1914 as an ordinary soldier, but soon got promoted to officer.

He followed Piłsudski at the time of the Pledge Crisis in November 1917 and was imprisoned until the end of the war.

In 1918 he joined the Polish Army and became Chief of Staff of the 9th Polish Infantry Division, in which he served in the 1920 Polish-Bolshevik War. He was transferred to the General Staff, where he worked mainly in intelligence.

He served in the Treasury for a few years in

1929-1932 and in the Polish parliament for three years, as well as being deputy president of one of Poland's largest banks. He also wrote several papers on the economy. He was thus supremely well qualified to take on the task of restoring Warsaw's economy after it had been badly managed.

On August 1st 1934 he was appointed by the government to become President of Warsaw, with many special powers.

He immediately set about restoring the finances, which were in a poor state. Initially, he was viewed with suspicion, but feelings towards him improved when he directed the money he saved towards public works.

He electrified the suburbs of Wola and Grochów, paved all the main roads out of Warsaw and connected the centre with the suburb of Zoliborz via a bridge over the northern railway line.

He beautified the suburb of Sródmieście by planting trees and flowers and he created a large park in Wola.

He expanded the city to the south and built many public buildings, including the National Museum.

Appointed in 1934 for a four year term, he was democratically elected for a second four years in 1938, although this would be cut short by the war.

He stayed in Warsaw during the Siege of Warsaw throughout most of September 1939 and took control of the administration at a time when there were shortages and people were being made homeless.

After Warsaw fell, he continued administering the city while joining an early form of the Underground Army, the AK. One of the things he provided to the army were thousands of blank ID cards and other official forms, such as birth certificates. These would later be used by the resistance.

Although he had many chances to escape from the city, he refused them all.

The Gestapo took him, and others, in early October 1939 as hostages prior to the visit of Hitler for a victory parade to celebrate the defeat of Warsaw.

He was released, but captured again at the end of October, when he was sent to the Pawiak prison.

In December he was offered a chance to escape, but turned it down as the reprisals would have been costly. What happened to him later that month is unknown. The most likely scenario is that he was shot by the Gestapo some time between December 21st and 23rd.

In 2003 he was voted to be the Warsowian of the Century by a large majority. Presumably Starynkiewicz was voted politician of the 19th century.

There is a statue of him in front of the Blue Skyscraper in Plac Bankowy.

Hearing his story, one wonders how many of today's politicians would have the same ability and courage as he showed.

Prawosławny w Warszawie (Orthodox)

Situated near the Rising Cemetery, this cemetery

has been used since 1836 although not officially consecrated until 1841. Remember that Warsaw was in the Russian partition at that time and that there would have been a growing number of Eastern Orthodox citizens.

In 1905 a new church was built and the former Roman Catholic church that had been converted to Eastern Orthodox in 1834 was returned to its former religion.

Burials in this Orthodox cemetery take rank into account. The more important you are, the nearer to the church you were laid for your eternal rest. In this hierarchy we have:

Generals, clergy and civil servants of rank;

lower rank officers, clerks and wealthy merchants;

soldiers and members of the bourgeoisie;

others.

No mention of politicians, who, on today's rating would probably be buried outside of Warsaw!

One very notable resident is Sokrates Starynkiewicz, whom we encountered earlier.

Red Army Cemetery

If you are eagle-eyed when travelling on the 175 bus from the airport to the city centre, then you might just catch a glimpse of the Red Army Cemetery. This is just before the stop for the University Medical School. It commemorates the Red Army soldiers who died in the liberation of Warsaw, or, rather, the removal of one occupying regime and its replacement with another.

The Russian offensive started on 14th January 1945, giving the Nazis plenty of time between the end of the Rising and the Russian offensive to destroy most of Warsaw and more of its inhabitants. At the start of the War, Warsaw had 1.3 million inhabitants. At the time of the Russian offensive the population was down to 153,000, some 10% of what it was.

Interestingly, the verb *to decimate* means to reduce something **by** 10%, not to reduce something **to** 10%, so the population of Warsaw was more than decimated.

As you might expect, the architecture in this cemetery is Communist Brutal with pedestals either side of the main drive showing brotherly comradeship between the Poles and the Russians. These are surmounted by statues of soldiers in fighting poses. All very stylised and built more for propaganda than reality.

At the focal point of the drive is a tall obelisk.

Between the pedestals and the obelisk the drive is flanked by graves to dead soldiers. More soldiers are buried at the sides of the obelisk. Some have been identified, but thousands ended up in mass graves.

It is sobering to see evidence of all these lives cut short through war, but the casualties of the three month wait are not buried here.

Museums

You will probably want to visit some of the sites mentioned so far, so the next few chapters give practical advice on how to get there.

Entries are provided with a location (usually a street), the name of a transport stop, trams, buses and subway trains that stop there, and directions on how to get from the stop to the site of interest.

National

Ul. Jerozolimskie
Muzeum Narodowe
Tram   7, 9, 22, 24, 25
Bus   111, 117, 158, 507, 517, 521

Walk east to the Poniatowski Bridge and the National Museum is on the right. It is a building in the form of a capital 'E'.

Military

Next to the National Museum, just before the Poniatowski bridge.

Rising

79 Ul. Grzybowska
Muzeum Powstania Warszawskiego

Tram 1, 11,22,24
Bus   105, 109 171,178,190

Although the address is Grzybowska, the entrance is on Ul. Przyokopowa. Just follow the red brick wall.

Diving

While in the area of the Rising Museum, at 88 Grzybowska is the Diving Museum, opened on 27th February 2006.

Państwowe Muzeum Archaeologiczne (Archaeological)

Ul. Długa
Ratusz Arsenał
Metro   Ratusz Arsenał
  Tram   13, 20,23,26, 15, 18,35
  Bus   190

Castle

Plac Zamek
Stare Miasto
Tram   4, 13, 20, 23, 26
Bus   160, 190, 527

The castle is the red building above you. Ascend the stairs either side of the tunnel, or go through the glass doors on the right of the tunnel to the escalator and lift.

Neon

Ul. Minska, Praga Południe
Gocławska
Tram   3
Bus   125, 135, Z-6, 311

Go north for 300 metres up Ul. Gocławska to Ul. Minska. Continue up the road opposite (slightly to your left) and go another 100 metres. The museum is the building on the corner on your left.

PRL Museum

The museum of life in the People's Republic of Poland.

Ul. Głucha off Ul. Minska
Gocławska
Tram   3
Bus   125, 135, Z-6, 311

Go north for 300 metres up Ul. Gocławska to Ul. Minska. Turn left along Ul. Minska for 100 metres to Ul. Głucha and turn left. Ahead of you, with small notice, is PRL. Go through the gates and follow the directions. Signing is as good as it was in communist times.

Rail Transport (Stacja Muzeum)

Ul. Towarowa off Plac Zawiszy
Pl. Zawiszy
Tram   1, 7, 9, 24, 25, 28, 73

Head up Towarowa from Plac Zawiszy on the left hand side until you come to the museum, some 150 metres from the roundabout on Al. Jerozolimskie at Pl. Zawiszy.

Katynskie, Oddział Martyrologiczny (Katyn)

Jana Jeziorańskiego
Cytadela
Bus 118, 185, 385

Jan Nowak-Jezioranski (1914-2005) was an emissary between the AK and the Polish Goverment in Exile. He was nicknamed the Courier from Warsaw. He took part in the Warsaw Uprising. After the war, he was the head of the Polish section of Radio Free Europe and later became a security advisor to both Presidents Reagan and Carter.

X Pawilionu Cytadeli Warszawskiej

Ul. Skazańców 25
Wybrzeże Gdyńskie
Cytadela   Bus 118, 185, 385

There is a walk of 600 metres or so between Pavilion 10 and the Katyn Museum.

Skwer Powstanców Styczniowych

Park located between the Citadel and the Vistula.

Just in case you visit the Citadel and want to know what this parkland is called.

Gasworks Museum

25 Ul. Kasprzaka
Krzyżanowskiego   Bus   103
Szpital Wolski   Bus   105,109,136, 155, 171,178,190,255

Located on the former Wola Gasworks site, built 1886-88 and opened as a museum in 1977.

Parks

Ogrod Saski (Saxon Gardens)

These are the gardens you are most likely to visit during a short visit to Warsaw as they are located near the Old Town and are very pleasant in the summer.
Plac Piłsudskiego
Plac Piłsudskiego
Bus 107, 116, 128, 175, 178, 180,222
Walk across the square to the Tomb of the Unknown Soldier and carry on to the gardens.

Uzadowski

Al. Ujadowskie
Piękna
Bus 116, 166, 180,195, 222

Lazienki

Al. Ujadowskie
Łazienki Krolewskie
Bus 116, 166, 180,195, 222

Wilanow

Ul. Wiertnicza

Wilanów
Bus E-2, 116, 130, 180, 264, 317, Z63

Pole Mokotowskie

Al. Żwirki I Wigury
Banach Szpital
Bus 128, 136, 175, 188, 504

Ul. Stefana Batorego
Stefana Batorego
Bus 119

Pole Mokotowskie Metro
Bus 130, 168, 174, 200

Skaryszewski

Al. Waszyngtona
Park Skaryszewski
Bus   102, 158, 521
Tram   6, 9, 24, 26

Al. Zieleniecka
Al. Zieleniecka
Bus   123, 138, 166, 509, 517
Tram   6, 7, 25, 26, 73

Szymanskiego

Ul. Elekcyjna
Monte Cassino
Bus   109, 154, 171, 184, 190, 197

Elekcyjna
Tram   10, 11,13, 26, 27

Krazinskich

Swiętojerska
Bus   180, 227, 400

Marshal Edward /Rydza-Smigly

Ul. Rozblat
Śniegockiejez
Bus   108, 162, 171.

Ul. Książęca
Książęca
Bus   108, 118, 127, 166, 171

Szczęśliwica Garden Park

Ul. Dickensa
Szczęśliwica
Bus   128, 157, 184, `86, 414, 521

Dolinka Szwajcarska

Ul. Fryderyka Chopina
off Al. Ujadowskie
Piękna
Bus 116, 166, 180,195, 222

A small, but attractive park. Ul. Fryderyka Chopina is opposite the bus stop.

As you walk up Ul. Fryderyka Chopina you will pass a monument to Stefan Rowecki (1895-2nd August 1944), known as 'Grot' (Spearhead) in the AK during the 1944 Uprising. He was the head of the AK and was murdered by the Gestapo on the personal orders of Himmler.

Kazimierozowski

Ul. Browarna
Browarna
Bus 105

A pleasant park named after the palace, which was built originally in 1637-1641. It was rebuilt in 1660 for King John II Casimir, after whim it takes its name. It was again rebuilt in 1765-68 for the Corps of

Cadets, established by King Stanisław II Augustus. It is

currently used by the University of Warsaw.

There is a monument in the park to the Secret Teaching Organisation of WW2.

Samuela Orgelbranda

Ul. Sowia
South of Mariensztac Square.
Named after the publisher of the Universal Encyclopaedia, Samuel Orgelbrand. He was a Polish Jew who lived from 1810 – 1868.

AK Rog

Romualdan Traugutta

Ul. Konwiktorska
Konwiktorska
Bus   178, 503
An indifferent park for such a famous figure.

Olympic Golf Club

This is not a golf club in the sense that we know it in England, but a cross between a driving range and a means of running competitions based on the driving area. This is because land for a proper golf course of 18 holes would be impossible to find in Warsaw.

Cemeteries

Powstańców Warszawy (Warsaw Rising)

Ul. Wolska
Sowińskiego
Tram   10,11,13,26,27
Bus   105, 197

Prawosławny (Orthodox)

Ul. Wolska
Cmentarz Prawosławny
Tram   10,11,13,26,27

Wolski

Ul. Wolska
Cmentarz Wolska
Tram   13, 27
Bus   194, 255,
Fort Wola
Tram   10, 11, 27
Bus   105, 197

Powązkowski

Ul. Powązkowski
Powązkowski   Tram   1, 22, 27
                     Bus   180, 327

Powązki IV Brama   Bus   180, 327

Zydowski

Ul. Okopowa
Cmentarz Zyowski
Tram   1, 22, 27
Bus   180, 400
Esperanto
Bus   107, 111, 180, 527

Bródnowski

Ul. Sw. Wincentego
Cmentarz Bródnowski
Bus   156, 169, 327, 409

Mauzoleum Zołnierzy Radzieckich

Ul. Żwirki I Wygury
Pruszkowska or Uniwersitet Medyczny
Bus   128, 136, 175, 188, 504 (request)

A Three Day Itinerary

If you have ready everything in this book so far, you will realise that you do not have the time to do everything justice in the typical three day weekend that most tourists spend in Warsaw. This is great news, because it means that you have to return and enjoy more of Warsaw!

I am setting out a suggested itinerary covering arrival on Friday early evening and departing Tuesday noon on a weekend sometime between May and September.

Friday Evening

With luck, it should be possible to get in a show at the Fountain Park, but you have to be organised.

Exchange some currency whilst at home. You will almost certainly get a better rate than at the airport. You will need some currency to buy transport tickets and something to eat.

Also, before you leave home, you should use the ZTM maps to work out precisely how you are going to get to your accommodation.

Buy your tickets at either the ZTM office, or the newsagents. I would suggest a 72 hour ticket and one 90 minute ticket for your return to the airport.

Follow the signs to the urban railway. You want either the S2 or the S3 if you are staying in the centre.

Going by rail avoids the Friday evening rush hour on the roads.

Go to your accommodation and book in.

If you have time, find somewhere to eat. There is a McDonalds at Centrum which I have often used when in a rush.

Go to the Fountain Park and enjoy the show.

Saturday

You need to remember that Nowe Swiat and Krakowskie Przedmiescie are closed to traffic at the weekend.

Saturday morning is a good time to visit the Old Town and exchange some of your currency for Złotys while enjoying the sights.

At some point in the morning it would be good to take a tour of the castle.

At noon there is the changing of the guard at the Presidential Palace, after which it is easy to get to see the grave of the Unknown Soldier at Plac Piłsudskiego and then to the 175 bus stop to catch the 175 to the Central Railway Station to go to the top floor of Złoty Teras for lunch.

After lunch would be a good time to go to the Information centre at the Palace of Culture and Science, where you can take in a view from the Viewing Terrace on the 31st floor. The information centre will be able to tell you of any events you might like to go to.

You now have time to do as you wish. Hopefully

you will have some ideas for reading the book so far.

Sunday

Two things to do today are:
visiting Wilanów;
taking in a Chopin concert in the park at either noon or at 4pm.

If you are energetic, you can walk the Royal Route as far as Ujadowski, otherwise go by bus and listen to the pronunciation of Plac Trzech Krzyzy.

You can eat at Wilanów.

Monday

Suggestions for Monday are tentative. There are so many things that you could do, yet time is running out.

There are many museums to see, but the Rising Museum, Jewish Museum and Kopernik Experience are probably the top three. You should allow the best part of a day for any one of them. To fill in the rest of the day, you could squeeze a visit to Praga to look at the bears and the cathedral.

There is the old Jewish Quarter or you may find inspiration from the earlier chapters in this book. The choice is very much yours according to your interests.

Whatever you choose to do, I hope you enjoy it and I hope that this book has been informative enough to allow you to make an informed decision.

Timeline of Polish History

It is easy to think that Polish history started at World War I, but it is possible to delve as far back as Iron Age and earlier.

Perhaps the best point at which to start is 966, for this is when Poland adopted Christianity. This is quite a bit later than England, which adopted Christianity with the Romans before they left for home.

It was a king who got converted – Mieszko I – so everybody else had to follow suit if they wanted to be in the king's good books. We know the exact date - 14th April 966, but not the place, although somewhere around Poznan in western Poland is the most likely place.

From 966 to 1370 the Piast dynasty ruled Poland. I mention this in case you come across references to it, but not much of note happened. (Well, it probably did, but this is not a detailed history of Poland.)

From 1386 to 1572 it was the Jagiełłonian dynasty. There is a nice story about its start that is worth repeating, because it had a lasting effect on Poland.

It was started by the marriage of Lithuanian Grand Duke Jogaila (Władysław II Jagiełło) to Queen Jadwiga of Poland This formed a strong union that lasted four centuries.

On 15 July 1410 the Battle of Grunwald was fought between the union and the Teutonic Knights and won by the Union. It shifted the balance of Power in Lithuania-Poland's favour for some time to come.

It was the largest battle ever fought in Medieval Europe and became a symbol of the defence of Poland and Lithuania against aggressors.

In the Jagiellonian period, Poland developed as a feudal economy with power increasingly in the hands of the landed nobility.

Of interest also is that the Black Death, which devastated Western Europe between 1348-49, the Germans blamed the Jews, who travelled east to the largely-unaffected Poland. With no persecution, they flourished and by the end of the Jagiellonian dynasty Poland was home to 80% of the world's Jews.

The last Jagiellonian monarch, the childless Sigismund II, believed he could keep the monarchy going by making it an elective monarchy, where the king was elected by the nobles, rather than by heredity. (Note that the peasants did not have a vote.)

The Union of Lublin in 1569 established the Polish-Lithuanian Commonwealth. This started a central parliament and local assemblies led by, from 1573, elected kings. Considering that the rest of Europe was ruled by absolute monarchies (Elizabeth I in England for example), this was a relatively democratic system.

In 1573 the Warsaw Confederation established religious freedoms, unlike anywhere else in Europe.

The Catholic Church countered with the Counter Reformation and had some success in bringing back converted protestants into the Catholic fold.

Most of the elected kings were foreigners, the first being Henry II of France, who stayed for a year before moving to become King of France.

He was followed by King Stephen Bathory from Transylvania.

Ivan IV of Russia in 1577 had designs on the area of the Commonwealth that is now roughly present-day Estonia. King Bathory, in conjunction with another famous Pole, Jan Zamoyski, took back the lands taken by Ivan.

King Bathory was followed by two kings from the Swedish Wasa dynasty – Kings Sigismund III (ruled from 1587 – 1632) and Władysław IV (reigned from 1632 to his death in 1648). It was Władysław who erected the column in Plac Zamek to his father – yes, the Sigismund Column. During Sigismund's time as king, there was an invasion by the Turks that was rebuffed.

The Swedish king, Gustavus Adolphus, attacked the area now in Estonia and lost it back to Władysław a couple of decades later.

Then there were the occasional defences against incursions by Russia.

It gets confusing around this time as there was a succession of elected kings. Ones to be aware of are John III Sobieski (ruled 1674 – 1696) combated many Ottoman invasions and provided stability after the Deluge.

The Deluge refers to the Russian invasion in 1654, followed by the Swedish invasion of 1655-1660.

Sobieski was skilled militarily and beat the Turks in 1683 at the Battle of Vienna, after which the Pope hailed him as the Saviour of Christendom.

Stanisław August Poniatowski was the last king of Poland, ruling from 1764 to 1795).

The Commonwealth declined due to infighting among the nobles and the nobility's reliance on serfdom and agriculture at a time when England, for example, was undergoing the Industrial Revolution.

One other character we referred to is Tadeusz Kościuszko. He was a veteran of the War of American Independence, who, by 1794 had come back to Poland and was incensed by the capitulation of the king to the demands of the Russians, Prussians and Austrians.

Catherine the Great, a former lover of King Poniatowski, set out to destroy the weak Poland and sent part of the Russian army to see them off. However, against a stronger force, Kościuszko's rag-bag army defeated them at the Battle of Racławice. This roused the Poles, who, a month later in April 1794 initiated the 1794 Warsaw Uprising (not the 1944 Warsaw Uprising). This uprising was led by Jan Kilinski.

Kościuszko abolished serfdom and gave civil liberties to peasants For the first time, peasants were regarded as being part of the nation, for prior to this the concept of nation was restricted to the nobility.

Kościuszko was wounded fighting the Russians in the Battle of Maciejowice on 10th October 1794 and captured by the Russians, who sent him to Saint

Petersburg.

On 4th November, with Kościuszko gone, the Russians won the Battle of Praga and in the looting which followed, the cossacks murdered 20,000 people.

Poland surrendered on 16th November and was partitioned the following year, a position it would occupy for the next 123 years.

All was not happy for those 123 years, for you can never dominate the Poles and hope that they will be happy.

The first uprising was in November 1830, also known as the Polish-Russian War of 1830-31. It started with two young Polish officers from the Army of Congress Poland's military academy. It was an uprising against the dominant Russian Empire and grew as army units from other parts of the empire were drawn in. However, Russian numerical superiority won and retribution was extracted. Poland became an integral part of Russia and Warsaw became little more than a military garrison.

A second uprising took place a generation later in January 1863.

The Polish nobility and the bourgeoisie hankered after the semi-autonomous state that had existed before the first uprising and saw a weakened Russia after its adventures in Crimea.

The underground National Government planned a strike, but the Head of the Civil Administration, Aleksander Wielkopolski, got wind of it and tried to avert it. He brought forward the conscription of young Polish activists into the Russian army. This act precipitated the uprising, the very thing that Wielkopolskie wanted to avoid, presumably because he had read his history and knew that you did not mess with the Russians.

With no international support, the rebels resorted to guerilla tactics, for which the standard counter measures were imposed – public executions and deportations to Siberia.

In addition, Alexander II hit the landed gentry hard by abolishing serfdom. This led to the breakup of estates and the destitution of the out-of-work serfs.

In 1918, Poland got back its independence, but lost it again with the invasion of the Nazis on 1st September 1939 and the invasion of the Russians on 17th September 1939. In the six years that followed, Poland lost 16-17% of its population, more than any other country. Warsaw lost 85-90% of its buildings.

Polish People's Republic

From 1945 to 1989, Poland was part of the Communist Bloc led by Russia. This came about as a result of the Yalta Conference, where the western Allies, not wanting to upset Stalin, agreed to recognise a Government of National Unity as the legitimate government, thereby not recognising the government in exile in London. Needless to say, the new government was rabidly pro-Soviet.

At the Potsdam conference in July-August 1945, Poland was shifted westwards. With the loss of all the Polish Jews and the fleeing of ethnic Germans into

Germany, the western border of Poland was moved west to the line of the Oder and Neisse rivers. The eastern border was moved west to what was called the Curzon line – a border drawn up shortly after the start of Operation Barbarossa, in which Germany invaded the Soviet Union and a line which roughly followed the border agreed by the Ribentrop-Molotov treaty of August 1939. It was named after the British Foreign Secretary of the time, George Curzon. Churchill tried to modify the line at the Yalta Conference, but Stalin was having none of it. So the city of Lwów became part of Ukraine. The inhabitants of the lost lands of the east (the Kresy) were resettled in the lands gained from Germany. Poland became ethnically homogeneous, with no significant minority. Even today, Poland is 94% ethnically Polish.

By now you will have realised that the Poles do not like being ruled by outsiders, so they rebelled, but not for a while, as there was too much to do to reconstruct the country, which, in 1952, officially became the People's Republic of Poland (PRL).

Following Stalin's death in 1953, the more liberal wing of the Communist Party took over in the form of Władysław Gomulka. He had been the leader of Poland until 1948, when the Russian masters dethroned him for being too liberal.

In the clampdown that followed, the Catholic Church was targetted, but, no matter what they did to him, Cardinal Wyszyński became a leader of the opposition, although he trod a careful line so that he did not instigate repressive action by the authorities.

In October 1956, there was the Polish October. This started with the workers in Posnan going on strike. The authorities reacted with brutality and 57 people were killed. In 1956 a Hungarian rebellion was brutally suppressed by Russian tanks.

In 1966 Poland celebrated 1,000 years of Polish Christianity, which did not please the authorities. I suspect that the vast number of stamps and memorabilia associated with the thousand years collected by my father, a religious man, had more than a tinge of rebellion connected to it.

By 1968 the authorities had become ever more censorious. In March 1968 they banned a Warsaw University production of a play written in 1824 by Adam Mickiewicz on the grounds that it was anti-Soviet. This was followed up after the June 1967 Arab-Israeli War with a clampdown on intellectuals and 'Zionists'. Many thousands of students were expelled from universities, as were lecturers and others who did not toe the new line of intolerance.

It was not only intellectuals who rebelled – there was significant displeasure among the workers.

In 1968 Alexander Dubcek launched reforms in the Prague Spring in Czechoslovakia. This led to an invasion by the Warsaw Pact countries, including the People's Army of Poland. This resulted in the Brezhnev Doctrine, whereby Russia could unilaterally enter any country of its satellite states if they deviated from the course of socialism.

In 1970, Gomulka made an agreement with West Germany. They would recognise the western borders of Poland. It only took 25 years, but at least it was done. The Germans also agreed to let anybody of German ethnicity living in Poland the right to emigrate to Germany and to provide pensions to those ethnic Germans who wished to stay in Poland.

When coming to Warsaw to sign the new agreement, Willi Brandt took the opportunity to visit the site of the Jewish ghetto, where he fell on his knees and asked for forgiveness for the horrors that the Nazis had bestowed on the Poles. It was a move to move Poland towards the west and slightly, ever so slightly, away from Russian domination.

But Poland's economy was in dire straits and the authorities massively increased the price of basic household items, including food, just before the peak buying period of Christmas. This led to demonstrations along the Baltic coast in the north, then spreading throughout Poland. Demonstrations create repression. Gomulka authorised the use of lethal force. People were killed. Resentment increased. Gomulka resigned, to be replaced in early 1971 by Edward Gierek.

Gierek brought in reforms, but was scuppered by the 1973 oil crisis in the west, where there was high inflation. Foreign goods disappeared from Polish shelves and the country's foreign debt increased. By 1976, poor management of the economy and the cost of servicing the increased debt, became onerous.

In 1971, Gierek had frozen basic prices at an artificially low level, but by 1976 supply could not keep up with demand and long queues formed outside all retail outlets. To reduce demand, Gierek raised prices by an average of 60% in mid-1976. This resulted in a massive wave of strikes and a backing down by Gierek as he rescinded the price rises and brought in ration cards. Relations between Gierek and Brezhnev deteriorated.

The miracle happened on the 16th October 1978 when a Polish Pope was elected. Pope John Paul II. To say that this electrified the nation is an understatement. He toured Poland in June 1979 to a rapturous poplar welcome. Half a million people attended a mass in Warsaw and it is estimated that ten million people throughout Poland attended one of his public masses.

He promoted the separation of social institutions independent of the government. Nothing too controversial, for he was aware how the wrong word could start a bloodbath.

The Polish Government in Exile, ignored since the end of the war, was still going and became more respected in the atmosphere of Polish assertiveness. There was also support from the exiled Polish community in America and Europe.

It was during his tour of Poland that the Pope met a man called Lech Wałęsa in a remote valley in the Tatra mountains within walking distance of Zakopane, the main tourist resort of Poland. (I went there on one visit for a few days and can thoroughly recommend it if you like mountain walking.) What they discussed we don't know, but they apparently got on well together.

By 1980 the government had to do something to

address the failing economy, so they agreed to put up prices gradually but persistently. The result was an outbreak of strikes starting in Lublin. It rapidly spread to the Gdansk shipyards and beyond.

The government had a choice between more repression or appeasement of the workers. They chose the latter and the Gdansk Agreement was signed in August 1980. The workers received many benefits, including the right to freely associate as trade unions, and all calmed down.

It was not long before, on 17th September 1980, that the trade union *Solidarność* was created. It soon became an amalgam of intellectuals and workers and became an effective opposition to the government. Ten million people joined the Union – more than four times as many as were members of the ruling party.

Lech Wałęsa was caught in the middle of a government eager to repress the workers and the workers who were seeking to act against the government.

In December 1981 the government unilaterally introduced economic measures. The union announced December 17th to be a day of protest.

But before the protest could begin, on 13th December the government set about repressing the workers and some were killed. To be fair to the president of the day, General Jaruzielski, he feared that an uncontrolled uprising could result in the entry of Russian tanks to quell the rising and that would result in untold deaths,

Martial Law was imposed and Solidarity was banned in August 1982. It went underground, but did not have the support it once had.

Poland's economic mismanagement continued.

After a while, market reforms were initiated, where companies could be created more or less along Western lines. They flourished but the rest of the economy did not. Rationing was used to share out scarce resources. Poland became an economic basket-case again.

In the late 1980's, Mikhail Gorbachev rescinded the Brezhnev Doctrine and opened a period of Glasnost (restructuring) and Perestroika (openness and transparency).

In Poland, nationwide strikes broke out in the summer of 1988. Things had to be sorted out.

Talks were held between government and unions and General Jaruzelski threatened to resign if the central committee did not relax its stance.

The Party agreed to let 35% of the lower house seats be contested, whilst retaining the other 65% for itself. But on June 4th 1989, at the same time as the Tienanmen Square slaughter was going on in China, the first round of elections was held, with the second round held on 18th June. When the results were announced it was dynamite. Solidarity had won all the seats it was allowed to have and in the upper house they won 99 out of the 100 seats.

The situation was intolerable and, after some shenanigans, Lech Wałęsa was elected President of Poland and took office on 22nd December 1990.

The Warsaw Pact was dissolved in July 1991. The Soviet Union finished in December 1991 and the last non-Polish troops left Poland in 1993.

Poland was free again.

In 2004, Poland became part of the European Union. There would appear to be two main reasons for this – Financial assistance and a need to be part of a bigger federation as a counter to the threat of Russia.

Poland was let down by Britain in 1939, when Britain declared war on Nazi Germany, but actually did nothing to come to the assistance of Poland. Indeed, it turned out that the Poles came to the assistance of Britain in the Battle of Britain and the taking of Monte Cassino not to mention the invaluable contribution to the decoding of the Enigma machine.

Poland was also let down at Yalta, when it shifted westwards and lost some of its former land area.

Although now part of NATO, this is a treaty organisation, and the fear is that history would repeat itself if Russia invaded, whereas to be part of a Union would likely bring swifter action.

Poland is now a sound economy, with GDP growing at some 4% pa. Its problem now is a shortage of workers. There are many suitable Polish workers in Britain, but most seem happy to stay, especially as they earn more in Britain. (In 2019 the average income in Poland is some £13,000pa, whereas in Britain it is nearer £30,000pa. What will happen when the salaries reach parity is anybody's guess.

Conclusion

Warsaw and Poland in general, are delightful parts of the world. All of Poland can easily be reached from Warsaw and travel is relatively cheap.

I hope that what you have read in this book gives you a deeper understanding of Poland and the Poles than the average tourist has and that this knowledge will let you gain much more from your visit. Or should I say 'visits', because, if you are like me, you will never tire of seeing what this country and its people have to offer.

I welcome any feedback that you might want to give. My email address is koniecznytony@gmail.com.

I look forward to hearing from you.

Alphabetical Index

1830 uprising..163
1st Tank Division..238
3rd May Constitution..86
Adam Czerniaków...170
Agricola..275
Agrikola..139
AK monument...275
Aleksander Wielopolski.....................................78
Aleksandra Zelwerowicza..................................55
Alvenslaben Convention in................................79
Andersa...53, 58
Andrzej Kicinski...239
Andrzej Renes..256
Anielewicza..177
Antoni Madalinski..69
Apollo Korzeniowski......................................247
Archaeological Museum...................................62
Archbishop's Palace...55
Bar Confederation..84
Barbican..38
Battle for Moscow..88
Battle of Białołęka..76
Battle of Bydgoszcz..72
Battle of Chełm..72
Battle of Dobre..76
Battle of Galicia...260
Battle of Grunwald..........................65, 134, 361
Battle of Grunwald monument........................134

Battle of Kaniów	260
Battle of Maciejowice	72, 363
Battle of Olszynka Grochowska	76
Battle of Praga	73
Battle of Raszyn	87
Battle of Szczekociny	72
Battle of Tannenburg	65
Battle of the Nations	88
Battle of Vienna	98
Battle of Warsaw	138
Battle of Wawer	76
Battle of Zielence	87
Battle of Zieleńce	87
Bazar Różyckiego	258
bear pit	262
Belweder Palace	139
Bishop Josef Rossakowsk	97
Bishop Josef Rossakowski	97
Blue Army	260
Botanical Gardens	136
Branicki	83
Breda	243
Brzozowa	37
Budexpo	275
cathedral	40
Chambois	242
Charles de Gaulle roundabout	112
Chłodna	172
Chłopicki, Josef	163
Chopin	109
Chrystian Piotr Aigne	113
Cielna	38

Citadel	246
Confederation at Targowek	85
Congress of Vienna in 1815	74
Copper Roofed Palace	42
Countess Emilia Plater	164
Czesław Wojciechowski	178
Dąbrowski	73
Długa	53
Duns	240
dward Rydz-Smigły	289
Edward M. House	266
Edward Szymański	318
Edward Wolanin	151
Emilia Plater	163p.
Empik	229
Esperanto	167
Father Ignaci Jan Skorupki	255
Feliks Dzierżynski	247
Filtry	204
Florianska	256
Foksal	111
Franciszek Bielińsk	165
Franciszek Szanior	264
Franz Kutschera	132
Frederick Chopin University Music School	111
Frederik Chopin.	
street	132
Freta	43
Gabriel Narutowicz	247
General Jósef Sowiński	77
General Romuald Traugutt	79
General Stanisław Maczek	240

Georges Sand..118
Ghetto Fighter..179
Ghetto Rising..57
Grossaktion Warschau...174
Grunwald Monument in Krakow.......................................266
Gunnersbury Cemetery...201
Hedwig..65
Heroes of the Ghetto..57
Holy Cross Church...105
Hotel Bristol..99
Ignaci Jan Paderewski..133
Ignacy Kłopotowsk...257
Indian Embassy...275
Jagiellonska...257
Jan Henryk Dąbrowski...73
Jan Kilinski..55
Jan Piekałkiewicz..195
January Uprising...77
Jarosław Dąbrowski...247
Jerzy Januskiewicz..54
Jerzy Sikorsk...239
Jewish Ghetto...62
Jewish Quarter..167
Jews...167
Joanna Rajkowska...112
Joanna Różewska..148, 229
Johann Christian Szuch..193
John II Casimir Wasa...33
Josef
 Poniatowski..86
Josef Piłsudski...137
Josef Chłopicki..75

Josef Conrad..111
Josef Haller..259
Josef Poniatowski..85
Josef Sowinski..319
Josef Sowiński..319
Josef Sowinski Park..319
Julian Niemcewicz..163
Kabaty..15
Kampinoski..15
Kanonia..39
Kantor..19
Kapitulna...54p.
Karol Tchorek..316
Katarzina Kraszewska..151
Katarzyna Kraszewska...110
Khmelnytski...33
Kilinski...53
Kingdom of Poland..74
Kłopotowskiego..256
Konieczny, Marian...270
Kościuszko..69p.
Kościuszko Uprising..69
Krakowskie Przedmiescie..21
66..97
Adam Mickiewicz statue..98
Brawarnia...102
Cardinal Wyszynski...100
church of the Assumption and Saint Joseph....................98
Herbert Hoover monument...98
Jan Twardowski...100
Josef Poniatowki..99
Madona of Passau..98

Palac Tyszkiewiczów 102
President's Palace 98
Krasinski 57
Kresy 138, 232
Krolewska 101
Krzysztof Jabłoński 153
Krzywe Kolo 39
Kubusia Puchatka 128
Lech Kaczyński 135
Leszno 27
Lindley 206
Little Insurgent 54
Louis Fitzgibbon 201
Ludwig Lejzer Zamenhof 167
Maksimilian Biskupski 60
Maria Skłodowska 38
Maria Wodzinska 118
Marian Konieczny 266
Marie Curie 43
Maria Skłodowska 38
Matejki 279
Maurycy Mochnacki 142, 163
Maurycy Mochnatski 75
Mazowie 29
Memorial to the Heroes of the Ghetto 334
Mendeleev 98
Mermaid 36
Mieczysław Apfelbaum 179
Międzynarodowa 323
Mieszko I 360
Mikołajczyk 298
Miła 179

Miodowa...55, 62
Money..
Kantor...19
Monte Casino...58
Monument to the Fallen and Murdered in the East........60
Mordechai Anielewicz..177
Most Swiętokrzyżka..106
Muranow...59
Museum of the University of Warsaw.....................103
Narutowicz..261
National Stadium..263
Nicolas Kopernikus...103
Nike...270
November Uprising..74
Nowe Świat...96
Nowolipkie...58
Nowomiejska..38
Okolnik...111
Operation Harvest Festival.....................................176
Ordynacka..109
Orthodox Cemetery..320
Pac, Michal Jan..115
Palac Kultury i Nauki...158
Pałac Paca..55
Palac Staszic...103
Palac Uruski...103
Palace of Culture and Science................................158
palm tree...112
Park Praski...325
Peace of Brest-Litowsk..260
Piotr Wysocki...163
Piwna...34

Saint Martins	34
Plac Bankowy	53
Plac Haller	259
Płac Krasinskich	57
Plac Piłsudskiego	101
Plac Powstancow Warszawy	128
Płac Trzech Krzyży	112
Plac Zamkowy	34, 96
Podwale	54
Polish First Armoured division	240
Polish Russian War of 1920	261
Polish Stock Exchange	113
Polish-Bolshevik war	241
Polish-Ukrainian war	188
Pomnik Małego Powstańca	54
Poniatowski	83
Poniatowski Bridge	88
Powązki	256, 283, 291
Prince Adam Czartoryski	163
Prince Adam Jerzy Czartoryski	75
Prince Franciszek Ksawery Drucki-Lubecki	75
Proclamation of Połaniec	71
Prudential building	128
Puławski	234
Radomiła Zofia Piątkowska	195
Radziwiłł	83
Ratusz Arsenał	27, 61
Ribbentrop-Molotov Pact	58
Righteous Among the Nations	55
Rita Chen	154
Roland Gabriel Narutowicz	293
Roman	

Dmowski	135
Roman Dmowski	135
Roman Polanski	245
Romuald Traugutt	247
Rondo Waszingtona	263
Rosemary's Baby	245
Royal Route	131
Russian Orthodox Church	262
Saint Aleksander	113
Saint Anny of Wilanow	142
Saint Augustine's	180
Schiller	55
Sierakowski	72
Sigismund	30
Sigismund II Augustu	66
Sigismund III Vasa	29
Skaryszew	264
Słupecka	225
Smolensk	135
Sobieski III monument	139
Sokrates Starynkiewicz	207, 322
St. Augustine's church	58
Stanisław II Augustu	67
Stanisław Maczek	240
Stanisław Mokronowski	71
Stanisława Augusta	324
Stare Miasto	27
Starynkiewicz	206
State Aviation Works	225
Statue of a dog	227
Stawki	59, 174
Stefan Starzyński	340

Stefan Tyszkiewicz......103
Stefan Zamoyski......201
Stoczek......164
Supreme Court......56
Swięta Anny......97
Świętojańska......40
Świętokrzyski bridge......89
Świętokrzyżka......106
Szczęśliwicki......326
szlachta......33
Tarnopol......231
Tesco......250
The Polish Officer......39
Third Partition......86
Thirty Years' War......32
Tomasz Wawrzecki......72
Toruń......103
Traugutt......79
Treblinka......174
Tylman of Gameren......135
Tylman von Gameren......57
Ujazdowski......131
Ujazdowski Park......133
Umschlagerplaz......174
Under the Giants......131
Union of Lublin......66
viewing tower......96
Voice of Poland......191
Wacław Śledziewski......178
Walerian Łuckasińskiego......263
Warecka......128
Warsaw Card......20

Warsaw Museum	37
Warsaw Rising Square	128
Warsaw Uprising of 1794	97
Weydlich	116
Wiejska	279
Wilhelmshaven	243
William Lindley	135, 206
Winnie-the-Pooh street	128
Władysław II	65
Władysław IV Wasa	33
Wojciech Żywny	117
Zagiew	178
Zamenhofa	167
Zapiecek	108
Zelwerowicz, Aleksander	55
Zielemiecka	325
Złoty	19
Zloty Teras	181
Zygmunt Puławski	224
Garrison church of the army in Warsaw	56
Krzysztof Komeda Trzcinski	244
Maksimilian Biskupski	60
Polish-Russian War of 1792	87
Łazienki Park	139, 193
Łukasz Krupiński	155
Śląsko-Dąbrowski bridge	38
Żelazowa wola	115

Printed in Poland
by Amazon Fulfillment
Poland Sp. z o.o., Wrocław